ADVANCE PRAISE FO

Reading Contemporary African American Drama

"*Reading Contemporary African American Drama* is a much needed volume that makes a major contribution to black identity formation studies. Playwright and novelist Alice Childress devoted her life to debunking stereotypes—misrepresentations—about blacks inside and outside of the American theater. It is only fitting that quintessential scholar/teacher Trudier Harris, who wrote one of the first comprehensive studies on Childress's plays and novels, should shepherd a volume that includes cutting-edge research on Childress and other black dramatists who have carved out a place for truth on the American stage. The essays in this volume explore the many ways in which contemporary dramatists reformulate black identity by interrogating historically racist praxis. What these essays have in common is an exploration of history wherein characters move forward toward self-discovery, self-definition, and self-fulfillment in plays by blacks since the 1950s."

Elizabeth Brown-Guillory, University of Houston;
Editor of Middle Passage and the Healing Place of History: Migration and Identity in Black Women's Literature

"*Reading Contemporary African American Drama* is an important reminder that history has never been a closed book for African American dramatists. By rejecting the long and troubling record of silent, biased, and inaccurate accounts of the African American past, dramatists from William Wells Brown and W.E.B. Du Bois to August Wilson and Suzan-Lori Parks have been able to rewrite history with an eye toward deconstructing old myths, giving voice to the nameless masses, and re-inserting the African American presence into the white space. The common bond that holds together this continuum of African American dramatists is the knowledge that history provides—for both writers and the characters—what August Wilson's characters who suffer from historical amnesia call a 'starting place.' This book on the role of history throughout the canon of African American drama is an extremely valuable 'starting place' for increased scholarship on the works of African American dramatists."

Sandra G. Shannon, Professor, Department of English, Howard University

Reading Contemporary African American Drama

AFRICAN AMERICAN LITERATURE AND CULTURE

Expanding and Exploding the Boundaries

Carlyle V. Thompson
General Editor

Vol. 15

PETER LANG
New York • Washington, D.C./Baltimore • Bern
Frankfurt am Main • Berlin • Brussels • Vienna • Oxford

Reading Contemporary African American Drama

Fragments of History, Fragments of Self

Trudier Harris, Editor
Jennifer Larson, Assistant Editor

PETER LANG
New York • Washington, D.C./Baltimore • Bern
Frankfurt am Main • Berlin • Brussels • Vienna • Oxford

Library of Congress Cataloging-in-Publication Data

Reading contemporary African American drama: fragments of history,
fragments of self / Trudier Harris. editor; Jennifer Larson, assistant editor.
p. cm. — (African American literature and culture; v. 15)
Includes bibliographical references.
1. American drama—African American authors—History and criticism.
2. History in literature. 3. Slavery in literature. 4. Self in literature.
5. Identity (Psychology) in literature. 6. African Americans—Race identity.
7. African Americans in literature. I. Harris, Trudier. II. Larson, Jennifer.
PS338.N4R43 812'.609896073—dc22 2006101456
ISBN 978-0-8204-8887-5 (hardcover)
ISBN 978-0-8204-8886-8 (paperback)
ISSN 1528-3887

Bibliographic information published by **Die Deutsche Bibliothek**.
Die Deutsche Bibliothek lists this publication in the "Deutsche
Nationalbibliografie"; detailed bibliographic data is available
on the Internet at http://dnb.ddb.de/.

Cover design by Lisa Barfield

The paper in this book meets the guidelines for permanence and durability
of the Committee on Production Guidelines for Book Longevity
of the Council of Library Resources.

29 Broadway, 18th floor, New York, NY 10006
www.peterlang.com

Printed in the United States of America

Contents

Acknowledgments

Atkinson, Brooks. "The Theatre: 'A Raisin in the Sun.' Negro Drama Given at Ethel Barrymore." New York: *New York Times*. Copyright, 1959. Reprinted by permission of the publishers. All rights reserved.

James Baldwin. *Blues for Mister Charlie*. New York: Dell, 1964. Reprinted by permission of The Permissions Company, Rights Agency for Howard University Press.

Wine in the Wilderness by Alice Childress. Copyright 1969. Used by permission of Flora Roberts, Inc.

Reprinted with permission of Scribner, an imprint of Simon & Schuster Adult Publishing Group, from *for colored girls who have considered suicide when the rainbow is enuf* by Ntozake Shange. Copyright 1975, 1976, 1977 by Ntozake Shange. All rights reserved.

Gwendolyn Brooks, "The Sundays of Satin-Legs Smith." Reprinted By Consent of Brooks Permissions.

Introduction

Cracking the Mirror of History

Or, Shaping Identity in African American Drama

TRUDIER HARRIS

In 1959, after the tremendous success of her much-awarded *A Raisin in the Sun*, Lorraine Hansberry was commissioned to write a script on slavery for NBC; it was to "initiate a series of ninety-minute television dramas commemorating the Centennial of the Civil War."[1] Hansberry completed the script and was paid for her work, but the project was never produced. It would be 1972 before even a scene from the drama found its way onto television. The censorship, Hansberry's literary executor and ex-husband Robert Nemiroff speculates, resulted from Hansberry's refusal to allow her characters to live out their expected roles as masters or those enslaved. Instead, she preferred to humanize both groups. Her potential mammy refuses to trade tending to her son for the life of her master, and the master tries desperately, in an effort that can only reap failure, to make slavery better than it could ever be.

That little-known and little-studied Hansberry creation, entitled *The Drinking Gourd*, explores a phenomenon reported historically and one that circulated often in African American oral tradition. An enslaved person surreptitiously learns how to read and/or write, a master or mistress discovers this "forbidden, unlawful" activity, and the enslaved person is punished with blinding or the severing of the writing hand. Hansberry pictures young Hannibal, who, enslaved on a plantation in an unnamed southern state on the eve of the Civil War and in a time of increasing numbers of runaways, wants as urgently to know what the black squiggles on white pages mean as he wants to run away to freedom in the North (his brother Isaiah has "followed the drinking gourd"—the handle of the Big Dipper that points to the North Star—and escaped to freedom). Hannibal unlocks the mystery of reading by exchanging his expertise on the banjo for lessons in literacy from Tommy, the ten-year-old younger son of his white master. Hannibal's refusal to work in the fields leads to his downfall when the black driver follows him to the hidden site where Hannibal meets Tommy. Having just completed a composition on "The Drinking Gourd," Hannibal is eager to have his "teacher" read the composition out loud. Surprising Hannibal during the demonstration of his newly acquired skill, Everett, Tommy's older brother, considers this development the most grating of insults. He has early accused his father, the "good" master, of running the plantation as a "resort for slaves."[2] "*Truly outraged*" (209) and without hesitation, Everett orders the newly acquired overseer to blind Hannibal. Such occurrences, real or imagined, are the stuff of which folklore, history, and literary texts are made.

By finding her imaginative point of departure in an event that makes clear the intersections of history, white supremacy, and African American positionality, Hansberry joins many of her literary brothers and sisters. From their beginnings in America, writers of African descent have found their subject matter in the historical events that shaped their lives. Playwrights are no exception. William Wells Brown, who penned the first play as we know it, entitled his effort *The Escape; or, A Leap for Freedom* (1858). Read at various gatherings but never produced formally, the play echoes slave narratives in selecting freedom of enslaved persons as its primary subject. Pauline Hopkins's (1880) *Slaves' Escape: or the Underground Railroad* (revised as *Peculiar Sam, or the Underground Railroad*) similarly focused on slavery; the play may have been inspired by Brown's work. The pattern of drawing upon historical events for dramatic representation continued in the twentieth century with the many plays that treated lynching in the 1920s and 1930s;[3] with Langston Hughes's treatment of miscegenation in *Mulatto* (1935), which was the first play by an African American that had a successful run on Broadway; William Blackwell Branch's *In Splendid Error* (1954), about John Brown's raid on Harper's Ferry; Alice Childress's *Trouble in Mind* (1955), about the difficulties of black actors and actresses getting substantive roles on the American stage; and with Adrienne Kennedy's *Funnyhouse of a Negro* (1965), which pictured Patrice Lumumba, Queen Victoria, and Jesus as the various "selves" of Sarah, a young black woman whose identity is so unsettled that she opts for a melodramatic solution to her identity crisis.

These playwrights had formidable tasks in accurately representing black subjectivity on American stages. The backdrop against which they worked had been shaped by the tradition of minstrelsy and buffoonery that is so powerfully documented in *Ethnic Notions*.[4] From the slapstick dancing of Jim Crow, through the black-faced minstrelsy era and through the Stepin Fetchit convention in early motion pictures, black people on stage and in the movies were presented in a plethora of stereotypical guises. *Ethnic Notions* documents the dandy, the mammy, the uncle, and the pickaninny; in addition, it showcases household products containing images of blacks in more stereotypical guises. Largely seen as existing for the entertainment of whites, blacks on stage and in the movies were expected to be loud, outrageously dressed, comically (though at times destructively) violent, and always humorous. A serious actor, such as Bert Williams, who would liked to have worked against that tradition, nonetheless found himself subjected to the same blackface and humorous conventions as his far lesser-talented counterparts.

Graduation to representation on stage without being subjected to blackface did not bring an appreciable difference in portrayals. The musical comedy tradition, to which such luminaries as Paul Laurence Dunbar and James Weldon Johnson contributed and which captured the imagination of Langston Hughes, invariably depended for its success upon the lighter side of African American existence. The broader the humor the better. Outlandish costumes and makeup were standard fare in shows that featured the cakewalk, dancing, and singing. Above all, "the Negro" was perceived to be entertaining.

Instead of falling prey to traditional stereotypes, many playwrights, including those represented in this volume, turned to other uses for history. Informed by black people's quest for freedom throughout their history in America, and specifically by Civil Rights activity of the mid-twentieth century, Hansberry, Childress, James Baldwin, Amiri Baraka, Ntozake Shange, Pearl Cleage, August Wilson, George Wolfe, Suzan-Lori Parks, and others cracked the mirror of history to reveal black folks who were not always grinning the Sambo grin.[5] They explore possibilities for black people to define themselves without assuming the stereotypical portrayals of history, but by transforming that history into meaningful fuel for forward progress. Hansberry's Hannibal does not die from his wounds. Rather, he succeeds in transcending slavery for the short time that he read and wrote. More important, he succeeds in transforming his mother's attitude. Rissa, usually Christian and long-suffering—and simultaneously proud and fearful when Hannibal reads from the Bible—steals her master's gun and gives it to Hannibal's girlfriend, who will lead the blind Hannibal and his young nephew (son of Isaiah) to freedom in the North. Everett, the villain who ordered that Hannibal be blinded, may attempt to obliterate the effect of Hannibal's reading and writing achievements, but they will always be written upon his mind, and he will assuredly miss the valuable property that Rissa has helped to escape from the plantation. Hannibal's achievements will also be written upon the minds and imaginations of the black people who remain in the quarters. They are witness to the fact that Hannibal defined himself in terms other than those coming from the warped imagination of his so-called master. That reformulation of identity might inspire them to similar attempts to define and free themselves. By refusing to accept the status of "slave" that has been carved out for him, Hannibal opens possibilities for self-definition that characterize many of the central figures of African American drama from the mid-twentieth century to the beginnings of the twenty-first century.

Overview

Reading Contemporary African American Drama begins with an essay on Lorraine Hansberry's *A Raisin in the Sun* (1959). A classic in American drama and an iconic touchstone in African American drama, there is barely a high school student who is unfamiliar with the play. Fewer, perhaps, are familiar with African American labor history and the up-by-the-bootstraps philosophy of Booker T. Washington. It defines black people, first of all, as manual laborers. If blacks learned to work with their hands, Washington believed, whites would recognize their essential place in the society and the economy and would gradually enable them to achieve greater things. The "dignity" of working with the hands, Washington posited, was just as significant as working with the mind. Both were crucial to the shaping of African American identity. In "'Education has spoiled many a good plow hand': How Beneatha's Knowledge Functions in *A Raisin in the Sun*," Rachelle S. Gold tackles the Washington philosophy and its shaping of identity in relation to Beneatha Younger, the questing college-student daughter in the play who embraces her African roots as well as her African American history. Washington's philosophy becomes a fertile ground for the exploration of Beneatha's character, for critics mainly ignore Beneatha in attempts to put forth Walter Lee or Mama Lena as the dominant character in the play. Gold illustrates what careful attention to the slightly shadowed character of Beneatha can reveal about the consequences of history, the shaping of identity, the purposes to which education is put, and the price of progress in mid-twentieth-century Chicago.

The history that informs Matthew Luter's "*Dutchman*'s Signifyin(g) Subway: How Amiri Baraka Takes Ralph Ellison Underground" is a history of influence. How does a writer define himself or herself against a tradition of writers? For Leroi Jones turned Amiri Baraka, creating space to be a writer meant rejecting other writers—or so he asserted anyway. Luter argues that for Baraka, like many of his contemporary African American writers who had the shadow of Ralph Ellison hanging over their heads, Ellison is indeed a major influence in spite of Baraka's protestations to the contrary. Luter bases his argument on an encounter in Ellison's *Invisible Man* (1952) that arguably could have served as the basis for Baraka's controversial *Dutchman* (1964). That encounter centers upon black male/white female interaction, which is shaped by a history of mythology, folklore, and factual occurrences, including the history of lynching. Dual identity issues, then—how to be a black male writer in America and how to be a black male in America—inform Baraka's creation. For Clay Williams, Baraka's protagonist, the space of a New York subway and a history of oppression restrict him in ways that force him, finally, to have his "Hannibal moment"—the moment of self-discovery, self-recognition, self-definition.

Richard Henry, in James Baldwin's *Blues for Mister Charlie* (1964), similarly has a fatal moment of self-discovery. Meredith M. Malburne posits, however, that death is only the beginning of Richard's significance in the play. Through applying theories of abjection in "No Blues for Mister Henry: Locating Richard's Revolution," she asserts that Richard's body in death has more significance than he would ever be able to reap in his actual lived life. Malburne therefore reads through Baldwin's history of race relations to illustrate how that history is far less despairing than an initial glance would make it seem. Certainly young black men ran the risk of being killed in the South, especially if they were in any way verbally or physically assertive, but the threats that loomed over their heads were not ultimately the dominant force in their lives. Just as Hannibal knew the consequences of learning to read and write, so does Richard know the consequences of challenging the man known as the most virulent racist in his hometown. Yet Richard issues the challenge, and the results, Malburne suggests, are much more complicated and far richer than previous critics have allowed for in their readings of this at times unwieldy drama.

African American women, too, try to define themselves against a historical backdrop of centuries of misrepresentation. It is bad enough when the images come from outside the culture, but what about those instances in which black people, both male and female, stereotype black women? How can an individual black woman fight back and try to define herself? Alice Childress offers answers to these questions in what Joy E. Cranshaw maintains is a subtle and at times slippery examination of the intersections of race, class, and gender in *Wine in the Wilderness* (1969). Often subdivided in discussions of African American literature, with race being the primary card played, these intertwining categories make it difficult for black women to assert their definitions of themselves. So is the case with Tomorrow ("Tommy") Marie, who, during a riot in an urban area, encounters other blacks who view her as "the messed up chick" fit only to fill the negative role in an artist's mind of what society has done to black women. Against a history of mammyism, uncouthness, and asexuality frequently identified with black women, Tommy attempts to show her definers that she can be just as middle class as they—in spite of her wig and her mismatched clothes. Childress's presentation and Cranshaw's exploration of it in "African Queens and Messed-Up Chicks: Representations of Identity in Alice Childress's *Wine in the Wilderness*" leave lingering questions: When will black people learn to appreciate their inherent beauty, not that wrapped in the packages of beauty as defined by the larger culture? Is it possible for well-educated black women to find black male partners? Can the gap between those blacks who handle English well and those who are prone to confuse subjects and verbs ever be bridged? And where is the ground on which class, gender, and race simply do not matter anymore? Can one ever escape the burdens of race and history?

One way of dealing with that problematic history, Ntozake Shange argues, is for "colored girls" of all ages to come together in bonds of comfort and support. In successive generations, the problems of history become the problems of childhood and are replicated in the warped adult psyches that Shange portrays. By examining Shange's refusal to compartmentalize childhood and adulthood, Pamela Hamilton, in "Child's play: Ntozake Shange's Audience of Colored Girls," suggests that the too-old-to-be child mentalities and the too-young-for-seeming-adulthood representations in *for colored girls who have considered suicide when the rainbow is enuf* (1976) reflect Shange's self-positioning as an African American griot of sorts who is determined that young black females not grow up as uninformed about life as she did. Through language/storytelling/narrative, action, movement/dance, color, symbolism, and imagery, Shange creates a world in which girls as young as twelve can enter to gather lessons for the difficulties of womanhood. By reconsidering a play usually thought to be exclusively for grown-ups, Hamilton invites viewers and readers to reposition Shange from her previously held slot of angry black woman to guide, teacher, counselor.

While narrative has its virtues, movement across vast expanses of American soil prove equally useful to black women in defining and redefining themselves. In "Flyin' 'Anyplace Else': (Dis)Engaging Traumatic Memory in Three Plays by Pearl Cleage," Benjamin Sammons explores how movement is crucial to the formation of identity. In *Flyin' West* (1992), Cleage draws upon the history of westward movement that resulted in the "Exodusters" and the founding of several all-black towns in the southwest; in *Blues for an Alabama Sky* (1995), she represents black Southerners relocated to New York who envision moving to Paris; and in *Bourbon at the Border* (1997), she follows Civil Rights workers from the Deep South to a residence in Detroit from which they can see the Canadian border. In each instance, black women injured psychically and physically try to find wholeness in ways that will enable them to escape the burdens of personal and communal history, whether that history is lynching in Memphis before moving west or violence in the South during Civil Rights demonstrations. Invoking trauma theory, Sammons explores how Cleage's characters attempt to find wholeness and reasons for moving toward the future in worlds where there is much more darkness than light in their circumstances.

History that other playwrights may draw upon casually was the raison d'etre for August Wilson's creative output. The dean of late twentieth-century African

American playwrights and winner of two Pulitzer Prizes, Wilson set the task for himself to create a cycle of plays about African Americans in the twentieth century, from their beginnings in the repressive South, to their hopeful but soon deflated migrations to the North, to their attempts to remake their lives and find work in the North. *Joe Turner's Come and Gone* (1988) revisits the peonage system, the new form of slavery that met black Americans after Emancipation and how it shaped the lives of blacks who migrated from the South to the North. John M. Hannah begins with this history and progresses toward a history of influence, specifically how Wilson's work was shaped by his admitted dependence upon Romare Bearden as one of the "four b's" of his creative imagination (Bearden, Baraka, Borges, and the Blues). In "'A World Made in My Image': Romare Bearden's Collagist Technique in August Wilson's *Joe Turner's Come and Gone*," Hannah undertakes a structural analysis of *Joe Turner* that illustrates meticulously how Wilson replicated the collage technique that dominates Bearden's work in his own conception of character and the structuring of *Joe Turner*. From the titles of artistic works to the naming of characters within those works, Wilson bowed to Bearden again and again in this play. Hannah's essay makes clear that even the most well-known and most well-studied of African American playwrights still invite unique and rewarding approaches to their work.

The same might be said of Hannah's approach to Lorraine Hansberry's influence upon August Wilson. Hansberry and Wilson are obviously the most written-about playwrights included in this volume, yet, though Hansberry preceded Wilson by at least two decades and influenced just about every other playwright who followed her, no scholar has undertaken a systematic examination of how the most decorated African American playwright of the late twentieth century might also have been influenced by Hansberry. Hannah undertakes this examination in "Signifying *Raisin*: Hansberry's *A Raisin in the Sun* and Wilson's *Fences*." In many surprising revelations, he considers a substantial number of ways in which Hansberry's influence upon Wilson is clear, though Wilson himself chose far more obscure playwrights to credit with influencing him. Mirroring Baraka's denial of Ellison's influence upon him, the revelations of careful reading make clear that Wilson knew Hansberry's *A Raisin in the Sun* intimately and that it shaped him deeply. Indeed, his identity as a playwright can be appreciated fully only in the context of Hansberry and *Raisin* as parts of his personal and collective history.

Wilson's domination of Broadway and his role as the darling of American drama critics was interrupted only with the arrival of Suzan-Lori Parks, a little-known playwright who swooped in and won the Pulitzer Prize for drama for *Topdog/Underdog* (2002). The story of Lincoln and Booth, two ominously named black brothers cramped into a single room in an urban area, the play garnered accolades for the power of the writing, the evocation of Abraham Lincoln, and the stars who graced Broadway to bring the play to life, namely Don Cheadle and Mos Def. What happens to identity when one is given a name that has major historical significance? Jennifer Larson answers that question in "Folding and Unfolding History: Identity Fabrication in Suzan-Lori Parks's *Topdog/Underdog*," for not only does Lincoln have the name of the signer of the Emancipation Proclamation, but he works in an arcade where he dons a Lincoln costume, impersonates the president, and watches himself being shot day after day by visitors to the arcade. Booth carries a gun—even at home—and is an expert at shoplifting, particularly fabulous suits. Thus clothes, Larson maintains, make and unmake these characters. Their shapeshifting into various costumes is often matched by a shifting or loss of identity. Who they are as black men with the names of famous white males makes for engaging interaction with their audiences as well as their readers. By unraveling the meaning of classic history to the shaping of their identities through the costuming/clothing that they use, Larson reveals that identity is ever-shifting, ever-unsettling, always as much as part of the exterior as it is part of the interior of human beings.

The performance of identity implied in *Topdog/Underdog* is equally relevant to *Venus*, Parks's 1997 play about the Venus Hottentot, a.k.a. Sarah Baartman, who was born in South Africa and brought to England and France for display of her buttocks and genitalia between 1810 and 1814. As an enslaved woman, it was doubtful that Baartman had any control over her fate. Yet Parks suggests that the history as given to us leaves out another possibility: Sarah Baartman, "The Venus," may have willingly gone to Europe and may have acquiesced in her own debasement for the sake of making money. In "'With Deliberate Calculation': Money, Sex, and the Black Playwright in Suzan-Lori Parks's *Venus*," Jennifer Larson attempts to untangle the implications of this exploitation/victimization paradigm and what it means not only for viewing or reading Parks's play, but what it means for the African American playwright who is similarly positioned in a world where success, or the ability to have one's plays viewed, may frequently depend upon acquiescence in exploitation. Larson's discussion suggests that history that seems so far away, therefore, is really no farther than Broadway or Hollywood.

History as the shaper of African American identity in dramatic representation, then, has been impressively transformed since the nineteenth century, but it is still evolving in the twenty-first century. The white master's notion of who Hannibal should be is echoed in America's conception of Baraka's Clay Williams and where a black man should be and what he should want. However, Parks merges boundaries to show the influence of a history identified with black people only in its mythological implications. Lincoln and Booth were the great actors; black folks were the recipients of Lincoln's largesse. Turning the tables on that history, so to speak, and showing possibilities—even negative ones—for it defining black character in different ways opens a space for black playwrights that portends even more experimentation as the twenty-first century moves along. For the playwrights included in this volume, history is the crucible from which they mold new versions of identity, the stable foot of the compass that keeps them grounded to their ancestors, and the ever-evolving potential for imaginative creation.

Notes

1. Robert Nemiroff, "A Critical Background," in *Lorraine Hansberry: The Collected Last Plays* (New York: New American Library, 1972, 1983), p. 143.
2. Lorraine Hansberry, *The Drinking Gourd*, in *Lorraine Hansberry: The Collected Last Plays*, p. 182.
3. See, for example, Mary P. Burrill's *Aftermath* (1919) and Georgia Douglas Johnson's *A Sunday Morning in the South* (1925) and *Blue-Eyed Black Boy* (1930). Angelina Grimke's 1916 play, *Rachel*, is also classified as a lynching play. See as well the volume on lynching plays edited by Judith L. Stephens and Kathy A. Perkins.
4. *Ethnic Notions*, distributed by California Newsreel, 149 Ninth Street/420, San Francisco, CA 94103.
5. For a study of the impact of Sambo upon American culture as well as upon the lives of black people, see Joseph Boskin, *Sambo: The Rise and Demise of an American Jester.*

Works Cited

Boskin, Joseph. *Sambo: The Rise and Demise of an American Jester.* New York: Oxford University Press, 1986.

Nemiroff, Robert. "A Critical Background," in *Lorraine Hansberry: The Collected Last Plays.* New York: New American Library, 1972, 1983. 143–62.

Perkins, Kathy A. and Judith L. Stephens. *Strange Fruit: Plays on Lynching by American Women.* Bloomington: Indiana University Press, 1998.

1

"Education has spoiled many a good plow hand"

How Beneatha's Knowledge Functions in *A Raisin in the Sun*

RACHELLE S. GOLD

Although few of even the most devoted of Lorraine Hansberry's admirers know it, most stage productions and published versions of *A Raisin in the Sun* (1959) omit a scene that features the Youngers' nosy neighbor Mrs. Johnson. Omitting this scene is unfortunate, for when Mrs. Johnson evokes Booker T. Washington with, "Education has spoiled many a good plow hand," she firmly situates herself in a tradition that privileges industry over scholarship. In contrast, Mama understands the world differently: "My husband always said being any kind of a servant wasn't a fit thing for a man to have to be [. . .] And my boy is just like him—he wasn't meant to wait on nobody" (Hansberry 103). As Mrs. Johnson, who responds by "rising, somewhat offended," sees it, the Youngers are "too much for me! You sure one proud-acting bunch of colored folks" (103). They are, in a word, ambitious, "getting ready to 'move on up a little higher'" (99). Prompted to leave the room by Mama's dismissive attitude, "Is that what old Booker T. said? [. . .] Well, it sounds like him. The fool" (103), Mrs. Johnson is aware that Mama has mocked her assertion. Before she exits, surveying the packed boxes, Mrs. Johnson reflects "You know, me and you ain't never agreed about some things, Lena Younger" (103). When this confrontation is omitted, a scene of clashing ideologies—representing the differing views of African American education embodied by these two black women—is lost to us. But these clashing ideologies, I would argue, do creep into the play, but through a different female character: Beneatha.

As representatives of many other clashing ideologies, it is natural that the Younger women themselves "ain't never agreed about some things." Yet, most critics agree that the female characters Ruth, Mama, and Beneatha, as well as the annoying busybody Mrs. Johnson in *Raisin* are as vibrantly depicted and as headstrong as Walter Lee. Brooks Atkinson, writing in *The New York Times* the day after *Raisin* opened on Broadway in 1959 at the Ethel Barrymore Theatre, praises the actresses for their portrayal of these characters:

> Since the performance is also honest [. . .] *A Raisin in the Sun* has vigor as well as veracity and is likely to destroy the complacency of anyone who sees it [. . .] As the matriarch, Claudia McNeil gives a heroic performance. Although the character is simple, Miss McNeil gives it nobility of spirit [. . .] Diana Sands' amusing portrait of the over-intellectualized daughter; [. . .] Ruby Dee's young wife burdened with problems [. . .]—bring variety and excitement to a first-rate performance. (27)[1]

Atkinson's review highlights the ways in which Hansberry's female roles, as portrayed by the actresses, come to represent character traits such as heroism, nobility, intellect, spirit, humor, and perseverance. He seems to be under the impression that because he perceived the performance as "honest" and full of "veracity" that the actresses are embodying the ideology of their roles. He equates the "first-rate"-ness of their performances with the fact that the dialogue seems to him, mistakenly or not, to have verisimilitude to black life, and that the strength of character of Mama or Beneatha or Ruth was the result of adhering to what he understands as the constituent and representative attributes of black womanhood.

Most scholars, however, focus exclusively on Mama as the locus for critiquing the family's discord and dynamics. This interest in Mama spans at least thirty-five years; for example, Ossie Davis, in "The Significance of Lorraine Hansberry" in *Freedomways* in 1965, reminds us that "everybody who walked into that theatre saw in Lena Younger [. . .] his own great American Mama" (399), and he paints her as a figure with whom audience members would feel comfortable and familiar (400). More recently, Trudier Harris devotes an entire chapter to Mama in her 2001 book, *Saints, Sinners, Saviors: Strong Black Women in African American Literature*, arguing that "Mama Lena Younger is as much a problem in the lives of her family as whites are, and her influence is more immediate and perhaps operates at a more insidious level [. . .] Mama Lena's good intentions are frequently overshadowed by the strong-armed methods she uses to achieve her objectives" (24).

Still, Mama and Ruth dominate the stage as central female characters, which might prompt an audience member to inquire into how a less central character who is not a primary plot-mover, such as Beneatha, figures into the play. Indeed, so many critics write about Mama that the preponderance of critical examination of her begs the question: why is there a dearth of scholarly work about her daughter? By way of a partial answer, we can look to Amiri Baraka (1987), who writing twenty-one years after Davis, summarizes Beneatha's situation: "She is already socially mobile, finding a place, as her family cannot, among other petty bourgeois aspirants on the rungs of 'education' where their hard work has put her" (14). While audience members do not dismiss Beneatha because of her class aspirations, it is noteworthy that both she and her mother are ambitious, but Beneatha is unaware of the sacrifices that are necessary for her to climb socially, while Mama is all too aware. In fact, Mama clearly understands that the $10,000, which signifies what her husband was forced to sacrifice, could very well be the means that lead to social mobility to which Baraka refers.

This chapter takes as its point of departure Baraka's observation that Beneatha is able to climb the ladder of upward mobility "on the rungs of 'education' where [her family's] hard work has put her" (14). In other words, Mrs. Johnson, mouthing the sentiments of Booker T. Washington, may be right; "Education has spoiled" Beneatha, but perhaps not in the way that Mrs. Johnson envisions it has. Arguably, because Beneatha embodies many of the complexities that Hansberry desired to portray, audiences see Beneatha as a character to whom we are attracted, while at the same time, about whom we raise serious questions. As we admire her altruism in her desire to heal the sick, simultaneously, we puzzle over her self-centeredness to send her robe to the cleaners and to buy a fifty-five-dollar riding habit. As we value her commitment to expressing herself through activities such as guitar, photography, and drama, we wonder at her inability to dedicate herself to one hobby or her seeming inability to comprehend her family's finances. She is at a critical nexus between new modes of expressing herself as being a black woman that resist categories and old ways of expressing herself as a black woman that confine her. When she substitutes the values she learned in her internal home sphere with the cultural and ideological values that she learns in college, an external sphere, her family finds her threatening. Compassionate and yet judgmental, she is both peripheral and central to the play's action. Her role juxtaposes the old and the new, and as a mixture of these two perspectives, she is complicated because of her paradoxical nature. Thus, the play introduces its audience to a corrupting element of education and engages the artistic and intellectual debate over the role of education in black communities.

Hansberry, too, some would argue, was spoiled by her education, some of which she received formally at the University of Wisconsin from 1948 to 1950, at the University of Guadalajara in 1949, and at Roosevelt University in 1950. She also learned less formally while studying art and writing at the New School for Social Research in the summer of 1950, as well as by studying African history and culture under W.E.B. Du Bois at the Jefferson School for Social Science in 1953 (Carter, 1991 viii). But Hansberry gained her political education, to a great extent, while working as a journalist for Paul Robeson's monthly newspaper *Freedom* from 1950 to 1953. Ben Keppel, in his book *The Work of Democracy: Ralph Bunche, Kenneth B. Clark, and Lorraine Hansberry and the Cultural Politics of Race* (1995), claims that "Hansberry spent her political and professional apprenticeship under FBI surveillance as an associate of Paul Robeson, the most known leader of the African-American left in the late 1940s and early 1950s" (179). Reared in a middle class home, Hansberry was influenced by her uncle, William Leo Hansberry, an Africanist at Howard University who introduced her to Robeson and Walter White when she was a young woman (Carter 8). Hansberry inherited a belief in the Du Boisian legacy of "The Talented Tenth" from her uncle and through her education, political activism, and artistry, made a distinctive contribution to the legacy in her own right. This is the educational and political background, then, that provides the back-story for the character who is to become Beneatha, modeled by Hansberry's own admission, after the playwright herself.

In an interview with Nan Robertson for an article in the *New York Times,* which appeared days before *Raisin* opened on Broadway, Hansberry describes Beneatha in this way: "[Walter Lee's] kid sister Beneatha—she's a mess. She's me eight years ago. I had a ball poking fun at myself through her. A precocious young female, very outspoken, way out. Says things like 'There is no God, momma. Shut up.' I never dreamed of being a doctor like Beneatha, but I don't disagree with anything she says" (X3). It is clear by this description that Hansberry's authorial feelings toward Beneatha are favorable and sympathetic. Beneatha, then, is the focus of this chapter, and it is Beneatha whose seeming contradictions Baraka describes:

> She is, on the one hand, secure in the collegiate world of "ideas" and elitism, above the mass; on the other, undeceived by the myths and symbols of class and status. Part militant, part dilettante, "liberated" woman, little girl, she questions everything and dreams of service to humanity, an identity beyond self and family in the liberation struggles of her people. (14)

Considering these contradictions and considering Hansberry's admission that Beneatha is the playwright herself at age twenty-one, why is she not a more central character? To rephrase a question that plagued the nuns in *The Sound of Music*: "How do you solve a problem like Beneatha?" One could posit that Beneatha, a mix of sympathetic and unsympathetic traits, is more than comic relief and an ideological agitator in the play. Does her education merely "spoil a good plow hand," and make her unfit for the domestic work that literally occupies her family? Or will she use her education in the way that Du Bois envisioned when he wrote in "The Talented Tenth" in 1903 that "The Negro race, like all races, is going to be saved by its exceptional men [. . .] From the very first it has been the educated and intelligent of the Negro people that have led and elevated the mass" (33–34)? While

Beneatha does imply that she would like to use her medical skills to heal people, it is unclear that she wishes to lead and "elevate the mass." Because she is not a man, she would have been omitted from Du Bois's vision. Noticeably, neither was Hansberry a man, and thus, she too would have been excluded from Du Bois's original views, yet she carved a space for herself as a female representative of "The Talented Tenth." As one of few women playwrights writing before the Black Arts Movement, she represented a fuller and more sophisticated picture of black womanhood than the male Black Arts Movement playwrights would later offer, a picture that included Beneatha as an example of a deeper and richer feminine character.

Although she did not graduate from college, Hansberry used the knowledge that she gained at the colleges she attended to advance her skills as a writer and to produce a play that addressed controversial topics, but which was disguised as a family drama. On March 1, 1959, Hansberry delivered a speech entitled "The Negro Writer and His Roots: Toward a New Romanticism" (1981), boldly advocating: "The question is not whether one will make a social statement in one's work—but only what the statement will say, for if it says anything at all, it will be social [. . .] The Negro writer has a role to play in shaming, if you will, the conscience of the people" (5, 10). Hansberry spoke to a major black writers conference convened by the American Society for African Culture a mere two weeks before *Raisin*'s Broadway premiere, and these sentiments express a profound passion about the role of the artist in society ("Negro Writer" 2). Her views, certainly shaped by the seriousness with which she approached her new responsibility in the literary limelight, reflect the way in which Hansberry used her education to compose an intensely political play which she hoped would move her own ethnic community forward. In contrast, because she is still a student, Beneatha has yet to achieve anything tangible with her political views, that is, a protest, a voter registration drive, an Emmett Till tribute. But Hansberry did: when *Raisin* was playing at the Schubert Theatre in January of 1959, she composed a letter to her mother:

> Mama, it is a play—that tells the truth about people—Negroes—life—and I think it will help a lot of people to understand how we are just as complicated as they are—and just as mixed up—but above all, that we have among our miserable and downtrodden ranks people who are the very essence of human dignity. (*To Be Young, Gifted and Black* 63)

In this way, Hansberry uses her play as a political tool to feature characters whose portrayals gesture toward humanity and defy the stereotypical caricature roles in productions such as *Porgy and Bess* (1935; revivals, 1942 and 1952) and *Carmen Jones* (1943).

Yet, Beneatha, as she appears to us in the play, seems a candidate unprepared to "elevate the mass." Throughout the play, Walter, Ruth, and Mama tease Beneatha about her distractibility and poke fun at her various suitors and hobbies. Despite her biology and African history classes, she has not yet put her education to any practical purpose. So, Mrs. Johnson's critique of Beneatha's educational pursuits seems quite understandable, "sometimes she act like ain't got time to pass the day with nobody ain't been to college. Oh—I ain't criticizing her none. It's just—you know how some of our young people gets when they get a little education" (102). An apt representative of Hansberry's vision that Negroes be portrayed in the theatre as "just as complicated as they [whites] are and just as mixed up" (63), Beneatha resists the simplistic categories that Mrs. Johnson's worldview affords, which allow her to be either a "good plow hand" or "one proud-acting bunch of colored folks" (103). However, instead of using the knowledge that she learns at college to assist her family, she uses her knowledge to insult her family members, to indulge her whimsical fancies, and to incite rifts within her family rather than to build bridges to understanding.

In writing Beneatha, Hansberry articulates a clearly expanded notion of not only a "new Negro," but also of a "new Woman." Indeed, Anne Cheney, in her book about Hansberry (1981), describes her in this way: "At twenty, Beneatha is very much the new woman: she is planning to become a doctor, she will delay marriage until she completes her training, she doubts God and various social institutions, and she toys with diverse forms of self-expression" (61). Also, Cheney offers an interpretation of her name: "Beneatha is an obvious pun, suggesting her contempt for many traditional ties" (61). Beneatha has opportunities open to her, namely education, delayed marriage to an educated man, professional autonomy and respect, economic advancement, sophisticated cultural entertainment, and international travel. In contrast, Ruth and Mama have not sought these opportunities, and while not openly hostile toward her, they realize that Beneatha has options that they have neither conceived of, nor imagined. Often, but not always, patient with her sassy sister-in-law, Ruth tries to keep Beneatha in her place by reinforcing the generational hierarchy. In the scene that ends with Mama slapping Beneatha, Ruth expresses dismay at Beneatha's ability to overstep boundaries: "Fresh—just fresh as salt, this girl!" (46).

Sharing Ruth's dismay, Mama, incredulous at Beneatha's announcement that she will be taking guitar lessons, asks "Lord, child, don't you know what to do with yourself? How long it going to be before you get tired of this now—like you got tired of that little play-acting group you joined last year? [. . .]. I just wonders sometimes why you has to flit so from one thing to another all the time" (47). Clear-sighted, Mama has a true vision of who her daughter is, naming her fault openly, but Beneatha does not want to admit that she "flits." In fact, there is something to be said for the fact that she aspires to be a Renaissance woman, perhaps inheriting Mama's predilection for "aim[ing] too high" (139), who is accomplished in a variety of hobbies. Framed more positively, Beneatha may be cultivating a range of activities that will allow her to "pass" as middle class, and so she has chosen guitar and drama, because they do not strap the family financially as much as the equipment-intensive hobbies of photography and equestrian training did. By redefining her lack of commitment to any hobby as "expression," Beneatha condescendingly dismisses Mama and Ruth's laughter, with "Don't worry—I don't expect you to understand" (48). This dismissal reinforces the gap that Anne Cheney explains in this way:

> The old world of Lena and the new world of Beneatha are separated by more than forty years of social and political change. The old world looks inward to the kitchen, the family, the home; the new world stares outward at college, medical school, Africa. Since the Younger family is searching for a center, a nucleus, the old and new world cannot orbit peacefully: like stray neutrons, the two worlds were destined to collide. In *A Raisin in the Sun*, Lena and Beneatha clash—sometimes violently. (61)

Beneatha refuses to concede that Mama is right in assessing her lack of commitment as a fault, because doing so would be an admission of fickleness or an admission of the failure of that larger world in which she has been sojourning. If she admitted that her mother's evaluation was correct, she would diminish the knowledge that she privileges by claiming to be a member of the college elite. By this, I mean that Beneatha adopts the cultural values that she learns from college and is in the process of substituting some of her home values with the values that she is learning from this external institution.

Beneatha is, as we know, a first generation college student, and Mrs. Johnson's remark about the value of an education is noteworthy, especially when one considers that Hansberry herself was a student of W.E.B. Du Bois and is a product of his vision of "The Talented Tenth." But both Du Bois and Washington—although they differed greatly in terms of which educational curriculum black students should study and with regard to how black and white people should interact socially—agreed that the education should benefit one's family and oneself. Perhaps because of her youth, Beneatha neglects the responsibility that is part of the privilege of being the first to attend college, and instead of benefiting the family with her knowledge, she belittles them.

Beneatha uses two modes of knowledge to separate herself from her family, one where she merely broadcasts her beliefs, without asking anyone to subscribe to them, and one where she elevates her belief system over theirs, which highlights how Hansberry demonstrates the lack of "understanding" between the generations in the play. For example, after fighting with Beneatha in act 1, scene 1, Walter laments the servile attitude he must adopt at work, "Mama, I don't know if I can make you understand [. . .] You just don't understand, Mama, you just don't understand" (73–74). Beneatha, after telling Mama and Ruth why she wishes to have so many hobbies, exclaims, "Don't worry—I don't expect you to understand" (48) and later dismisses Ruth's inquiry about what kind of qualities a man needs to have to satisfy her, "You wouldn't begin to understand. Anybody who married Walter could not possibly understand" (49). Later in the scene, she explains her atheism: "Mama, you don't understand. It's all a matter of ideas, and God is just one idea I don't accept" (51). Mama is intensely aware of the gap as she intimately shares with Ruth after slapping Beneatha: "There's something come down between me and them that don't let us understand each other [. . .] the other done commence to talk about things I can't seem to understand in no form or fashion" (52). These scenes emphasize the rifts in understanding and show how being misunderstood is one of the major, but perhaps overlooked, themes in the play.

Insulting Her Family: The Triumph of Censure over Sympathy

Through Beneatha's sharp tongue and harsh criticism of Walter, Mama, and Ruth, Hansberry demonstrates how Beneatha does not use her education as a way to enlighten her family, but rather to insult them. Immediately after Beneatha first enters the stage, sensing Walter's disapproval about her career path, when he feigns interest in her schooling, she sarcastically responds to his question, "Lovely. Lovely. And you know, biology is the greatest. I dissected something that looked just like you yesterday" (36). After they bicker about her desire to become a doctor and his irritation that she might accept some of the insurance money, Walter laments "Nobody in this house is ever going to understand me" (38) and Beneatha retorts with "Because you're a nut [. . .] you are a nut. Thee is mad boy" (38). Walter doesn't know that she is quoting from *Antigone,*[2] but she does continue her volley of verbal assaults on him as he exits, "And then there are all those prophets who would lead us out of the wilderness—into the swamps" (38).[3] In this way, she berates him, and although some could argue that she is just teasing and that she has learned to bicker by watching Mama and Walter Lee, Ruth and Mama register their jibes as verbal sparring: Ruth chides Beneatha: "Don't be so nasty, Bennie" (36), and Mama observes "My children and they tempers" (40). In addition to Greek drama class where she is studying *Antigone*, Beneatha must also be taking a Freudian psychology class as evidenced from another insult she hurls at Walter: "Brother is a flip—let's face it" (49), and Mama is puzzled. Ruth clarifies "She's saying he's crazy," but Beneatha corrects: "Not crazy. Brother isn't really crazy yet—he—he's an elaborate neurotic" (49).

She also ridicules her mother when she comments on the little plant that Mama sees as a representation of herself. Making fun of her wish to move her plant to the new house, she asks in a dismissive way: "Mama, you going to take *that* to the new house? [. . .] That raggedy old thing?" (121). Mama successfully defends herself by reminding Beneatha, who "flits" from one hobby to the next, with "It expresses ME!" (121). In this way, Mama is able to deflect the power of Beneatha's insult by using the word "expresses," which is the same word Beneatha uses when claiming what her hobbies do for her. This paradoxical and comic exchange highlights the fact that both Beneatha and Mama are privileging their individual desires over the family unit, which is a departure from the preference for privileging communal needs in the black community. By "flipping the script" in this way, Mama prevents Beneatha's censure from stinging. Later in the play, she employs this technique regarding her lack of knowledge about Africa.

By berating Walter, Beneatha attacks her brother's failure of judgment with these taunts: "There he is! Monsieur le petit bourgeois noir—himself! There he is—Symbol of a Rising class! Entrepreneur! Titan of the system! [. . .] . I look at you and I see the final triumph of stupidity in the world!" (138). She adopts Marxist terms and French vocabulary, learned through her college classes, and uncharitably labels Walter. Wounding his feelings in order to make him feel small, Beneatha showcases her education and wears it like a crown, all the while maintaining a degree of self-righteousness and a self-satisfied attitude with her clever turns of phrase. She chastises her brother soundly when he loses the money that was never hers, but which she, nonetheless, feels some claim to defend. She is vocal and astute about her critique of black men, yet even though he does not understand what she is saying, he understands that the tone is insulting. In this way, instead of using her education to assist her family, she distances herself from her family and uses her education as a wedge to further separate from them.

In another example, after Bobo discloses Willy Harris's disappearance, Beneatha lashes out at Walter as she recounts her tale of self-pity to Asagai. She insults Walter's judgment as she implicates him, "He made an investment! With a man even Travis wouldn't have trusted with his most worn-out marbles"(132). Blaming Walter for her woes, she reduces him to having a childlike intellect, comparing and harshly judging him to be ineffectual and inept. Later, after Walter articulates how he will perform his "step-n-fetch-it" routine for Lindner, Beneatha is disgusted at Walter's planned performance "That is not a man. That is nothing but a toothless rat" (144). Twice, she repeats her view that "He's no brother of mine [. . .] I said that that individual in that room is no brother of mine [. . .] Love him? There is nothing left to love" (145). Unlike Mama who can compassionately forgive Walter for losing the money, Beneatha unleashes her wrath on him and her desire to wound overcomes her ability to put the situation in perspective, as her mother does: "There is always something left to love. And if you ain't learned that you ain't learned nothing" (145). This is another example of Mama using Beneatha's words to "flip the script" and just as before, when she challenged Beneatha's use of the word "expresses," she calls into question the value of what Beneatha has learned, asserting the value of love over anger.

Indulging Her Fancies: Beneatha's Self-Absorption

In the directorial notes, Hansberry describes Beneatha in this way: "She is about twenty, as slim and intense as her brother. She is not as pretty as her sister-in-law, but her lean, almost intellectual face has a handsomeness of its own" (35). Then, the playwright tells us most notably about the way Beneatha speaks: "Her speech is a mixture of many things; it is different from the rest of the family's insofar as education has permeated her sense of English—and perhaps the Midwest rather than the South has finally—at last—won out in her inflection" (35). Her first utterance in the play: "I am going to start timing those people" (35), referring to the bathroom users, expresses both irritation about her living condition and a disgruntled attitude toward her neighbors. Instead of saying "I'm gonna start timin' dem people" which might be the expected locution from a person speaking African American Vernacular English in 1959, Beneatha's language use reveals exactly what Hansberry indicates: her preference for a more standardized pronunciation.

In act 1, scene 1, Walter asks a question designed to provoke Beneatha, after he confronts her about the insurance check that Mama is going to receive: "You such a nice girl—but if Mama got that money she can always take a few thousand and help you through school too—can't she?" (37). Beneatha replies: "I have never asked anyone around here to do anything for me!" to which Walter retorts: "No! And the line between asking and just accepting when the time comes is big and wide—ain't it? [. . .] I don't want nothing but for you to stop acting holy 'round here. Me and Ruth done made some sacrifices for you—why can't you do something for the family?" (37). Perhaps because he is not grateful for what Ruth and Mama have done for him, he projects his attitude onto his sister and perceives Beneatha as ungrateful for Ruth and Mama supporting her endeavors. Regardless of Walter's motivation for asking the question, his inquiry is a reasonable one considering that all the other adults in the household work, yet Beneatha does not bring any income in to either defray household expenses or pay for her costly hobbies. In fact, she does not seem to contribute to the family in traditional ways, such as chores, but Hansberry is silent about other ways in which she might help at home.

Rather, Beneatha engages in indulgent luxuries, such as the photography equipment, guitar lessons, and equestrian classes mentioned above, perhaps because she thinks that she is superior to her family members, perhaps because of the education, or because she is too self-centered to think about the way in which her spending choices affect the family. What might shock any reader who considers the financial situation of a family living in a 1959, Southside Chicago apartment where tenants must share a bathroom is that when Mama asks Beneatha where her robe is, Beneatha tells her that it is "in the cleaners" (40). This choice reflects her lack of consideration for her family's economic circumstances. Her mother and sister-in-law work to support her expenses, but Hansberry does not address why Beneatha does not work to subsidize her tuition or to contribute to the rent or why having a garment cleaned is preferable to washing it at home.

To further support the notion of Beneatha's self-centeredness, I look to Elizabeth Brown-Guillory, whose article "Black Women Playwrights: Exorcising Myths" (1987) portrays Beneatha typifying "the evolving black woman" (235). Brown-Guillory calls attention to *Raisin*'s conclusion: "the play ends without Beneatha making a serious commitment to anyone or anything except her dream of becoming a doctor. Preoccupied with taking care of herself, Beneatha rejects the idea that her happiness or completeness hinges upon guidance or support from a man" (235).[4] Unlike Mama and Ruth, Beneatha, who knows she is a product of the working-poor, wants to have all the extracurricular experiences of the middle and upper classes. Also, she rejects traditional roles prescribed for black women. She behaves as if she has the leisure to "express herself" through her avocations, which is a sign not only of the family's potential for advancing their socioeconomic status, but also a sign that the "new Negro woman" will be able to experiment with modes of expression that were heretofore reserved for men and for the middle and upper classes. Earlier in the play, Mama quickly calls Ruth back to reality about the woman's race, gender, and class status in society and how unchangeable she believes it is; indeed, Beneatha is not deluded enough to think that the insurance check will alter her class status because she understands that class boundaries are less permeable than Mama and Ruth think they are. Suggesting that Mama use some of the money to take an international cruise, Ruth offers: "Shoot—these here rich white women do it all the time" and Mama counters with "Something always told me I wasn't no rich white woman" (44).

Unlike her mother, Beneatha does not see why she should be denied the privileged experiences that come with a higher-class status, and because she is spoiled, she permits herself the desire to have as full a collegiate experience as anyone else, black or white, male or female. Defensive about the questions that Mama puts to her about her experiments with photography, acting, guitar, and horseback-riding, Beneatha replies "I don't flit! I—I experiment with different forms of expression—[. . .] People have to express themselves one way or another" (48). After Mama inquires about what exactly she wants to express, Beneatha, according to the directorial remarks, "angrily" responds "Me!" (48). Part of the reason for her defensive reply is that after she says "Me!", the stage directions indicate that "Mama and Ruth look at each other and burst into raucous laughter" (48). Because they laugh at her, Beneatha is forced to become keenly aware of the gap in experience between the life that she leads at school and the life that Ruth and Mama lead at home. A few lines later, Ruth, prompted by Mama's attempt to change the subject by asking about whom Beneatha will be dating that evening, mocks Beneatha. Beneatha says "George Murchison" and Mama, thinking perhaps she has found a way to connect with her daughter about her beau, innocently asks, "Oh—you getting a little sweet on him?"(48). Instead of letting Beneatha respond, Ruth interrupts, "You ask me, this child ain't sweet on nobody but herself—(*Underbreath*) Express herself!" (48). From this interaction, we can glean that Ruth is resentful of, or at least bothered by Beneatha's focus on herself and that Mama is skeptical of Beneatha's ability to remain committed to one enriching activity exclusively and to one man. Since Beneatha changes her hobbies frequently, perhaps, Mama may wonder, she will change her mind about her interest in becoming a doctor? Ruth's comment can be read as an indication that she pauses over the fact that Beneatha is not sacrificing much, yet she is reaping the enjoyment of a life of leisure, while the other women work to support the recreational activities that she so casually changes from one semester to the next.

When she retorts, "Don't worry—I don't expect you to understand" (48), Beneatha patronizes Ruth and Mama and asserts that her knowledge is more valuable than their knowledge. Expressing her preferences and opinions, she is arguing the perspective that artistic self-expression is vastly more important than consistency in one's actions or hobbies and more important than physical labor. By disregarding the fact that her mother is providing her with some insight about her character, Beneatha is oblivious to her mother's prompting that she look seriously at her tendencies. Yet, she desires self-expression, not self-reflection. Unlike Beneatha, Ruth and Mama "know" what it takes to run a household, and Beneatha, who does some chores on the weekends, seems to be disinclined to work. In the scene in which Mama slaps Beneatha, Ruth gently critiques Beneatha's resistance to work, "I wish certain young women 'round here who I could name would take inspiration about certain rugs in a certain apartment I could also mention" (46). Decidedly opinionated, Beneatha has no plans to clean homes, or cook for people; she leaves the domestic sphere to go to college, to learn African dance, and to go to the theatre, which are also ways of leaving the family. At the end of act 1, after Walter has asserted that "Money is life," Mama laments: "You my children—how different we done become" (74). Like his sister, Walter rejects what Mama has to say: "You just don't understand, Mama, you just don't understand" (74). So, when each representative of a different generation perceives his or her knowledge to be superior, a gap in understanding will always remain.

Critics have praised Beneatha as sassy, savvy, knowledgeable, and college educated. Yet, it is noteworthy that while Mama and Walter, it can be argued, progress and develop as characters in the play, Beneatha, in the directorial parenthetical notes, is just where she was at the beginning of the play, petulant and argumentative. The note tells us that she responds "Angrily, precisely as in the first scene of the play" when she yells at Walter, "What have you got to do with who I marry!"(150). Catered to by her family, Beneatha, even as an outspoken woman who represents what the future may hold for black society and education, is spoiled and indulgent.

Beneatha's knowledge represents conflict between herself and her family members as well as how that knowledge is rooted in her intellectual training at college. Like Richard Rodriguez who writes in his autobiographical work, *Hunger of Memory* (1982), about becoming alienated from his Mexican immigrant family as a first generation college student, Beneatha's political and religious views separate her from the people she loves. As illustrated in the scenes in which she indulges, insults, and incites rifts, her knowledge reifies that she prefers the core values advocated at the university over the core values that she inherited from her home sphere. In order for "The Talented Tenth," of which Beneatha is the fruition of a Du Boisian perspective, to succeed, the elite and well-educated need to often throw off the home values and dissociate with some of the cultural views that incubated them. Beneatha's ideas, at twenty-one, are not homegrown; they initiate as a result of her education. In fact, more often than not, Beneatha asserts her knowledge in order to differentiate herself from her family members.

Sometimes, however, Beneatha does share her view, in a neutral and inoffensive way. She merely tells her family how she feels, but the sense is that these ideas just exist. The knowledge seems innocently offered, rather than thrown in their faces. One might interpret her comments about her views on marriage, her awareness of birth control, and her assessment of Lindner in a very innocuous way and assume that she offers them in a spirit of show and tell—a "Here is what I learned at college today" type attitude. Keeping in mind notions of understanding and misunderstanding, Beneatha uses knowledge regarding six different topics, half of which are presented benevolently and half of which are presented antagonistically.

Telling and Showing: Beneatha's Broadcasts

First, in terms of her views of marriage, she questions not when, but "if" she will get married: "I'm not worried about who I'm going to marry yet—if I ever get married [. . .]—Oh, I probably will [. . .] but first I'm going to be a doctor" (50). Independent and headstrong, she rejects Asagai initially and questions whether she will get married, which was a nearly scandalous notion in 1959. Yet, when women were often economically dependent upon marriage, she still wishes to contemplate romantic relationships, for she believes, "there is more than one kind of feeling which can exist between a man and a woman" (62). Asagai counters with "No. Between a woman and a man there need be only one kind of feeling. I have that for you" (62). While she protests what she initially perceives as his lustful intentions, she refuses to merely accept what she thinks is a sexual proposal, defending her virtue by dismissing him: "I'm not interested in being someone's little episode in America" (63). Yet, at the same time, she allows herself to be smitten with Asagai's marriage proposal "Mama, Asagai asked me to marry him today and go to Africa—[. . .] (*Girlishly and unreasonably*) To go to Africa, Mama—be a doctor in Africa" (149–50). She wants to be able to flirt with notions of delaying marriage or avoiding it all together; yet, Ruth, Mama, and Asagai derail her notions of alternative types of relationships quickly.

Second, instead of expressing full joy and exuberance over Ruth's pregnancy, which would be a normal response, especially within the black folk community in 1959, she expresses shock, asks where the child is going to live, and is surprised that Ruth and Walter didn't "plan it" (58). By indicating that she understands the intricacies of birth control: "Did you plan it or was it an accident?" (58), she indirectly discloses to Mama and Ruth that she knows how to plan a pregnancy. Although the play is situated in a time before the pill and before *Roe v. Wade*, she knows how to avoid getting pregnant.

Third, she reads Karl Lindner accurately, but even as she offers her suspicions, both verbally and nonverbally, she conveys a sense of pride about the fact that she was the first one in the family to figure out that Lindner is not a benevolent neighbor. She is sassy and self-assured, showcasing her astuteness. When confronted with Lindner's explanation of what the Clyborne Park Improvement Association does, and before he offers the family money not to move there, the stage directions indicate that she "is watching the man carefully" (115). Later, after Lindner claims "that our Negro families are happier when they live in their own communities" (118), according to the directorial notes, Beneatha responds "with a grand and bitter gesture" uttering this ironic retort: "This, friends, is the Welcoming Committee!" (118). By this time, Ruth and Walter have figured out what Beneatha has already intuited. Lindner, trying to salvage the conversation, makes "A very generous offer" and an indignant Beneatha responds with "thirty pieces and not a coin less" (119).[5]

Beneatha's experiences dealing with middle-class white people at her college teach her to be more skeptical about what news Lindner could wish to share with the family on their home turf. Thus, the fact that she does not work as a domestic or a chauffeur, in this case, is an asset rather than a deficit, in that she has learned the ways that institutional racism can rear its ugly head and how to read between the lines for the rhetoric of bigotry, disguised as praise of racially segregated housing: "but you've got to admit that a man, right or wrong, has the right to have the neighborhood he lives in a certain kind of way" (117). Again, misunderstanding plays a central role in the scene. Lindner even tries to make overtures to solidarity by representing his community as "hard-working, honest people who don't have much but those little homes and a dream" (117). Interestingly, he is the one who feels misunderstood: "There is always somebody who is out to take advantage of people who don't always understand" (117), and after Walter tells him to leave, Lindner says, "Well—I don't understand why you people are reacting this way" (119). In this way, Beneatha's accurate suspicion of Lindner shows her skepticism of white institutions, but she does not demean her family, as the examples that follow show her doing.

Yelling and Shoving: Inciting Political Gaps and Religious Rifts

Unlike the benign examples I just mentioned, some of Beneatha's remarks are made purposefully to divide her family and to highlight the rift between her belief systems and theirs. By showcasing her opinions, she is enforcing a separation between an "us" to which Beneatha belongs and a "them" to which the rest of the Youngers belong. Her intention with her remarks about George's family, her knowledge of Africa, and her proclamation of atheism are designed to elevate her status as the astute, worldly, and savvy one in a family of domestics and servants. Three examples show the ways in which Beneatha's knowledge incites rifts in her family that enforce a hierarchy between what she understands and what they understand about the world. It is her formal education that grants her knowledge about the class barriers in the United States, about her African identity and colonialism, and about atheism.

First, unlike Ruth and Mama, Beneatha is aware of the class barriers that exist in her relationship with George. In fact, Beneatha is shrewd enough to know that George is unlikely to marry her because she is from a different class; he is not downwardly mobile. Because Beneatha and her family are upwardly mobile, Ruth and Mama believe that George could help them as they rise from the ghetto; yet, Beneatha knows that George reaps no benefit in that equation. She clarifies:

> if the Youngers are sitting around waiting to see if their little Bennie is going to tie up the family with the Murchisons, they are wasting their time.[. . .] Besides, George's family wouldn't really like it.[. . .] The Murchisons are honest-to-God-real-live-rich colored people, and the only people in the world who are more snobbish than rich white people are rich colored people. I thought everybody knew that. (49–50)

Here is another way in which Beneatha subordinates her family's knowledge of the world and critiques what they understand by elevating the value of what she understands.

George agrees with Mrs. Johnson's perspective in that he envisions college not as a place to gain knowledge, but as an economic stepping stone to ease into the business world, completely disconnected from learning—which is the polar opposite from the way that Beneatha imagines it. This difference in collegiate expectations is related primarily to class in that George needs to jump through the hoop of college in order to inherit his father's business; his class position is stable. He desires greater wealth, but not greater knowledge. On the other hand, Beneatha thinks of college as a way to expand her mind, to express herself creatively, and to develop her ideas. When George, being brutally honest and tactless, tells her, "I don't go out with you to discuss the nature of 'quiet desperation' or to hear all about your thoughts—because the world will go on thinking what it thinks regardless" (96–97). Beneatha replies, "Then why read books? Why go to school?" George, who according to the directorial notes expresses "artificial patience" and then counts on his fingers, responds, "It's simple. You read books—to learn facts—to get grades—to pass the course—to get a degree. That's all—it has nothing to do with thoughts" (97).

Beneatha is stunned by this revelation and sees that the gap that separates her worldview from George's is nearly as wide as the gap that divides her from her family. Her views fit neither in George's upper-middle-class, bourgeoisie world, nor in her family's lower-class world; residing in a kind of no-man's land, Beneatha exists in a marginal space, not fully buying into the cultural values of the class to which she is supposed to aspire and not satisfied with the class to which she currently resides. It is as if the experience of college provides a bridge between the realm that she can claim and the realm that she dwells in; it is a kind of passing. Yet, despite the social lubricant of learning to speak correctly, and her adoption of middle-class avocations, she is not wholly comfortable in either realm. She rejects the shallowness, elitism, and superficiality of George's world and rejects the pat answers that religion provides to her mother; her family understands her aspirations, but not fully, for they may think that George can help her realize her dreams of becoming a doctor by providing her with the social class for which that profession will be a natural outgrowth. But they do not realize that he cannot satisfy her intellectually or emotionally.

After this clear articulation of how he understands the role of knowledge in his worldview, Beneatha has little to say beyond: "I see. Good night, George" (97). When her mother questions whether she had a nice time or not, Beneatha tells her she did not because "George is a fool—honest" (97), and Mama counters with "Well—I guess you better not waste your time with no fools" (98).[6] Before exiting to the room that they share, Beneatha looks at her mother and thanks her "for understanding me this time" (98) which implies, of course, that she often feels misunderstood.

Second, regarding Mama's knowledge of Africa being confined to Tarzan and saving people from heathenism, Beneatha treats her mother rudely and pleads with her, assuming she will embarrass her upon meeting Asagai, "Well, do me a favor and don't ask him a whole lot of ignorant questions about Africans. I mean do they wear clothes and all that—[. . .] I'm afraid they need more salvation from the British and the French" (57). Mama responds, intimating that her feelings have been hurt, "Well, now, I guess if you think we so ignorant 'round here maybe you shouldn't bring your friends here" (57). By insulting her mother's knowledge, Beneatha congratulates herself for what she knows about Africa, information that she prizes more highly than her mother's feelings or her mother's good intentions of donating money to the missionaries.

Third, when Mama and Beneatha are discussing her future professional plans, Mama tells Beneatha "'Course you going to be a doctor, honey, God willing." Beneatha replies that "God hasn't a thing to do with it" (50). Mama is shocked: Beneatha counters with "Well—neither is God. I get sick of hearing about God. [. . .] I'm just tired of hearing about God all the time. What has He got to do with anything? Does he pay tution?[. . .] It's all a matter of ideas, and God is just one idea I don't accept.[. . .] There simply is no blasted God—there is only man and it is he who makes miracles!" (50–51). Beneatha's atheism is not homegrown; it must initiate as a result of her education. She imposes her college-influenced ideas about atheism on Mama and blasphemes in her mother's house in reference to her disbelief or skepticism about the existence of God. She should believe in God based on the way she was reared, but her collegiate experiences and readings in politics encourage her to question God's existence.

Beneatha bridges knowledge that she learns from college with knowledge that she learns from her status as a triple minority (poor, black, and female), and she is a force of incredible power, boldly expressing both her religious views and her civil rights values. Beneatha represents many anxieties that white audiences might have about the evolving type of Negro that she embodies. She is a budding feminist, educated, knowledgeable about her African heritage, skeptical about religion's role as a pacifying force, and sensitive to how class barriers restrict her from certain social relationships. She seems to be a central character, yet is really rather marginal to the main plot. She is paradoxical on both structural and theoretical levels. Complex and charismatic, her position in the play is murky. She is loveable and frustrating, unimportant, yet pivotal. She is absolutely one of the most memorable characters, vital to the character development, and yet she is irrelevant and expendable to the main conflict in the play. Walter Lee losing the money to Willy Harris could easily be accomplished without Beneatha being in the play at all.

As I have shown, Beneatha uses her knowledge for self-expression and self-promotion rather than for the family's gain. Her hobbies are only for self-development; she does not sacrifice any of her desires, and they do not enrich the family in any way. I am convinced that Beneatha's youth and inexperience contribute to her desire to be a "know-it-all." She has a privileged position in the family as the lone representative who goes out to meet well-educated whites, and she learns a great deal in that environment.

In the social and the political critique that Hansberry offers, it seems as if Hansberry is providing in Beneatha a self-critique or a critique of a Du Bois/Washington educational curriculum debate. She is certainly commenting on the full spectrum of how education "has ruined many a good plow hand" (103) in Beneatha's case, or at least according to the neighbor Mrs. Johnson in the original version. Mrs. Johnson feels slighted by Beneatha, who, politely but "crisply," responds to Mrs. Johnson's inquiry about school.

She considers herself superior to other family members, yet she herself does not occupy a central space as far as what action is necessary for dramatic tension to be heightened. Is she a caricature of a Du Boisian "Talented Tenth" personage? Why is she so difficult to categorize? Although she provides comic relief and window dressing, which seem like slight contributions to the play, she offers valuable insight as a politically idealistic woman who would like to heal the sick. Preferring to occupy a space as a character who is conflicted about the competing ideas in her head and in her heart, she refuses to be defined by any one of her characteristics, instead. Are we ambivalent about the fact that she is narcissistic and altruistic; she flits, and yet wants to be taken seriously?

Beneatha's dual moves of enforcing an ideological separation and elevating her own status enable her to demonstrate that both she and her preferred knowledge source, white higher education, are superior. The gap speaks for itself, and the threat is that the longer Beneatha attends college, the wider the rift will become, so that Mama's pronouncement "You my children—but how different we done become" (74) seems truer and truer. Ironically, the means by which Beneatha will step higher to an elevated socioeconomic status requires that she reject the views of the very people who have enabled her to attain that education. Beneatha uses her knowledge as a way to differentiate herself from her family, but one mode is rather neutral and one more intentionally incendiary. She does contribute in positive ways, but they are less clear, and involve her solidarity with Walter Lee and Ruth when Lindner offers the payoff.

Informed by her exposure to ideas from college, Beneatha continues to think and respond argumentatively, oppositionally, and defiantly as she confronts Lindner in the scene I have just described, but she wields that sassiness and assertiveness when dealing with Asagai's intentions toward her, George's political and personal behavior, and Mama's religious beliefs. Presented as a curious thinker who really does want to heal people, Beneatha is an idealist and a political realist, an ethnic outsider at college, and an ideological outsider in her own family. As a woman trying creatively to explore the complexities of relationships between women and men, she too is a traditionalist, paradoxically tied to the courting rituals of her time, yet, thoughtfully considering alternatives to those conventional relationships.

Beneatha is often described in praiseworthy terms, despite the fact that she is indulgent, instigates discord with her mother and brother, and introduces subversive ideas into her family sphere. She delights viewers with her intelligence, charm, wit, as well as her political optimism and naiveté. Yet, if one scratches the surface and examines the character more closely, one finds a less central figure, whose self-centeredness betrays a lack of sensitivity to her family's limited financial resources, an ignorance about how much her mother and sister-in-law do to support her monetarily, and a resentment that Walter Lee and Ruth are going to have a baby, which will further crowd the already crowded apartment. In all of these ways, Beneatha is paradoxical, ambiguous, and contradictory, exemplifying the clashing ideologies that inform and are woven through the play. If Booker T. Washington is right and it is true that education "has ruined many a good plow hand," Mrs. Johnson may be right about Beneatha as well. Or perhaps Asagai is correct when he suggests, upon looking at Beneatha, "This is what the new world hath finally wrought" (137).

Notes

1. Atkinson, Brooks. "The Theatre: '*A Raisin in the Sun*.' Negro Drama Given at Ethel Barrymore." *New York Times*. Copyright, 1959. Reprinted by permission of the publishers. All rights reserved.
2. "Thee is mad" from Sophocles' *Antigone*, the Chorus, line 914.
3. Curiously, Beneatha refers to Jesus' time in the wilderness, while earlier in the play she claims to be an atheist.
4. It is ironic to consider that Hansberry herself was being supported by her wealthy Jewish husband, Robert Nemiroff, who after he had earned a sizable sum of money in music publishing, made it possible for Hansberry to stay home and devote herself exclusively to writing, rather than to the newspaper, editing, and sewing work she had done earlier to support herself.
5. It is curious, here, to note that Beneatha, who claims "I don't believe in God. I don't even think about it" (51) would use a biblical allusion to Judas Iscariot selling Jesus to the Roman soldiers as the metaphorical reference to Lindner trying to buy her family out of moving into Clyborne Park.
6. Interestingly, Beneatha calls George a fool, and Mama agrees. In the omitted scene, Mama uses the same word to describe Booker T. when she talks to Mrs. Johnson.

Works Cited

Atkinson, Brooks. "The Theatre: '*A Raisin in the Sun*.' Negro Drama Given at Ethel Barrymore." *New York Times*. March 12, 1959. 27.

Baraka, Amiri. "*A Raisin in the Sun*'s Enduring Passion." In *A Raisin in the Sun* and *The Sign in Sidney Brustein's Window*. Ed. Robert Nemiroff. Expanded Twenty-Fifth Anniversary Edition. New York: Plume, 1987. 9–20.

Brown-Guillory, Elizabeth. "Black Women Playwrights: Exorcising Myths." *Phylon*. 48.3 (3rd Quarter, 1987): 229–39.

Carter, Steven. *Hansberry's Drama: Commitment and Complexity*. Urbana and Chicago: University of Illinois Press, 1991.

Cheney, Anne. *Lorraine Hansberry*. Boston: Twayne Publishers, 1984.

Du Bois, W.E. B. "*The Talented Tenth*." *The Negro Problem: A Series of Articles by Representative American Negroes of Today*. New York: James Pott & Co., 1903.

Hansberry, Lorraine. *A Raisin in the Sun* and *The Sign in Sidney Brustein's Window*. Ed. Robert Nemiroff. Expanded Twenty-Fifth Anniversary Edition. New York: Plume, 1987.

———. "The Negro Writer and His Roots: Toward a New Romanticism." *The Black Scholar: Journal of Black Studies and Research*. 12.2. (1981): 2–12. (First publication of a speech Hansberry delivered on March 1, 1959, at the American Society of African Culture).

Harris, Trudier. *Saints, Sinners, Saviors: Strong Black Women in African American Literature*. New York: Palgrave, 2001.

Keppel, Ben. *The Work of Democracy: Ralph Bunche, Kenneth B. Clark, and Lorraine Hansberry and the Cultural Politics of Race*. Cambridge: Harvard University Press, 1995.

Nemiroff, Robert. (Adapted by) *To Be Young, Gifted and Black: A Portrait of Lorraine Hansberry in Her Own Words*. New York: Samuel French, Inc., 1971.

Robertson, Nan. "Dramatist against Odds." *New York Times*. March 8, 1959. X3.

Rodriguez, Richard. *Hunger of Memory: The Education of Richard Rodriguez*. New York: Bantam, 1982.

2

Dutchman's Signifyin(g) Subway

How Amiri Baraka Takes Ralph Ellison Underground

MATTHEW LUTER

At the end of chapter 11 of Ralph Ellison's novel *Invisible Man* (1952), Ellison's unnamed narrator has been dismissed from the Liberty Paints factory hospital following shock treatment and will soon begin boarding with Mary Rambo after being banned from his previous lodging at the Men's House. Disoriented and afraid, he takes a dimly remembered subway ride to Harlem:

> Out of the grounds and up the street I found the bridge by which I'd come, but the stairs leading back to the car that crossed the top were too dizzily steep to climb, swim or fly, and I found a subway instead.
>
> Things whirled too fast around me. My mind went alternately bright and blank in slow rolling waves. We, he, him—my mind and I—were no longer getting around in the same circles. Nor my body either. Across the aisle a young platinum blonde nibbled at a red Delicious apple as station lights rippled past behind her. The train plunged. I dropped through the roar, giddy and vacuum-minded, sucked under and out into late afternoon Harlem. (250–51)

At the end of the ride, the narrator is still unsettled and woozy, but since chapter 12 begins "When I came out of the subway," readers have no indication of what, if anything, transpired on the train. A few key details in this brief scene, however, point to another major work in the African American canon—Amiri Baraka's play *Dutchman* (1964).[1] Though the images are not precisely the same (the woman on Baraka's subway, for instance, is a redhead, not a blonde), the salient features of this brief scene—white temptress, unassuming black man, subway, apple—are the same.

What is a critic to make of this: parody or coincidence? Is Baraka mining this passing moment in Ellison's novel for dramatic material for his own use, claiming to reveal what might have transpired on the subway ride over the chapter break? And if so, why might Baraka gravitate toward this scene in particular over other episodes in *Invisible Man*? In this chapter I argue that Baraka's play is an attempt at revision of Ellison in order to advance an alternate aesthetic that more directly attacks white (especially white liberal) racism and that offers his own explanation of the relationship between black art, political action, and the role of the individual. To reveal his disdain for Ellison's politics and aesthetic, which struck Baraka as too Eurocentric, Baraka employs the techniques that Henry Louis Gates has articulated in his description of the tradition of motivated Signification in African American literature. Furthermore, Baraka employs the New York subway as setting not only in order to respond directly to Ellison by using Ellison's images, but also because the subway functions as a site wherein individuals must conform to the predetermined will of the majority, against which they are nearly powerless to resist.

Though readers familiar with both works might find the intertextual echo unmistakable after rereading Ellison's text, this connection has been mentioned in previous criticism only once to my knowledge. In a typically brief piece in *Notes on Contemporary Literature* (1985), Nicholas Canady points out the repetition, further extending the connection in the process to Ed Bullins's play *A Minor Scene* (1966) (2). I propose that this connection is a largely unexplored possibility because the idea of Baraka directly responding to Ellison through *Dutchman* is at odds with the popular image of Baraka the revolutionary playwright. Baraka has long been viewed as the consummate iconoclast of African American literature, offering the tradition something entirely new and rejecting prior black writing as too Eurocentric and bourgeois. This image, propagated by Baraka and largely accepted by many critics, has proven quite durable. As a result, critics who write about Signification, the often playful but usually ideologically informed revision of prior African American works by later writers, have largely excluded Baraka from most Signifyin(g) lineages.[2]

Baraka has long cultivated an image of himself as far removed, both aesthetically and ideologically, from earlier African American writers. His earliest statement regarding his ambivalent relationship with his literary forebears is the essay "Myth of a Negro Literature" (1962), in which Baraka characterizes previous work by black writers as "of an almost agonizing mediocrity" (*Home* 105). While he expresses a love for the blues and jazz that will continue to help define his life's work, Baraka faults Jean Toomer, Richard Wright, Ralph Ellison, and James Baldwin (among many others) for creating work that, even as it may take into account black music or folk traditions also, aspires only to a middlebrow respectability, not the high art status of

Herman Melville or James Joyce (106–7). Only a year later, Baraka would turn to another group with a kind of double consciousness, calling for consideration of "the great Irish writers," who "[taught] the mainstreamers their own language, and revitalize[d] it in the doing," as a useful model for "Black Writing" (1963) in the essay of the same name (*Home* 164). By the time of *Dutchman*'s premiere, Baraka was drawing heavily from Antonin Artaud, French theorist of the "theatre of cruelty."[3] And when *Dutchman* finally took the stage at New York's off-Broadway Cherry Lane Theater in 1964, Baraka's play took the place of a Harold Pinter work and was performed alongside works by Samuel Beckett and later, Edward Albee.[4] It is an odd contradiction: early on, at least, Baraka bemoans the Eurocentricity of African American writing but finds himself drawing from white writers and theorists in his own early plays. In doing so, he cultivates a reputation as an artistic free agent.

Such a take on Baraka's career, though, oversimplifies this writer who is nothing if not difficult to pigeonhole.[5] Clearly he is not out to reject all black writing, as evidenced by later essays in which a deep respect for Baldwin surfaces, in part as a contrast to Baraka's continued opposition to Ellison's aesthetic. By the 1980s, Baraka even writes with surprising approval of Lorraine Hansberry's *A Raisin in the Sun* (1959), long considered a quintessentially assimilationist play and therefore a likely candidate for Baraka's disgust ("*Raisin*"). Still, it would be tough to dismiss entirely the idea of Baraka the maverick, especially since critics who speak of Baraka's re-employment of elements of the works of prior writers come tantalizingly close to acknowledging his Signification on his African American predecessors but never quite admit that Baraka riffs on writers within his own ethnic tradition.

Henry Louis Gates's construction of how Signification works in African American texts could easily describe *Dutchman*. Black writing, he claims, "is often characterized by tertiary revision," a literary reinterpretation that involves three texts: "texts that provide models of form [usually Western, Gates says], texts that provide models of substance [often prior African American texts, he continues], and the text at hand" (121–22). For Baraka, then, models of form come from Artaud especially, but also arguably Albee and Beckett, while the model of substance is often Richard Wright. All of this is in keeping with Gates's subsequent and central assertion that "black writers read and critique the texts of other black writers as an act of rhetorical self-definition" (122). *Dutchman* functions in just this way: as a response to Ellison that co-opts a scene from *Invisible Man*, albeit a minor one, in order to critique Ellison's worldview.

Gates calls such a move "motivated Signification," and his explanation of how the strategy works helps explain the means through which *Dutchman* achieves its literary-historical ends. Motivated Signifyin(g) "functions to redress an imbalance of power, to clear a space rhetorically" (124), or to fill in a lacuna, like the one in

Invisible Man. The later writer critiques the earlier writer's inability to read the figurative other than as the literal (124), evidenced by Ellison's narrator's stylized and symbolically significant underground lair, in contrast with Ellison's depiction of the subway as a relatively literal and unpoliticized space, unendowed with the figurative power it gains in *Dutchman*. In Baraka's play, the subway space itself, not just the interaction that takes place there, is politicized, and hence figurative. Baraka subtly revises the major tropes of Ellison's scene, changing one visible detail, the white woman's hair color, in order to signal a crucial difference—a revision.

Such a revision, Gates argues, "alters fundamentally the way we read the tradition, by defining the relation of the text at hand *to* the tradition" (124). Indeed, such an interpretation of *Dutchman* as site of motivated Signification requires that we view Baraka not so much as the African American literary tradition's revolutionary free agent, but as a writer in constant dialogue with Ellison just as he is with beat poets, Artaud, or jazz/blues musicians. "If black writers read each other, they also revise each other's texts. Thereby they become fluent in the language of tradition," Gates continues (124), and Baraka certainly knows his Wright, Baldwin, and Ellison, even as he maintains an ambivalent, slippery relationship with them.

Curiously, Gates hardly mentions Baraka in *The Signifying Monkey* (1988), though, which seems a surprising omission of a writer so central to contemporary African American writing. In a chart that helps Gates present relationships of Signification visually, Baraka is on the same axis temporally as Ishmael Reed, Toni Morrison, and Alice Walker and the same axis thematically as Richard Wright and Sterling Brown—but he is directly connected to no one (112). The implication is that Baraka somehow operates outside of the flow of Signification. Later in the text, Gates allows Kimberly Benston's reading of Baraka's "Crow Jane" poems through W. B. Yeats's "Crazy Jane" poems as an example of Signifyin(g) (123). That is the closest we get to Baraka doing any motivated Signifyin(g) within Gates, and in this instance, no other African American text is involved. Nita Kumar reminds us, though, that Gates is among those critics who are unsatisfied by the Black Arts Movement's proposition that art and action are inextricably connected (271). Such an antiessentialist position leads Gates both to the consideration of race as driven by tropes and not by ready-made categories and to an explicit alignment with Ellison. "The blackness of black literature is not an absolute or a metaphysical condition, as Ellison rightly maintains," Gates writes (121). He continues to define as "blackness" "specific uses of literary language that are shared, repeated, critiqued, and revised" (121). Therein is a possible explanation for Gates's dismissal of the possibility of Baraka's Signifyin(g) on other African American writers. If Baraka sees literary blackness as intrinsic and not performative, then he must be simply uninterested in the tropes that comprise Gates's figures of Signification. The lack of interest, then, could be mutual.

William J. Harris draws heavily from Gates in his book-length study of Baraka, explaining that Baraka's "jazz aesthetic" is founded on concepts of reinterpretation that share much of Gates's Signification. Harris argues, though, that Baraka Signifies primarily on white writers, especially William Carlos Williams, Ezra Pound, and Allen Ginsberg (16). While acknowledging the trajectory of Signification that runs from Wright to Ellison to Reed, Harris claims that Baraka seems to operate far outside of that solely African American lineage (22–23). "Baraka's changes are unique among the contemporary avant-garde," Harris claims, "because he is consciously transforming white forms into black ones" (17). Harris allows room for parody and revision of white writers in Baraka's work but dismisses the idea that he could do the same with black predecessors. This widespread rejection of the possibility of Baraka's Signification on black writers contributes to the long-standing image of the playwright as unconnected to—or at least, exceedingly difficult to place within—a larger arc of African American literary history.

My argument for the need to recognize Baraka's motivated Signifyin(g) would be built around a set of moot points, of course, were it not for the contentious relationship that existed between Baraka and Ellison for decades.[6] If their ideological and artistic differences are a war between two opposite aesthetics, Baraka fires the first shot with "Myth of a Negro Literature." In "Philistinism and the Negro Writer" (1966), however, readers find a surprising if indirect repudiation of parts of the earlier essay as Baraka calls *Invisible Man* "[t]he most finely constructed archetypal, mythological novel, utilizing perhaps a Kafkaesque sense of what the world really has become" (59). Where the earlier essay faulted black writers for using literature as a means by which they could rise to the middle class, "'Philistinism and the Negro Writer' revises that image to one of bourgeois black writers forced by American racism to create mainstream art" (Watts 163). The newly Black Nationalist Baraka briefly stops faulting African American authors for using white forms and instead seems willing to embrace any writer who embraces his own blackness.

Perhaps Baraka's clearest and most cohesive response to *Invisible Man* is also his briefest. This reply also helps display how his opinions about Ellison's novel are deeply informed by Baraka's changing politics. In a 1978 interview Baraka points out that *Invisible Man* "rejects Nationalism and Marxism [. . .] in favour of individualism, and individualism can't mean anything for the oppressed people" (*Conversations* 115).[7] This concise, impersonal, intellectually cohesive argument is further revised, however, in a pair of essays appearing in *Daggers and Javelins* (1984), a work characterized by Jerry Gafio Watts as predictable, "caught in a fifty-year time warp," and full of "unsophisticated 'Marxist' claptrap" (437, 443). The attack on *Invisible Man* here is more strident and at times supported with dubious chronology. Baraka claims Ellison's work is accepted by a white literary mainstream primarily because it moves African American writing away from Wright's protest work and into a less threatening direction. Watts notes, though, that Baraka gets his literary history wrong here: Baraka says that the establishment embraces Ellison only after Baldwin's *Blues for Mister Charlie* (1964) and the questioning of nonviolence therein gets rejected. This argument is tough to accept, given that *Invisible Man* won the 1953 National Book Award, more than a decade before the premiere of Baldwin's play (440–41).

In Watts's estimation, Ellison functions by now as a straw man for Baraka: of course he can attack Ellison in an essay that claims to discuss "revolutionary literature," especially when Baraka's real concern is protest literature, a camp with which Ellison never did align himself (441). To further confuse things, Baraka now refers to "Myth of a Negro Literature" as "an early and somewhat confused essay" (*Daggers* 326). At this point Baraka never fully repudiates the argument of the earlier essay; instead, he adds to it by claiming that all non-white-males' and all nonrevolutionary literatures suffer due to an enduring but conservative tendency to elevate "backward" writers like Henry James and Nathaniel Hawthorne (326).

Whether readers view Baraka's changeability as natural artistic development, frustratingly stubborn inconsistency, or slippery Signification on his own prior works, the distinct phases of his career (Beat poet, Black Nationalist, third-world Marxist) complicate our ability to read a clear trajectory of how Baraka responds to *Invisible Man*. In all phases, though, Ellison's novel remains a key text against which Baraka defines himself. Perhaps the best conclusion is that he never fully rejects or embraces *Invisible Man*. Instead, a deeply ambivalent relationship with Ellison's work drives Baraka to respond to it directly: he Signifies on it in order to show some amount of respect for it but also to right its perceived wrongs.

Of course, Ellison has responded to Baraka's work as well, and the differences of opinion displayed through Ellison's review of Baraka's book of music criticism *Blues People* (1963) illuminate the two writers' varying views of what black art should aspire to be. Ellison claims that the blues are "an art form" and not about "obvious political protest" (*Shadow* 257)—clearly Baraka would disagree, given that his book is largely about the sociopolitical significance of blues music. Furthermore, Ellison claims that major black jazz and blues artists are not as separatist as Baraka would allow, arguing that even antiestablishment bop artists want "their fair share of the entertainment market" as much as they want to express themselves (*Shadow* 252). The for-us-by-us and future Marxist Baraka would disagree here too. In fact, Ellison's claim that the "'concord of sensibilities' which has been defined as the meaning of culture allows for much more variety than Jones would admit" seems to prefigure decades of critiques of Baraka's writing about African American literature as overly prescriptive (*Shadow* 252). While Benston accuses Ellison of a deliberate oversimplification of Baraka's book, advanced in order to serve his own explanation of the blues ("Tradition" 343), the contrast between the two attitudes toward the blues remains critically useful.

The *Blues People* controversy is about far more than music, though. At its core the discussion is whether African American art should be defined more in American terms, as Ellison would have it, or in African terms, for which Baraka advocates. Benston sets up this binary via a contrast between "the changing, ever-becoming activity fundamental to African culture and the formalistic impulse of Western art" ("Tradition" 338). Baraka draws this contrast himself between process and product in "Hunting Is Not Those Heads on the Wall" (1964), explaining the difference between what he calls noun-centric and verb-centric art. "Art-ing is what makes art, and is thereby more valuable" than mere thought, he explains, creating a verb, "art-ing," that can encompass both process and product (*Home* 175). Ellison faults Baraka for not being product-oriented enough, for "giv[ing] little attention to the blues as lyric, as a form of poetry. He appears to be attracted to the blues for what he believes they tell us of the sociology of Negro American identity and attitude" (*Shadow* 248). Ellison, more interested in the noun, looks to the blues as text. Baraka, drawn to the process, or verb, sees the blues as act.

In Baraka's mind, of course, the act of art is still informed by thought. As Clay articulates it in *Dutchman*, that thought is often murderous. The central idea of Clay's tirade is the relationship between art and action, as expressed in his claim that "If Bessie Smith had killed some white people she wouldn't have needed that music" (35). For Clay, art replaces violence and vice versa since black artists have so sublimated their rage at white institutions. Benston agrees that "even the 'blackest' musical expression, according to Clay, sublimates what it reflects, erecting barriers to full psychic realization as it mediates insight and gesture" (*Performing* 207). Baraka seems to agree with the character he has created. "Even in our art we are using symbols," he has explained, "[b]ut to be direct is to invite death" (*Conversations* 257). Ellison, Baraka would argue, is not being direct at all in a novel like *Invisible Man* since he hides his main character behind anonymity and his artistic identity as an African American writer behind an overly Eurocentric aesthetic. Clay, however, invites death through his directness, but ultimately "chooses death by being content with words" (Sanders 144). Conversely, Lula's decision to act is rational, a murder that can be seen as self-defense, given that Clay has revealed a murderous rage (Sanders 145). Clay argues that violence, in self-defense or not, can be rational. At the end of his diatribe, he foresees the day that white people will be killed by blacks in rebellion who will "murder you . . . and have very rational explanations" (36).

Central as it is to Baraka's plays, violence is not the only meaningful thought behind effective art in Baraka's aesthetic. Direct but encoded criticism of his predecessors—arguably motivated Signification in its purest form—plays an important role in *Dutchman* also. Ellison, hopelessly Eurocentric in Baraka's mind, admits that while race is a concern in his work, it is far from being the only concern—he shares with Baraka a desire to utilize his own early influences in his own work. In the introduction to *Shadow and Act* (1964), Ellison explains that "the act of writing requires a constant plunging back into the shadow of the past where time hovers ghostlike" (xix). Ellison's language of haunting implies that for him, literary ancestors are inescapable. For Ellison, this reconsideration of history's (and literary history's) effects on the writer was inextricably tied to the imperative he felt to define the role of Euro-American literature within his set of influences and artistic practices. In sorting this out, he experienced what he calls "a struggle to stare down the deadly and hypnotic temptation to interpret the world and all its devices in terms of race" (xix). Having resisted this temptation, Ellison viewed himself as free to draw influence from anyone, hence his claim that "while one can do nothing about choosing one's relatives, one can, as artist, choose one's 'ancestors.' Wright was, in this sense, a 'relative,'" as was Hughes. Ernest Hemingway, T. S. Eliot, André Malraux, Fyodor Dostoyevsky, and William Faulkner were ancestors (*Shadow* 140). Eliot, especially, was a touchstone for Ellison: while at Tuskegee, Ellison read T. S. Eliot's *Waste Land*, which he recalls "seized my mind," and Ellison's "conscious education in literature" consisted of reading the works cited in Eliot's infamous footnotes (*Shadow* 159–60). When Lula belittles Clay's self-definition in *Dutchman* as a "black Baudelaire," Lula's derision can be read as an encoded critique of Ellison's appreciation for Eliot. While it would be tough to call *The Waste Land* entirely Eurocentric, Baudelaire is certainly present there. Compared to Ellison, Baraka is not as forthright in discussing his ancestors, though his attacks on writers whose work he finds distasteful are well documented. It is a shrewd, if misleading, move on Baraka's part, since it allows him to write unencumbered by the psychic weight of a lineage that he has chosen to take on his shoulders himself. It may not, however, lessen the impulse toward critical assessment of ideological opponents.

If Baraka feels such an imperative to respond to Ellison with an aesthetic and political critique, then why use the admittedly minor scene at the end of chapter 11 of *Invisible Man* as the theoretical site for such a piece of motivated Signification? What prevents *Dutchman* from taking place in a setting resembling Liberty Paints, or Ellison's narrator's underground home? I propose that the subway is the only place for the type of argument Baraka wants to make, given the existing trope of the underground space in African American literature (a trope which allows Signification to take place) and the cultural, political, and theoretical associations of the subway itself.

A brief look at the cultural history of the New York subway is a useful starting point. Two details here are important: since its inception, the subway is a space fraught with anxiety, although the causes and effect of that anxiety have changed over the course of the twentieth century. Furthermore, the subway, more than any other cultural institution, has come to represent New York City as a whole in the public imagination, within the city and elsewhere. Michael Brooks, in his outstanding study of the changing cultural image of the subway, *Subway City: Riding the Trains, Reading New York* (1997), reminds us that early in the century, the comparison of the subway to Dante's hell was common in the popular press, equating a ride through the subway with a journey into a menacing underworld (1). The trains were quickly embraced, though, even as they came to be plagued by overcrowding and did not receive air conditioning for decades. The subway "as a symbol [. . .] starts by expressing faith in the city's future and, once built, quickly becomes a handy rhetorical tool for expressing discontent with its present" (Brooks 3). For better or for worse, this ambivalent relationship between New Yorkers and the subway continues to this day, but things have shifted considerably since the early part of the twentieth century, when the subway was a technological wonder but still vaguely threatening.

Eventually, as Garrett Zeigler reminds us, "the subway effectively 'settled' New York, turning it from a collection of loosely integrated neighborhoods into a cohesive and powerful economic unit" (290). And while a typically modernist simultaneous celebration and suspicion of industrialization did lead to some anxiety regarding a trip through what Baraka calls "the flying underbelly of the city" (3), only in the mid-twentieth century did riders begin to fear that the underground tunnels could be a genuinely dangerous space (Brooks 193). If the subway seemed ominous in its early years, this was largely due to its novelty and the unfamiliarity of underground travel. Later, the object of fear becomes other subway passengers, or as Zeigler explains, "The fright emphasis, then, shifts from the train to its occupants" (293).

Complicating this fear is the fact that the subway represents the city itself. The New York subway can function as a synecdoche, "a vital part of the physical city which can easily be made to represent the urban whole," Brooks asserts, expressing a symbolic quality of the subway that can have wide-ranging implications (2–3). If the subway has made nearly all points in New York equally accessible, and the subway can serve as a convenient stand-in for the city, then "[a]ll places become equally accessible, therefore specific place no longer matters" (Zeigler 287). As a result, events associated with the subway, even if the train in question is actually beneath the surface far, far across town, are much closer to home psychically. Brooks explains: "To most New Yorkers a murder at the corner of Westchester Avenue and Castle Hill Avenue happens in a far distant place but one on the Pelham Bay line is next door" (194). A violent act on a subway car, then, no matter who it involves, where it actually occurs, or how unusual the circumstances, seems equally possible under any other given set of circumstances too.

Therein lies one reason the violence in *Dutchman* is so chilling for audiences both then and now: that train could be anywhere, and its space is open to all, no matter that the action is literally beneath the surface, dramatizing those tensions that similarly lie beneath the surface of American race relations.[8] Even worse, there was no plan for dealing with subway violence in 1964, the year of *Dutchman*'s premiere. Brooks recalls the 1965 murder of a Brooklyn teenager, which he describes as the first "actual murder on the subway" to capture large amounts of public press, noting that in that year, the New York Transit Authority tried out "a pathetic system in which a tollbooth attendant, aware of a crime in progress, would press a pedal with his or her foot, thus setting an amber light blinking on the street level" (194). Add this very practical concern to the list of potentially frightening aspects of Baraka's play, and the reasons *Dutchman* must take place on the subway become clearer: the New York subway circa 1964 is a place both familiar and novel—or as Leslie Sanders says, "historical and mundane" (140)—governed by generally understood rules but supporting no viable enforcement of them.

Given that the subway, then, is a space fraught with interaction that has potential to be exciting or violent, benign or malignant, and that New York in the 1960s was becoming arguably *the* international center for economic and cultural exchange, it should not be surprising that artists and writers began to turn to it as much for subject as for image. It also became a prime space for enacting a literary theme central both to the African American and the larger American literary traditions—the conflict between the individual and the community. The role of the individual is not only the central concern of *Invisible Man* with which Baraka has deep reservations, it is also the point at which the two major critics of subway culture from whom my argument draws, Michael Brooks and Garrett Zeigler, differ in crucial ways. Artists and writers of the subway, Brooks claims:

> recognized that the challenge the crowd poses was ultimately political. At a time when democracy was threatened from within by a vapid consumerism and from without by the rise of dictatorships, they sought to vindicate the crowd, to assert its essential dignity.
>
> All of these writers and artists conceived the crowd as possessing a certain cohesion. For all their careful attention to individuals, they shared a conviction that the crowd could be thought of in the singular. It was ultimately one crowd, not two indifferent or hostile ones colliding in a common space. But even the unified crowd contained divisions of class, race, ethnicity, and gender that could not be ignored. (158–59)

To this argument I raise two objections: first, Brooks downplays here the important role that the subway plays for African American writers who want to depict difference, for whom the subway crowd is anything but cohesive. My second objection, borrowed from Zeigler, is that such a construction leaves little room for individuals to assert selfhood. It becomes far too easy for the individual to be subsumed into an anonymous crowd.

Even after largely eliding the implications of the subway's crowd mentality for African Americans (or for that matter, any non-white-males), Brooks does offer multiple examples of early- and mid-twentieth-century writing by African Americans, such as Rudolph Fisher's "The City of Refuge" (1925), James Weldon Johnson's *Black Manhattan* (1930), and Langston Hughes's *The Big Sea* (1940), that depict the train ride to Harlem, a district thriving in part due to its new accessibility via subway, as a kind of exodus to a promised land (185). Furthermore, the history of the trope of the underground space as a place of refuge in African American literature has relevance to *Dutchman*'s subway setting. In addition to Ellison, Baraka recalls Richard Wright's "The Man Who Lived Underground," whose protagonist Fred Daniels, framed for murder, disappears into the sewers, where, in David Pike's words, "he finds himself with ready access to everything that had been refused him above" (21). While stealing, he existentially rationalizes his thefts by asserting that he steals things (including cash and diamonds) not for the sheer value of them and that he would have no problem with being stolen from in return. He winds up wallpapering his underground lair with money, displaying the worthlessness he sees in bourgeois concerns. In the end, however, Daniels is shot by police who either refuse to believe him when he confesses what he has and has not done, or otherwise, think him insane. Like Clay in *Dutchman*, Daniels winds up murdered for asserting what is, for both characters, irrefutable truth.

Wright's story paves the way for Ellison's narrator to disappear into his underground lair, covered not with money but with light bulbs, hence including a striking image of inescapable whiteness while letting Ellison's narrator, like Wright's, attack white-controlled capitalists by stealing electricity.[9] Furthermore, Ellison offers another significant scene, earlier in *Invisible Man* than the one which I propose serves as the starting point for *Dutchman*, in which the protagonist confronts the alleged democracy of the subway space. Not long after arriving in New York, the narrator takes a crowded subway to Harlem, and on the ride he finds himself pressed against a white woman, a physical arrangement that, even though accidental, he knows could easily lead to a lynching in the South. "I wanted desperately to raise my hands to show her that it was against my will," he thinks, and only after freeing one arm does he notice that "when I took a furtive glance around no one was paying me the slightest attention. And even she seemed lost in her own thoughts" (158). After leaving the train, he reminds himself calmly, "But you're up North now" (158). Here Ellison, like James Baldwin in *Another Country* (1962) and *If Beale Street Could Talk* (1974), places a black protagonist on the subway to, in

Michael Brooks's description, "explore situations where racial separation is overtly absent but psychologically present" (185). In Ellison's narrator's case, Brooks continues, his "position in the racially segregated south had been comparatively simple [. . .] in comparison with the new forms of invisibility that he is beginning to experience in the urban north" (186).

This unexpected complexity of social relations on the subway emerges in large part because the subway is a democratic space, but only allegedly. There is no first class or coach on the subway—everyone pays the same fare and shares the same space. And while African Americans were not employed on the subway until the 1950s (Brooks 183), New York subway cars have never been racially segregated by law. None of this means, of course, that the subway has ever been as democratic a space as it may first appear. Baraka's allusion in *Dutchman*'s opening stage directions to "The subway heaped in modern myth" (3) refers not only to the iconic status of the trains themselves, but the modern American myth that a desegregated space is automatically a race-neutral space. Again referencing the latent tensions that drive *Dutchman* and underlie the play's dialogue, Brooks calls the subway "a place of repressed resentments" (183).

Within the text of the play, Lula, in particular, attempts to convince Clay that this allegedly democratic and deracialized space can actually come to be. As part of her elaborate seduction, Lula encourages Clay to pretend with her "that you are free of your own history. And I am free of my history. We'll pretend that we are both anonymous beauties smashing along through the city's entrails" (21). She recognizes that for that to be true, both characters would have to do some quite serious pretending, especially in any universe Baraka creates, in which history and identity are always present and defined by interracial and intraracial conflict alike. Leslie Sanders agrees, referring to the play as a "reenactment of a script written by history and by an innately corrupt white society" (120). Implicit in Lula's line is the fact that such democratic equality, if it could exist at all in *Dutchman*, would be a sham. Of course, Lula hardly seems to value democracy all that highly anyway, as evidenced by her interjection, "yea for America where he [Clay's father] is free to vote for the mediocrity of his choice!" (20).

Connected to this issue of democracy and the relationship between individual power and the subway crowd is Garrett Zeigler's analysis of the subway space in "The Politics of the Third Rail" (2004). Drawing from Michel de Certeau's *The Practices of Everyday Life* (1974; translated 1984), Zeigler argues that urban phenomena like underground mass transit, though appearing to serve the needs of commuters, actually exist to serve the needs of the city and thereby allow no space for individuals to assert autonomous selfhood. Pedestrians above ground are able to resist this consuming flow, Zeigler says, by taking unofficially alternate routes, window shopping, or idling in busy places (285). But, he continues:

> The overarching economies of space and movement that designate the subway do not seem to be subject to the same possibilities of irrationality, individuation, and resistance that mark city streets. After all, one cannot window-shop on the subway, as even to look out the windows is a redundant and useless act [. . .] To idle onboard the subway is impossible: Although a passenger can certainly ride the trains merely to pass the time and with no discernible destination, once the doors of the car close, he or she is enmeshed in a spatial flow that nothing can be done to alter. The passenger on the subway has no choice but to take the route prescribed by the transit officials, the path exactly as it has been laid out on the Map. The only alternate routes possible are those that have already been put in place by the subway's planners: to change trains or take an indirect route is merely to choose a card from a stacked deck. (285–86)

The subway, then, is oddly deterministic and analogous to the ritual element in Baraka. Many readers and critics see a fatalistic inevitability in *Dutchman*: no matter how vehemently Clay resists Lula's teases and asserts his own selfhood and blackness, the play's considerable tensions seem to require everything to boil over in violent conflict. Just as subway lines can end only at predetermined terminals, the plot of *Dutchman* can only end with spilled blood.

Yet even though Clay tries to claim selfhood, Zeigler reminds us that the individual hardly matters at all to the subway as a system, especially as a system that ultimately serves the needs of the city—the masses—and not any passenger in particular. In other words, if Clay and Lula are to ride together "along the city's entrails" as Lula proposes, of course they will be "anonymous beauties"—with the emphasis on "anonymous." Exacerbating this problem further is that common pedestrian modes of rebelling against the preordained traffic flow are not an option when pedestrians choose to become subway passengers. The tunnels, trains, and stations prohibit resistance because they are overdetermined spaces (Zeigler 288). Even passengers on a railroad train, which will (one hopes) stay on well-established tracks, find more freedom and individual space than subway riders: they can switch cars, stretch their legs, watch scenery go by. The subway does not allow this.

As a result, codes of subway etiquette are both cause and effect of what Zeigler calls "a heightened interiority on its subjects, who lack the optic power of rail travelers [who can actually watch scenery when they look out the windows] but who retain [. . .] an elusive strength of individuation" (286). The implication: subway riders who acknowledge the etiquette of the space, which discourages conversation among strangers or even casual eye contact, are forced into an inward gaze (286), which takes the shape of self-reflection or some essentially solitary activity like reading. At the beginning of *Dutchman*, Clay is abiding by these codes strictly: he reads, as a productive middle-class member of subway society might, but also, the stage directions read, "*Occasionally he looks blankly toward the window on his right*" (3; italics Baraka's). When he sees Lula, "*He smiles then; more comfortably confident, hop-*

ing perhaps that his memory of this brief encounter will be pleasant" (4), but the encounter he foresees can take place only because their eye contact constitutes an implicit agreement that he and Lula will break the accepted codes of etiquette together. "*It is apparent that she is going to sit in the seat next to Clay,*" the stage directions continue, "*and that she is only waiting for him to notice her before she sits*" (5).[10]

Lula also violates subway etiquette by not withdrawing into her own world: she starts conversations, and most notably, sits next to Clay on a largely empty car. Her continued disdain for these codes of behavior, externalized by her screams and dancing, embarrasses Clay, and as long as Lula knows she is embarrassing him, she continues her antics in order to make Clay complicit in her rebellion (30–31). By the end of the play, Clay winds up killed not just for speaking the truth, as Fred Daniels does in Wright's story, but for racializing the allegedly ahistorical, democratic space of the subway, which, if the synecdoche works, represents New York and potentially the United States as a whole.

Given the location of Clay's death and its cultural and theoretical significance, it is only apropos, then, that some critics have viewed Clay's speech as a failed attempt at individuated resistance to the totalizing current of a hegemonic white society. Hence Clay's fierce statements along the lines of "Don't you tell me anything! If I'm a middle-class fake white man . . . let me be. And let me be in the way I want" (34) are most appropriately articulated in the subway, a natural site of negotiation of individual identity. If *Dutchman* really is, as Baraka claimed in 1964, "about the difficulty of becoming a man in America" (*Home* 188), it is worth noting that such an encapsulation of the play's plot and themes, even from a playwright who, both before and after *Dutchman*, questioned the value of individualism, highlights a single character and his individual identity.

Clay's problem, as Zeigler explains, is that the overdetermined subway space cannot allow for individuation, so his attempt is doomed to fail. Indeed, Philip Roth's review of *Dutchman* explains that Clay's "life is no more clearly defined for having been acted upon so violently" (Roth 12). Clay "suffer[s] from an inability to enact what [he] perceives" (Benston *Imamu* 17). Most significantly, critics who realize the hopelessness of Clay's attempted resistance sometimes couch their readings in language that also seems to reference the unalterable course of public movement of which Zeigler writes. Kimberly Benston claims that Clay's speech leads to death because it "fails to flow into the [tide] of a collective consciousness and hence collides catastrophically with an intractable world that will not satisfy it" (*Imamu* 5). Jerry Gafio Watts explains that Clay oversteps the boundaries allowed for black self-expression in white society, even as the white majority may be aware of repressed black rage. "Whites merely demand," Watts argues, "that such anger remain repressed, for all that matters to them is how blacks navigate public space" (71). And Baraka himself explains Clay's speech in a 1991 interview: "Clay is being told either you will join us or you are going to be iced. [. . .] It's a matter of being told you are going to ride on this train with us, you're going to go precisely where we allow you to go, you're going to ignore those inner feelings and play the game—or you're going to be killed" (*Conversations* 257). In each reading, Clay has attempted the tragically impossible: aggressive individuation within an overdetermined, racialized space whose movement cannot be resisted successfully.

Well after the curtain closes on *Dutchman*, though, the issues it raises remain on the cultural radar. The popular image of the subway as an urban crucible of sorts is still with us. Jokes about unsafe or just dirty subway cars are a longtime standby of New York standup comics, even though statistically, the subway is quite safe.[11] Especially in the 1970s, the subway served as the ultimate site of violent standoffs in popular film.[12] Continued negotiation of the relationship between the space allowed for individual expression within the crowded cultural space of the subway takes place in the 1970s into the 1980s in the form of subway graffiti, a highly individualized and aggressively countercultural art form that seeks to disrupt the subway's status as a purely functional environment. For Zeigler, graffiti was the visible marker of "a city that had lost control of its planned spaces" in the latter decades of the twentieth century (295). It was no coincidence, then, that the most common subjects of graffiti art were tags, artists' aliases that allowed them to assert selfhood and gain individual notoriety, albeit anonymously so as to evade law enforcement. These artists' primary impetus for choosing such an unusual artistic outlet, they often explained, was rebellion against urban anomie (296). The short-lived art form served as "the very definition of a tactical appropriation of ordered space—it gives legibility to the individual rendered invisible by the totalizing perspective of the planned subway" (296).

These simmering tensions all came boiling over in late 1984 and early 1985, however, with the high-profile and divisive incident involving Bernhard Goetz's vigilante-style shooting of four teenagers who approached Goetz for money on the subway. Just as in the public controversy over what to do about graffiti, discourse involving the Goetz shooting was and still is marked by questions regarding the place of the individual and more notably, intense racialized encoding.[13] Like *Dutchman*, these later incidents prove the truth of Michael Brooks's assertion that the subway "will always figure [. . .] as the place where democratic hopes meet their severest trial" (224).

Ultimately, *Dutchman* could only take place in a subway car. The sense of imprisonment on a path not of one's own making and the conflict between the will of the individual and the community, two societal and personal forces closely associated with this mode of transportation, help cause the tensions that boil over in *Dutchman*'s edgy and climactic final moments. It seems only fitting, then, that the play itself would not spring forth fully formed from Baraka's brow, but instead would be born out of similarly edgy ideological tensions with a literary predecessor. A reading of *Dutchman* based on Henry Louis Gates's idea of motivated Signification does more than simply allow critics of African American literature to trace Baraka's lineage. Such an interpretation forces a critical reappraisal of the popular image of Baraka as the quintessential literary maverick. Kimberly Benston states that "Baraka, like every great revolutionary poet, has realized that he can only begin to say what he is, or wishes to become, by saying what he is not" ("Tradition" 344). If the claim is true that every good writer must define himself in opposition to members of the prior generation, then Baraka's message has come through loud and clear, ever since the days of his earliest and most resounding success. Amiri Baraka may not be the iconoclastic revolutionary who many still assert that he is, but quite decidedly, Amiri Baraka is not Ralph Ellison.

Notes

1. Amiri Baraka was still known as LeRoi Jones at the time of *Dutchman*'s original production and publication. Since this chapter will draw from essays by and interviews with the writer from all periods of his career, I will refer to him throughout as Baraka. One quotation from another critic who refers to him as Jones has remained unchanged.
2. Here and elsewhere in this chapter's references to the African American literary practice of Signification, I borrow the capitalization and bracketed *g* from Henry Louis Gates's *The Signifying Monkey* (1988).
3. See especially Baraka's often anthologized "The Revolutionary Theater" (*Home* 210–15).
4. For insight into the Baraka-Albee connection, see Philip Roth's take on *Dutchman*'s similarity to Albee's *The Zoo Story* in the May 28, 1964, *New York Review of Books* and the heated letter exchange between Baraka and Roth in the July 9, 1964, issue. For his part, Baraka claims to have known Albee and benefited from his support even though the two "have never agreed about anything that I know of" (*Conversations* 144).
5. Indeed, part of the difficulty of writing about Baraka in any stage of his career is the multitude of political and aesthetic positions he has taken over the years. The organization of the William J. Harris-edited *LeRoi Jones/Amiri Baraka Reader* (1991) provides a helpful periodization of Baraka's major ideological concerns.
6. Any attempt to reduce Ellison and Baraka's career-long ideological conflicts to a binary "X vs. Y" conflict with no shared middle ground in between is complicated by Kimberly Benston's reminder that the two writers share more interests and recurring images than many are used to acknowledging ("Tradition" 335). Benston points to common themes and images like "the explicitly Dantesque descent to literal and psychological undergrounds" and "the individual's encounter with tradition" (336). What's more, the two share more influences than either would likely care to admit: five years before Baraka did the same, Ellison looked to Irish writers as models in "Some Questions and Some Answers," even naming some of the same poets as Baraka (*Shadow* 266).

7. For his own part, Ellison admits in the introduction to *Shadow and Act* to his early "attraction (soon rejected) to Marxist political theory" (xxi).
8. Indeed, one of the most often quoted comments from a contemporary review of *Dutchman*'s original production reads the play using language that calls attention to that which lies beneath the visible surface. Howard Taubman observed that if Baraka's play is in fact an accurate reflection of a widely shared African American cultural point of view, then "there's more rancor buried in the breasts of colored conformists than anyone can imagine" (46).
9. See Gates 105–7 for an explanation of Ellison's Signification on Wright.
10. In Leslie Sanders's reading of this scene, Clay "would have understood the danger immanent in the encounter" (142) if he were not so far removed from the South and hence able to see a latent menace in association with a white woman. This reading's emphasis on a black male character's unspoken anxiety at encountering a white woman on the subway owes much to the earlier subway scene from *Invisible Man* discussed above—further evidence that Ellison provides valuable material for critical contrast with *Dutchman*.
11. See Brooks 194–96 for a discussion of New York newspapers' practice of reporting the statistical safety of the subway while using threatening images and headlines that seem to contradict their articles' text.
12. Pike offers close readings of two of the most prominent films of the 1970s to feature subway violence, *The Taking of Pelham One Two Three* (1974) and *The Warriors* (1979), as well as a long list of recent films that include crucial subway-set scenes (12–14, 41–42).
13. Chapter 9 of Brooks's book (190–205) provides a multifaceted discussion of the cultural significance and role of the image of the subway in the Goetz case, focusing specifically on the *New York Post* coverage of the case. Interestingly, Brooks quotes portions of Goetz's taped depositions in which Goetz too expresses anxiety about urban anomie.

Works Cited

Baraka, Amiri. *Conversations with Amiri Baraka*. Ed. Charlie Reilly. Jackson: University Press of Mississippi, 1994.

———. "A Critical Reevaluation: *A Raisin in the Sun*'s Enduring Passion." *A Raisin in the Sun* (Expanded 25th Anniversary Edition) and *The Sign in Sidney Brustein's Window*. Ed. Robert Nemiroff. New York: New American Library, 1987. 9–20.

———. *Daggers and Javelins: Essays, 1974–1979*. New York: Morrow, 1984.

———. *Dutchman and The Slave*. 1964. New York: Perennial, 2001.

———. *Home: Social Essays*. 1966. Hopewell, NJ: Ecco, 1998.

———. *The LeRoi Jones/Amiri Baraka Reader*. Ed. William J. Harris. New York: Thunder's Mouth, 1991.

———. "Philistinism and the Negro Writer." *Anger, and Beyond: The Negro Writer in the United States*. Ed. Herbert Hill. New York: Harper and Row, 1966.

Benston, Kimberly. "Ellison, Baraka, and the Faces of Tradition." *boundary* 2.6 (1978): 333–54.

———, ed. Introduction. *Imamu Amiri Baraka (Leroi Jones): A Collection of Critical Essays*. Englewood Cliffs, NJ: Prentice-Hall, 1978.

———. *Performing Blackness: Enactments of African American Modernism.* New York: Routledge, 2000.

Brooks, Michael W. *Subway City: Riding the Trains, Reading New York.* New Brunswick, NJ: Rutgers University Press, 1997.

Canady, Nicholas. "Ellison, Baraka, and Bullins: A Setting and Two Characters." *Notes on Contemporary Literature* 15.3 (1985): 2.

Ellison, Ralph. *Invisible Man.* 1952. New York: Vintage, 1995.

———. *Shadow and Act.* New York: Random House, 1964.

Gates, Henry Louis, Jr. *The Signifying Monkey: A Theory of African American Literary Criticism.* New York: Oxford University Press, 1988.

Harris, William J. *The Poetry and Poetics of Amiri Baraka: The Jazz Aesthetic.* Columbia, MO: University of Missouri Press, 1985.

Kumar, Nita. "The Logic of Retribution: Amiri Baraka's *Dutchman.*" *African American Review* 37 (2003): 271–79.

Pike, David L. "Urban Nightmares and Future Visions: Life Beneath New York." *Wide Angle* 20.4 (1998): 9–50.

Roth, Philip. "Channel X: Two Plays on the Race Conflict." Review of *Dutchman*, by Amiri Baraka. *New York Review of Books* 28 (May 1964): 10–13.

Sanders, Leslie Catherine. *The Development of Black Theater in America: From Shadows to Selves.* Baton Rouge: Louisiana University Press, 1988.

Taubman, Howard. "The Theater: *Dutchman.*" Review of *Dutchman*, by LeRoi Jones. *New York Times* March 25, 1964: 46.

Watts, Jerry Gafio. *Amiri Baraka: The Politics and Art of a Black Intellectual.* New York: New York University Press, 2001.

Wright, Richard. "The Man Who Lived Underground." *Eight Men.* Cleveland: World, 1961. 27–92.

Zeigler, Garrett. "The Politics of the Third Rail." *Space and Culture* 7 (2004): 283–301.

3

No Blues for Mister Henry

Locating Richard's Revolution

MEREDITH M. MALBURNE

Richard Henry, the African American protagonist of James Baldwin's *Blues for Mister Charlie* (1964), is undeniably problematic. Indeed, the play opens with the gunshot that signals his murder at the hands of white Lyle Britten. As the play oscillates between flashbacks of Richard's life before the murder and the aftershocks that follow his death, Richard becomes defined by his arrogant, defiant, rebellious behavior that teeters precariously between angry insubordination and suicide in his Deep South hometown. Is Richard Henry, as many critics have suggested, no more than a stereotypical provocateur, a cardboard cut-out whose final telos is nothing more than a meaningless, avoidable death at the hands of a white bigot? Is he so predictably problematic that he negates any possibility for fruitful critical discussion?

In order to save Richard Henry from literary oblivion, since he cannot, after all, be saved from death, one must see Richard as both the object of significant historical weight and the small but significant seed of potential revolution. Richard Henry is, according to Baldwin, loosely based on Emmett Till. Like Emmett, Richard's death is dually tragic; not only do both Emmett and Richard *need* to die under the weighty rules of Southern "justice" (and they are both, indeed, murdered), but they are also, ironically, able to accomplish significantly more through their inevitable deaths than they could be expected to accomplish through their lives.

This chapter begins by reclaiming Richard. Using Baldwin's text and the historic precedent that surrounds and guides the play, I seek to relocate Richard as a *multidimensional* and complex character who is neither the suicidal maniac nor the sarcastic savior some critics have tried to make him. By reading Richard, and by reading Lyle, as characters that Baldwin wished to make human rather than uncomplicated *types*, both characters can begin to become more than simply radical representations of black and white. The second half of this chapter uses the psychoanalytic criticism of French critic Julia Kristeva's *The Sense and Non-Sense of Revolt* (2000) and *The Powers of Horror* (1982) in order to better understand the reasons behind the behavior reclaimed in the first section of the chapter. Through a clearer understanding of the reasoning behind the characters' anger, idiosyncrasies, and extremism, the reader can seek to understand them in lieu of dismissing them. Using Kristeva's theories, then, the reader can begin to see how Richard, as a reflection of Emmett, breaks with traditional Southern conformity, permanently alters the father/son cycle that threatens to repeat a racist history, rekindles demands for racial equality, and creates an opening—however small—for the possibility of revolution.

Very few critics have chosen to tackle Baldwin's *Blues for Mister Charlie* at all, while fewer still give serious critical attention to the character of Richard Henry. As scholar Nicholas K. Davis notes in his article "Go Tell It On the Stage: *Blues for Mister Charlie* as Dialectical Drama" (2005), "The most distant reverberations are the continued omissions of *Blues* from such recent and important revisionist studies as Dwight McBride's *James Baldwin Now*[1] and D. Quentin Miller's *Re-Visiting James Baldwin: Things Not Seen*,[2] which cite the play only once apiece, both times in passing" (Davis 31–32). Baldwin's play did not fare significantly better with contemporary critics either. His play is rarely mentioned and, when it is, both the play and Richard are often disparaged as artless, angry, and detrimentally antagonistic.

In 1967, Loften Mitchell offered a relatively kind condemnation of the play and of Richard in *Black Drama*, stating: "The playwright took great pains not to romanticize his black characters nor his white ones—sometimes too much. His leading character is hardly idealized" (Mitchell 201). Tom F. Driver, one of the play's biggest supporters and author of "The Review That Was Too True to Be Published" (1964), further explained the "hardly idealized" Richard, calling him "rebellious and unstable to the point of courting death" (Driver 292). Calvin C. Hernton (1970) notes that reviewers in the *Village Voice* were "saying that Richard got lynched because he 'asked for it'" (Hernton 111), a point John Simon (1975), supports: "Richard taunts Lyle and his dim, mousy wife, Jo, to the point where Lyle kills him" (Simon 48).

What is it about Richard that is so aggravating, so polarizing? Carolyn Wedin Sylvander, author of *James Baldwin* (1980), discusses Richard's "inability to adjust to the racial realities of the Southern town of his birth" by arguing "He is not humble, soft-spoken, or discreet, and he inevitably gets into trouble with Lyle Britten and his wife, Jo, who are representative of white townspeople who can't imagine what has gone wrong with all the 'good niggers' they grew up with" (Sylvander 99). Lyle Britten supports Sylvander's evaluation, saying Richard "might as well have been a northern nigger. Went North and got ruined and come back here to make trouble—and they tell me he was a dope fiend, too" (Baldwin 13). Richard's friends and family, however, present him as both spiritual and spirited; he is remembered at first through two songs—the hymn "His Eye is on the Sparrow" and the blues song "Midnight Special" (Baldwin 16–17). He quickly becomes rooted, therefore, in the black church and the black blues tradition; the reader is readily aware of his Southern community connections.

Such connections are reinforced through the presence of Richard's father, Reverend Meridian Henry, and his grandmother, Mother Henry. The reader meets both characters before s/he meets a living Richard. Both Meridian and Mother Henry begin the play by representing the "simple," "warm-hearted and good natured" blacks the town expects (Baldwin 49). Even after the murder of his only son, Meridian addresses Richard's friends, just back from a protest, warning them that "We can't afford to become too distrustful" (Baldwin 6). Mother Henry offers a similar turn-the-other-cheek mentality when speaking of the white townspeople: "I used to hate them, too, son. But I don't hate them no more. They too pitiful" (Baldwin 16). While the white characters tend to see Richard as defiant, his family and friends—all black—often present him as someone more multidimensional, perhaps projections of themselves. Richard becomes, in these initial presentations, a somewhat similar mix of spirituality and moral superiority.

Richard is not quite the character either side presents, however. Indeed, Richard's first appearance is all the more shocking considering his family and his friends who, despite angry talk among themselves, seem to remain peaceful protesters. Richard, driven home from New York after losing his chance at fame and fortune to a drug addiction, tells Mother Henry he "can't get over" having to return to the "ass-hole of the world, the deep, black, funky South" where he is surrounded by "all these nowhere people" (Baldwin 17–18). His first appearance is angry and frustrated as he insults his surroundings and his family. He is disrespectful to his grandmother and father, telling the former, "It's easy for you to talk, Grandmama, you don't know nothing about New York City," and speaking of the latter: "I didn't want to come back here like a whipped dog. One whipped dog running to another whipped dog. No, I didn't want that. I wanted to make my Daddy proud of me—because, the day I left here, I sure as hell wasn't proud of *him*" (original emphasis; Baldwin 18, 20). Convinced that whites murdered his mother while his father did nothing to avenge her death, Richard tells his grandmother:

> I'm going to treat everyone of them [whites] as though they were responsible for all the crimes that ever happened in the history of the world—oh, yes! They're responsible for all the misery *I've* ever seen, and that's good enough for me. It's because my Daddy's got no power that my Mama's dead. And he ain't got no power because he's *black*. And the only way the black man's going to *get* any power is to drive all the white men into the sea. (original emphasis; Baldwin 21)

Shortly after his tirade, Richard produces a gun in front of his grandmother. Although he surrenders the weapon to her, his seething hatred is obvious. In his introductory scene, Richard appears to flail against anyone and anything he can find: the South, the town, the townspeople, his grandmother, his father, his religion, and the white community in general.

Richard's opening hatred is both quelled and fed by the appearance of his old friend Juanita. With Juanita, Richard becomes increasingly honest and raw. He divulges the secrets of his illnesses—both his addiction to drugs and his obsession with white women. The two become united as he "started getting high" to keep from strangling "some pasty white-faced bitch" (Baldwin 29). Yet, while Richard begins a form of detoxification through his interactions with Juanita, he also finds a new reason to feed his hatred of whiteness. It is from Juanita and her friend Pete that Richard learns of Lyle Britten, and his original encounter with Lyle quickly descends into what could be considered male posturing, if only the stakes were not so high. Lyle jostles Juanita in Richard's presence as he walks by the couple (the intentionality of the act is unclear); already aware of Lyle's reputation as a murderer, Richard boldly (and some critics argue, stupidly) stares Lyle down. Between two men of the same race, such a situation would be less dangerous or would be resolved immediately. Between Lyle and Richard, the situation becomes deadly, as Richard himself knows: "They can rape and kill our women and we can't do nothing. But if we touch one of their dried-up, pale-assed women, we get our nuts cut off" (Baldwin 25).

Intrinsic to this scene is much of the historical weight Baldwin adeptly juggles throughout *Blues*. As Tom F. Driver notes, this play is not about civil rights in the common form; it does not deal with issues of economics or constitutionality (Driver 292). Instead, Baldwin "has described racial strife as *racial* strife, warfare between the black people and white people that is rooted in their separate ways of experiencing life, the difference symbolized in their sexuality" (original emphasis; Driver 292–93). Richard's defiance and arrogance never stray far from the "threat" of black male sexuality. Indeed, Richard's very attitude, the way he "walks and talks like a man who is aware of his dignity and inherent equality as a human being," is read with a "sexual meaning: it is perceived as sexual assault" (Hernton 112). Although it may be empowering to read Baldwin as suggesting that "Negros . . . even studious ones, make love better. They dance better. And they cook better. And their penises are longer, or stiffer" (Roth 41), such a suggestion is not without consequences.

While Baldwin's focus is not simply, as one reviewer noted, "'an attempt . . . to give the Caucasians in the audience a white inferiority complex,'" such a "complex" has certainly been noted by white viewers (unknown reviewer quoted in Littlejohn 73). That "inferiority complex" was often, as it is in this play, combined with the fear of the rape of a white woman by a black man: "if you [a white woman] was to be raped by an orang-outang out of the jungle or a *stallion,* couldn't do you no worse than a nigger" (original emphasis; Baldwin 50). Such "fears" often became excuses that quickly led to the grounds for murder, for "Southern justice," in the form of lynching.

Richard's initial confrontation with Lyle quickly establishes him as a troublemaker, a sexual being who does not seem to "know his place," but it is his second confrontation with Lyle that seals his fate. Richard enters Lyle's store to insult Lyle's wife, his economic standing, and his manhood. Richard speaks to Lyle's wife, Jo, in a mocking manner that is so unexpected, she does not immediately understand what is happening. Referring to two bottles of Coca Cola, he states: "Did you put them in this box with your own dainty dish-pan hands? Sure makes them taste *sweet*" (original emphasis; Baldwin 72). When neither Lyle nor Jo has change for a twenty dollar bill, Richard moves the verbal attack first to the Britten's economic failings and then out of the public sphere of the store and into the personal space of the Britten home; he states "I thought white folks was rich at *every* hour of the day," and then continues, "I only said you was a lucky man to have so fine a *wife.* I said maybe she could run *home* and look and see if there was any change—in the *home*" (original emphasis; Baldwin 72, 73). Richard's second comment is doubly offensive. He comments on a white man's wife, *and* he reemphasizes Lyle and Jo's economic status through the repetition of and emphasis on the word *home.* Jo must work outside the home in her husband's store to maintain their income; Lyle cannot provide for his family in a way that would allow Jo the luxury of raising her son in the comforts of the home.

What began as covertly defiant behavior becomes outwardly aggressive when Lyle demands Richard leave the store *without* his drinks and *without* change for his twenty dollar bill. Richard counters: "You don't own this town, you white motherfucker. You don't *even* own twenty dollars" (original emphasis; Baldwin 74). Richard's touting of his cash—more than the Brittens can change—makes him not only a suspected better *lover* because of his skin color, but he also becomes a better *provider.* Violence does, and must, ensue. Amid the scuffle, Richard further questions Lyle's manhood, calling him a "no-good, ball-less peckerwood" (Baldwin 74). The insult is carefully placed and ironic given Richard's earlier statement made at the mention of Lyle Britten: "They can rape and kill our women and we can't do nothing. But if we touch one of their dried-up, pale-assed women, we get our nuts cut off" (Baldwin 25). Here he turns the tables; the white man, it seems, is self-castrated either by the white woman, his own hatred, or simply by his whiteness. After emerging from the scuffle victorious, Richard cannot simply walk away. Whether Richard recognizes it or not, his fate, after insulting Lyle and his wife, is most likely already sealed. He delivers his final death knell, however, by raising the one issue not yet overtly stated: "Look at the mighty peckerwood! On his *ass,* baby—and his woman watching! Now, who you think is the better man? Ha-ha! The master race! *You let me in that tired white chick's drawers, she'll know who's the master!* Ha-ha-ha!" (my emphasis; Baldwin 75). Richard raises the taboo, the pervasive threat of black masculinity: the rape of the white woman. Such a taboo was ever-present, as Arthur Raper noted in 1933:

> Regardless of the cause of a particular lynching, there were always those who defended it by the insistence that unless Negroes were lynched, no white woman would be safe, this despite the fact that only one-sixth of the persons lynched in the last thirty years were even accused of rape. Regardless of the accusation, an example must be made of the accused Negro for the sake of womanhood. (Raper 20)

Richard, acutely aware of such a fear/excuse, throws that fear directly in the face of Lyle and Jo.

It is easy to see, through this scene, how critics can read Richard Henry as the harbinger of his own murder. There is a part of any reader that simply wants to quiet Richard, to ask him not necessarily to quell his hatred, but rather, to save his own life. There are other critics, however, who find a form of smug vindication in Richard, who question *why* he should have to be quiet to save his own life in the face of historical and ongoing race injustice and race hatred. Richard exudes, for these critics, a form of strength and freshness (all connotations included) evident in his final, quiet, raw, and honest conversation with Lyle: "No, I ain't drunk. I'm just tired. Tired of all this fighting. What are you trying to prove? What am *I* trying to prove?" (original emphasis; Baldwin 118). Such critics may recognize Richard's seeming death drive, but exalt him for his brutal honesty. Calvin Hernton is one critic who appreciates Baldwin's "realistic" grappling with such events and precedents: "We 'liberals' in America always want justice to win out in the end. Well, in the South there is no justice when it comes to the Negro. And Baldwin wrote it as it really is. The murderers of countless Emmett Tills are still running amuck throughout the entire South" (112). Hernton, like most readers, does not see or recognize Lyle's view of "justice," for indeed, Lyle feels that he has rendered white justice: "I had to kill him then. I'm a white man! Can't nobody talk that way to *me!*" (original emphasis; Baldwin 120). Unlike Lyle, Hernton sees *no* justice—and no hope for justice—in Baldwin's *Blues.* In lieu of justice, then, Hernton finds truth and defiance. Darwin T. Turner (1977) sees Richard's life as offering hope, or at least vindication, in a similar fashion—"Furthermore, the play appealed to many young blacks because Richard Henry was the first black stage character in their lifetime to attack white society boldly" (Turner 191). If Baldwin cannot give us justice, such critics would argue, he can give us Richard's boldness. The inevitable question remains: is it impossible to have both?

In order to be true—in order to bear witness—to the historical precedent of this play, Baldwin cannot, in fact, easily blend modern conceptions of justice and boldness. Much of the guiding history in this play revolves around Emmett Till. Emmett Till, the 14-year-old boy on whom Richard is loosely based, was alleged to have whistled at or spoken to a white woman in her husband's store, where Emmett and a friend stopped for a drink after picking cotton all day. Richard, too, emerges with a friend after allegedly "toting barges and lifting bales, that's right, we been slaving, and we need a little cool. Liquid. Refreshment" (Baldwin 71). While Richard directly provokes Jo and Lyle in ways Emmett Till never would have, the scenario is eerily repetitive; Baldwin offers the reader a revisionist understanding of history. Richard claims to have been "slaving," a clear reference to Emmett Till's cotton-picking. Richard makes "inappropriate" comments to a white woman; he is accompanied by another male friend. And the reader must know at this moment, even if s/he had not already witnessed Richard's murder at Lyle's hands, that this scene can only have one conclusion. Baldwin's ending has therefore been chosen for him:

> What other way—authentically—could Baldwin have conceived his piece, considering the material he had chosen? For it is not only a dramatic use of the Emmett Till lynching, but it is also a distillation of all the maimed and lynched, all the brutish sadism of three centuries of the Negro's American experience. It *had* to be a nightmare to be authentic, and it *had* to be a blues, a *Blues for Mister Charlie.* (Turpin 195)

This feeling of necessity—of being unable to write the play in any other way—is supported by Nicholas K. Davis:

> The present moment in Baldwin's writing is thus always two undivorceable things: a culmination of pre-existing patterns that can only now be appreciated, and a decisive, epiphanic break in the protagonist's life where genuine change seems within reach, even though a later moment of history or memory will see this, too, as an embedded moment within a revised larger pattern. Free will and historical fatalism cannot be separated in Baldwin, who refuses to dispense with either of them, however much each seems to diminish the claims of the other. (34)

Thus, Baldwin's "material" is both the historical precedent of the Emmett Till lynching and the historical burden of race relations in the United States. Indeed, while Richard is clearly parodying his own race's history (he has, as far as the reader knows, been nowhere near a cotton field), Baldwin is *not* parodying the Emmett

Till situation. Instead, Baldwin attempts to create a fatalistic cry for a boldness that simultaneously struggles against injustice while calling forth additional injustices: because no one here—Richard and Emmett included—deserves to die, violence and death must ensue in order to attempt to end future violence and death.

While the historical precedent of this play weighs heavily on all the characters—none more than Richard—I argue that Richard's death—or more specifically, the events surrounding his death—offers the only real sense of hope in the play. Embedded in Baldwin's struggle between both strength/suicide and fate/free will stands Richard who, for better or for worse, is a character who attempts to create a space for an altered history. His changing of history becomes his own small revolution. Using the psychoanalytic theories of Julia Kristeva, the reader can begin to see the space Richard creates.

Baldwin begins to create such a space with the opening of the play, a moment of *starting* that corresponds with Richard's moment of *ending*; in *Blues,* the opening scene portrays Lyle Britten dumping Richard's body in the weeds: "And may every nigger like this nigger end like this nigger—face down in the weeds!" (Baldwin 2). Kristeva, in the *Powers of Horror,* illustrates what happens at this critical juncture when the living face the dead:

> refuse and corpses *show me* what I permanently thrust aside in order to live. These body fluids, this defilement, this shit are what life withstands, hardly and with difficulty, on the part of death. There, I am at the border of my condition as a living being. My body extricates itself, as being alive, from that border. Such wastes drop so that I might live, until, from loss to loss, nothing remains in me and my entire body falls beyond the limit—*cadere,* cadaver. If dung signifies the other side of the border, the place where I am not and which permits me to be, the corpse, the most sickening of wastes, is a border that has encroached upon everything. It is no longer I who expel, 'I' is expelled. The border has become an object. How can I be without border? . . . The corpse, seen without God and outside of science, is the utmost of abjection. It is death infecting life. Abject. It is something rejected from which one does not part, from which one does not protect oneself as from an object. Imaginary uncanniness and real threat, it beckons to us and ends up engulfing us. (Kristeva, *Powers of Horror* 3–4)

Although the encounter with the corpse is brief, its importance is magnified simply because it opens the play. Faced with a corpse immediately, then, the reader/viewer (but most especially the viewer) is forced to face the abject, defined by Kristeva as that which "disturbs identity, system, order. What does not respect borders, positions, rules. The in-between, the ambiguous, the composite" (*Powers of Horror* 4). Facing the abject, the reader/viewer feels the shrinking of personal borders and boundaries. His/her own life becomes frailer, suspect, removable, destroyable. Since Baldwin opens the play with Richard's death, the abjection—the border breakdown—is even more insidious. The viewer has no understanding of Richard's character or his potential crime. S/he has only a white man carrying a dead black body and dropping it in the weeds. This scene is duplicated at the end of the play when the audience sees, through a flashback, Lyle kill Richard a second time. For a second time, the audience is reminded of the breakdown of boundaries and quickly comes to understand that Lyle drops "such wastes" so that his "I," his sense of self and race, "might live."

Adding to the difficulty of the opening scene are the opening words. Lyle augments the feelings of abjection. Not only is there a corpse, the "utmost of abjection," but there are also the words of Lyle which scream of abjection: "And may every nigger like this nigger end like this nigger—face down in the weeds!" (Baldwin 2). Linking language with the naming of the abject, Kristeva writes that "emotion, in order to make itself heard, adopts colloquial speech or, when it acknowledges its hatred straightforwardly, slang," and thus, Lyle's repeated use of the word "nigger" becomes his acknowledgment of his hatred (*Powers of Horror* 191). Kristeva continues: "The vocabulary of slang, because of its strangeness, its very violence, and especially because the reader does not always understand it, is of course a radical instrument of separation, of rejection, and, at the limit, of hatred" (*Powers of Horror* 191). Thus, Lyle uses slang to continue separating himself from Richard, from abjection (both in the form of Richard being a "nigger" and in the form of him being a physical corpse).

Lyle names his abjection as he also defines himself against it. Kristeva states that "The abject has only one quality of the object—that of being opposed to *I*" (original emphasis; *Powers of Horror* 1). For Lyle, Richard is "opposed to *I*." Lyle defines himself, his whiteness, in opposition to Richard, as evidenced by a similar form of repetition in a speech found at the *end* of the play when Lyle addresses Parnell: "What's the matter with you? Have you forgotten you a white man? A white man! My Daddy told me not to *never* forget I was a white man!" (original emphasis; Baldwin 117). With the somewhat ironic use of the double negative aside, Lyle completes the cycle of abject and object construction he began in the opening of the play. Lyle opens the play decrying Richard's blackness—his abjection—over the dead, black body; Lyle closes the play affirming his own prideful whiteness—himself as constructed object—in contrast or opposition to such blackness.

Indeed, Baldwin's entire play can be seen as operating within a neat, if complicated, circuit. Tom F. Driver notes that the play fails ultimately to be comic or tragic; it offers no answers or solutions to the issues raised, and it provides no catharsis. Instead, the play shows a movement from "'liberality' to warfare" (293). While the play is neither comic nor tragic, it is also nonlinear; Baldwin's play is, in fact, a circle, or more adeptly—a cycle. The play begins with the murder of Richard, moves through the events leading up to Richard's death, and concludes with a final explanation of the murder and an expected failure of the white jury to convict the white killer. There can be no surprise ending for the ending is already known. The ending is known, of course, both because the audience has already seen the murder and the murderer, and because of the historical weight of the play: if Emmett Till had to die, then Richard, too, must perish.

But Baldwin does offer a subtle breaking of the cycle through Richard. While it is clear that Lyle sees Richard as abjection, as opposite to *I*, the reader can also see *Richard* as seeing himself as abjection, as what Kristeva terms a "deject," thus stepping outside the realm of the expected, breaking borders, and refusing to admit accepted boundaries. Kristeva calls the deject one "by whom the abject exists" and one "who places (himself), *separates* (himself), situates (himself) and therefore *strays* instead of getting his bearings, desiring, belonging, or refusing" (original emphasis; *Powers of Horror* 8). Thus Richard cannot stay, physically, in one location—moving from the South to New York and then planning to leave the South again, this time with Juanita. He separates himself from his family by denouncing his father's weaknesses, turning away from God, and refusing the morality his family teaches: "We don't see things the same way, Grandmama. I don't know if I really *know* right from wrong—I'd like to, I always dig people the most who know *anything*, especially right from wrong!" (original emphasis; Baldwin 18). Richard attempts to find roots in the South, with his family, by handing over his gun to his grandmother and by reestablishing a relationship with Juanita. Ultimately, however, he remains an outsider, an other.

It seems, at times, that Richard tries very hard to maintain such an othering. But, indeed, that is part of being a deject; one must "situate" oneself and one must "stray." Both verbs require a form of conscious thought and decision. Thus Richard taunts his own friends and acquaintances, creating a distance: "I got a whole *gang* of white chicks in New York. That's *right*. And they can't get enough of what little Richard's got—and I give it to them, too, baby, believe me" (Baldwin 25). He similarly attracts and repels his own family, at once disrespecting and loving his grandmother while disrupting and recreating a relationship with his father. Critic Emmanuel S. Nelson, in "James Baldwin's Vision of Otherness and Community" (1983), claims the following regarding this very relationship between Richard and his friends and family:

> In the beginning Richard perceives the humiliations of his racial past as signs of weakness and tries to define himself in opposition to that collective experience. But as the play moves along, he becomes increasingly sensitive to the beauty and strength that have come out of the appalling suffering of his people. It is in his gradual identification with the collective, communal Black experience from which he had originally alienated himself that he finds his self and strength. (123)

Contrary to Nelson's statement, however, Richard does not ultimately find beauty, strength, or identification in his community. Instead, he finds only an indescribable internal resistance that can only be explained by his role as deject. Thus, while Nelson may very well be deriving his argument from Richard's attempts to establish relationships within the community—with Juanita (whom he possibly impregnates), his father, or his grandmother—such forays into the community do not limit his ability to stand as deject. Indeed, by continually *resisting* "that collective experience" and by needling and at times *augmenting* the "appalling suffering of his people," Richard consistently redefines his position as chosen outsider.

Richard's small moments of effective communication with friends and family do not limit his role as deject for, as Kristeva notes, the deject is "Situationist in a sense, and not without laughter—since laughing is a way of placing or displacing abjection" (*Powers of Horror* 8). Richard's laughter, then, displaces abjection when he reaches out to his family, but places abjection—on himself and the white community—when he laughs at Lyle and Jo in their store, or when he uses sarcasm even while Lyle shoots him: "Okay. Okay. Okay. Keep your old lady home, you hear? Don't let her near no nigger. She might get to like it. You might get to like it, too. Wow!" (Baldwin 120).

Indeed, Richard's laughter is consistent not only with his role as deject, but also with the role of rebel—another related position that places him outside the boundaries of normal and acceptable behavior. In *The Sense and Non-Sense of Revolt* (2000), Kristeva argues that *some* form of revolt or rebellion is indeed *necessary* to happiness as "happiness exists only at the price of a revolt" (*Sense and Non-Sense* 7): "None of us has pleasure without confronting an obstacle, prohibition, authority, or law that allows us to realize ourselves as autonomous and free" (*Sense and Non-Sense* 7). Richard takes pleasure in pushing the boundaries beyond the normal levels of rebellion or revolt. While Juanita, Mother Henry, Meridian, and the local black community carry signs of protest at organized meetings, Richard's only happiness comes from a more blatant, unexpected, raw form of protest. Richard is, using Driver's words, the embodiment of "the breakdown of 'moderation'" in an unstable and unequal environment in the play (292). More than simply a "breakdown of 'moderation,'" however, Richard takes real enjoyment in humiliating whites, even at the very moment of his own murder: "You can't eat because none of your sad-assed chicks can cook. You can't talk because won't nobody talk to you. You can't dance because you've got nobody to dance with—don't you know I've watched you all my life? *All my life!* And *I* know your women, don't you think I don't—better than you!" (original emphasis; Baldwin 119). Richard's only true joy comes from such interactions, where ironically, facing death, his "confronting" of "authority" "allows" him to feel "autonomous and free" (Kristeva, *Sense and Non-Sense* 7).

Seeing Richard as deject helps the reader to understand his erratic behavior which otherwise becomes paradoxical, as Carlton W. Molette notes in "James Baldwin as Playwright" (1977):

> Richard Henry thinks he must destroy "Mister Charlie" in order to achieve his own salvation. On the other hand, he knows that the system is programmed to destroy him if he attempts to destroy the man. He knows that he cannot realistically expect to beat the whole system singlehandedly. So he knows that his act of destruction perpetrated against "Mr. Charlie" will inevitably result in his own destruction. Yet he wants to live. He is not suicidal. Still a third paradox. (187)[3]

Richard is the non-suicidal deject who nonetheless asks to die because, as Kristeva describes, "He has a sense of the danger, of the loss that the pseudo-object attracting him represents for him, but he cannot help taking the risk at the very moment he sets himself apart. And the more he strays, the more he is saved" (*Powers of Horror* 8). Richard's "pseudo-object" can be seen as death, or it can be seen as Lyle (and while they are related, they are not identical). Either way, both represent abjection, to which Richard is drawn. He and Lyle thereby enter a symbiotic relationship; they define themselves against each other, they constantly struggle to maintain separate identities in each other's presence, and they experience similar emotions of rage, hatred, violence, and disgust. It is true that Richard provokes Lyle, but Lyle clearly needs little provocation, especially given that this is not, indeed, his first murder of a black man. The historical weight of racism in the play determines which abjection must be removed, but it is this very danger of removal that excites Richard. The danger, the moving away from the acceptable boundaries of his community, makes him feel "saved," useful, and powerful. Thus, while his actions may result in his moving from deject to abject (a corpse), it is the act of setting himself apart—the crossing of and denying of boundaries—not the death, that drives him.

Richard's desire to set himself apart centers largely around his desire to break the father/son cycle that begins to repeat itself in *Blues*. While Richard moves up North to join his aunt following his mother's death (or murder, if the reader chooses to accept Richard's opinion), he returns home after getting into trouble with the law regarding his drug use. He immediately begins a relationship with his old friend/girlfriend, Juanita, telling his father, "Lord, if I'd stayed here, I guess I might have married old Juanita by now, and we'd have a couple of kids and I'd be sitting around like this *every* night. What a wild thought" (original emphasis; Baldwin 34). The thought is not so wild, however, as Meridian tells Richard "You can still marry Juanita. Maybe she's been waiting for you" (Baldwin 34). Richard admits to considering such an option only *after* Meridian admits to having considered marrying Juanita himself, although he has "never spoken of it to her" (Baldwin 35). Richard's plans for the future, then, become a symbol of his continuing a cycle. He would, like his father, remain in/return to the South, live a more reserved life (since he certainly could not survive a life in the South otherwise), and marry a beautiful woman similar to his mother. Indeed, Juanita is *so* similar to his mother that she almost *is* his mother, or at least his step-mother. Baldwin thereby reemphasizes, all too clearly, what Richard *almost* does—he almost selects a life identical to his father's.

But what is gained from breaking the cycle? Turning again to Kristeva's later work, *The Sense and Non-Sense of Revolt*, the reader can begin to see the impact of Richard's rebelliousness, of his role as deject. Kristeva paraphrases Sigmund Freud's *Totem and Taboo,* commenting on the oedipal complex present in "all humans" (*Sense and Non-Sense* 12). According to Freud, all men originally lived under the rule of a dominant head of the horde who "demanded total submission from his sons and prohibited access to women, the sexual enjoyment of whom he reserved for himself" (Kristeva, *Sense and Non-Sense* 12). The sons eventually revolt, killing the father and eating him in a totemic meal, thus coming to identify with the totem they have consumed. Guilt and repentance bind the brothers and "the dead father became stronger than the living one had been" (Freud 143), forcing them to obey and reinforce the same laws that originally drove them to murder.

Richard, then, has a number of options related to this particular form of revolt or rebellion. He clearly sees his father as a figurehead of a *type* of power; Meridian's control over his son stems from Meridian's perceived legacy of debilitating *powerlessness.* This lack of power—this inability to avenge his wife's death or effectively raise his son—becomes a controlling force over Richard. Richard remembers his father's reaction to his mother's death: "But he wasn't there, he didn't know, he couldn't say nothing, he couldn't *do* nothing. I'll never forget the way he looked—whipped, whipped, whipped, whipped!" (original emphasis; Baldwin 20). He later tells his father of his own reaction, "You didn't want me to look at you and be ashamed of you. And you didn't know what was in my eyes, you couldn't stand it, I could tell from the way you looked at me sometimes. That was it, wasn't it?" (Baldwin 35). In order to escape the despotic *dearth* of power that binds Richard to his father, Richard could choose, in the way of Freud, to murder the father. Such a reaction is too consistent with the father's perceived lack of power to truly form any sort of rebellion, however. Richard could choose to remain in town with Juanita, or flee town with her, but he is still haunted by the imposing image of his "whipped" father and possibly murdered mother. Richard attempts drugs, music, moving North, and sleeping with white women, but he is consumed nonetheless by a powerful rage against *anything*—a rage that must ultimately be directed at *something.* In order to escape his father's cycle of non-action, in order to escape his father's *legacy* of failure, Richard must do what his father will not: Richard must fight Mister Charlie, even if it means his own death. Richard is driven by the need to replace powerlessness with power—the power of decision and "manly" action—but his rebellion is ironically tied to the continuation of powerlessness, in this case, his own death.

Twisting the Freudian concept, then, Richard murders—directly or indirectly—himself in lieu of murdering the father. Alternatively, the reader can see Richard as murdering the father *in himself,* the father figure he was starting to become by considering life choices similar to those Meridian chose earlier. Either reading, however, has the same outcome: Richard leaves his *father* behind, bound by guilt and repentance, to perpetuate the cycle the son has begun. Following Richard's murder, Meridian begins to question his own faith in both God and eventual change, and he begins to blame himself for the murder of his son and wife: "If you're a black man, with a black son, you have to forget all about white people and concentrate on trying to save your child. That's why I let him stay up North. I was wrong, I failed, I failed. Lyle walked up the road and killed him" (Baldwin 40). Meridian's guilt and anger grow as the play progresses: "Yes! I *am* responsible for the death of my son. I—hoped—I prayed—I struggled—so that the world would be different by the time he was a man than it had been when he was born. And I thought that—then—when he looked at me—he would think that I—his father—had helped to change it" (original emphasis; Baldwin 104). But Meridian realizes he misplaced his faith and his belief in the inevitability of change, and sees his own slow realization as leading to his son's death. That guilt creates Meridian's moment for personal change, and raises his demands for societal change, even if that means challenge and strife:

> I am a man. A *man*! I tried to help my son become a man. But manhood is a dangerous pursuit, here. And that pursuit undid him because of *your* guns, *your* hoses, *your* dogs, *your* judges, *your* law-makers, *your* folly, *your* pride, *your* cruelty, *your* cowardice, *your* money, *your* chain gangs, and *your* churches! Did you think it would endure forever? that [sic] we would pay for *your* ease forever? (original emphasis; Baldwin 103)

Meridian's shift, motivated by guilt and repentance, includes warning Parnell about the future violence that will strike the town while questioning his prior conviction not to arm (Baldwin 37). As reviewer Tom F. Driver notes, Meridian's shift is one of the most important movements in the play: "He has long been a spokesman and a bargainer for civil rights. He becomes an agitator ready to take up arms" (292). His changing convictions, however, cannot assuage his guilt: "Would God—would *God*—would God I had died for thee—my son, my son!" (Baldwin 43). Ultimately, however, like the story of Christ he references, Meridian cannot die for his son. It is, in fact, his son who must die to alter the life of his father.

Meridian's changes are consistent with Freud and Kristeva's understanding of the result of the father/son rebellion:

> In the Freudian fable, the father embodies the position of authority, value, and law against which the sons rebel. Their revolt consists in this: they identify with the father and take his place, an integration that constitutes the collective pact, the inclusion forging the link that will be the *socius*. Thanks to this, the brothers no longer feel excluded but rather have the imaginary certainty of being identified with the power that, prior to the revolt, oppressed them. (Kristeva, *Sense and Non-Sense* 23)

Richard enacts this rebellion even if he changes the rules. By challenging the white "father"—the possessor in this story of all the power, Richard binds his own black father to the aftermath of his choices. Meridian can "no longer feel excluded" and must instead choose to interact with and lead his congregation in new ways; he begins to keep his son's gun "In the pulpit. Under the Bible. Like the pilgrims of old" (Baldwin 120). Meridian thereby joins himself to a new community—to the community of the founders of the United States who had to fight for independence and recognition. Such a move also positions Meridian to begin to identify "with the power that, prior to the revolt, oppressed them." He begins to match a violent reaction to a violent oppression. Intrinsic to Meridian's shift is his new distrust of Parnell, his demands for a confession from Lyle (albeit outside the court house), and an understanding of the need to arm himself for future challenges.

Meridian's shift toward violence, unfortunately, runs the risk of eliminating one of his previous strengths, a strength Richard clearly lacks: the ability to survive. Meridian moves from a position of survival into a more violent posture, reflecting the revolution of his son. However, as Freud and Kristeva both note, the sons (or in this case, the ones left behind) often remember and commemorate the revolt, but such a movement seeks "to mimic this revolt" but "not to reproduce it exactly" (Kristeva, *Sense and Non-Sense* 13). Thus, like the outwardly moving ripples in a pond, the reader can expect (or at least hope for) such a revolution to spread while losing some of the power of the initial assault.

Richard's revolt, in the form of defying white expectations, affects more than just Meridian; it also affects his surrounding black community, most clearly articulated in the changes evident in Juanita. If she is indeed pregnant, she will clearly be *visibly* changed, but she is also poised to raise a son similar to Richard: "I hope I'm pregnant. I *hope* I am! One more illegitimate black baby—that's right you jive mothers! And I am going to raise my baby to be a man. A *man*, you dig? Oh, let me be pregnant, let me be pregnant, don't let it all be gone! A man. Juanita. A man" (original emphasis; Baldwin 94). Juanita has moved from herding Richard away from danger—"Just stay out of white places" (Baldwin 30)—to creating a son in his image (even if such a creation is only in her mind):

> And we tried to make plans to go, but he said he wasn't going to run no more from white folks—never no more!—but was going to stay and be a man—a *man*!—right here. And

> I couldn't *make* him see differently. I knew what he meant, I knew how he felt, but I didn't want him to die!" (Baldwin 99)

In both instances, Juanita repeats "a *man*" several times as she is, in her own mind, redefining what it means to be a man, to be a black man. Meridian, it should be noted, uses the same repetition later, as he too begins to redefine manhood: "I am a man. A *man*! I tried to help my son become a man" (Baldwin 103). Such repetition echoes Lyle's use of repetition in the opening scene of the play. Juanita and Meridian demonstrate the essential shift in the play, however, as Lyle's "nigger" is redefined as a "man." Thus, Juanita hopes to have a son who can, bound by the legacy he has been left, continue to refuse "to run" from "white folks." Such a refusal, she hopes, will become increasingly nuanced and supported so as to continue the rebellion without ending more black lives.

Much of this redefinition of manhood that Meridian and Juanita emphasize revolves around Richard's denial of the "automation" that has settled into his small southern town. As Kristeva notes, people, "faced with the religious and political impasses of our time," often find that "an experience of revolt may be the only thing that can save us from the automation of humanity that is threatening us" (*Sense and Non-Sense* 7). For Kristeva, the lack of real political power, manifested in the desire for figureheads and scapegoats, combined with a consumer culture that makes entertainment more important than growth or development, form a complacent, rebellion-less society. For Richard, surrounded by a town of people who protest and struggle only within certain boundaries, such automation is suffocating. The expectations of such automation are clear: people fulfill their roles based on color, or they forfeit their lives or reputations. Thus, Lyle kills Old Bill and Richard for questioning his right to behave in any way he sees fits because of his color, and Parnell becomes "*worse* than a nigger" for his attempts to defend the reactions of the black community to Richard's murder (original emphasis; Baldwin 53). Meridian, Juanita, Mother Henry, and even Papa D. attempt to force Richard into a form of automation by trying to talk him out of his hatred, telling him to put away his pictures of white women, and attempting to convince him to leave town. Admittedly, they wish to save his life. To do so, however, for Richard, is to assume a role of passivity that he outwardly denies. As Kristeva explains:

> Furthermore, on the social level, the normalizing order is far from perfect and fails to support the excluded: jobless youth, the poor in the projects, the homeless, the unemployed, and foreigners, among many others. When the excluded have no culture of revolt and must content themselves with regressive ideologies, with shows and entertainments that far from satisfy the demand of pleasure, they become rioters. (*Sense and Non-Sense* 7)

Richard, faced with a family and friends who want him to be "normalized" in order to survive, feels excluded and unsupported. Raging against the boundaries that attempt to corral him, not content with "shows and entertainment" of the white dominant culture, he becomes a violent rioter who seeks to upset the "normalizing order."

Ironically, Richard, like Emmett Till, upsets the "normalizing order" most effectively through his death. Emmett Till, horribly tortured and murdered by a white store owner and his brother, became, by many accounts, a catalyst for the Civil Rights Movement in America. Emmett's mother insisted on having an open casket for her mutilated son's funeral so that America could bear witness to such brutality ("The Untold Story"). Pictures of the body were published in *Jet* magazine in 1955, sparking outrage. Emmett Till's murder, while undoubtedly tragic, sparked a cause that reached well beyond his own life or murder. In a similar way, Richard's murder can be seen to accomplish more than his life would have. Richard's attempts to infuse his own sense of defiance and rebellion into his friends and family are repeatedly thwarted as Mother Henry tells him to "just try not to *go* so much, try to calm down a little," and Papa D. tells him to put away the pictures of white women he carries with him: "I thought you had good sense" (original emphasis; Baldwin 18, 27). Meridian and Juanita, too, maintain their views on race relations while Richard is alive, opting for religion and patient protest until after the murder. It is only after Richard is killed that Juanita wishes to grow out her hair "the way God arranged it in the first place" while hoping to raise her son to militancy (Baldwin 37). And it is only after the murder that Papa D. breaks his relationship with Lyle, turning on him while on the witness stand. Meridian, too, turns his faith away from acceptance and toward anger. These changes, while small, are the beginnings of a stronger sense of self-awareness and race pride. They are the seeds for a later, stronger revolution.

Like Richard Henry and Emmett Till, James Baldwin also found a way to upset the "normalizing order"—this time the order of 1960s American theater—with *Blues for Mister Charlie.* In a 1984 interview, James Baldwin spoke about his controversial essay "Everybody's Protest Novel," his views on victimization novels (such as, in Baldwin's opinion, *Native Son*), as well as his role as a writer, asserting, "I was convinced then—and I still am—that those sort of books do nothing but bolster up an image" (Baldwin, *Conversations* 237). It was an image Baldwin was unwilling to support or sanction: "it seemed to me that if I took the role of a victim then . . . they could pity me and add a few more pennies to my home relief check" (Baldwin, *Conversations* 237). It is clear, given Baldwin's views on victimization, that Richard Henry cannot be simply a victim. He is, by Baldwin's own assertion, not pitiable. He must be, on some level then, multidimensional, culpable, and human; we are meant to read his murderer, Lyle, in much the same way. Both characters are presented as possessing overpowering emotions, deep beliefs in autonomy, and a strong sense of "justice." While Baldwin was clearly bound by the historical precedent that surrounds this play, he did not choose to simply provide an Emmett Till, a victim, who is too young and too naïve to make rational, adult choices. Richard makes his choices—regardless of what the viewer/reader thinks of them, or *him*. His choices reflect those of a deject, a rebel, who desires nothing more than to step outside the lines of a racially troubled society. In doing so, he pays the ultimate price. But it is not a price without reason or consequences. Richard chose revolution and his choice influences a community, however subtle those influences may be. By reading Richard through Julia Kristeva's psychoanalytic criticism, the reader can begin to acknowledge Richard's sacrifice; the reader can begin to set him free.

Notes

1. See Dwight McBride, ed. *James Baldwin Now.* New York: New York University Press, 1999.
2. See D. Quentin Miller, ed. *Re-Visiting James Baldwin: Things Not Seen.* Philadelphia: Temple University Press, 2000.
3. Carlton W. Molette. "James Baldwin as Playwright" from the collection *James Baldwin: A Critical Evaluation*, edited by Therman B. O'Daniel. Washington, DC: Howard University Press, Copyright, 1977. Reprinted by permission of the publishers. All rights reserved.

Works Cited

Baldwin, James. *Blues for Mister Charlie.* New York: Vintage Books, 1964.

———. *Conversations with James Baldwin.* Ed. Fred L. Standley and Louis H. Pratt. Jackson: University Press of Mississippi, 1989.

Davis, Nicholas K. "Go Tell It On the Stage: *Blues for Mister Charlie* as Dialectical Drama." *The Journal of American Drama and Theatre* 17.2 (Spring 2005): 30–42.

Driver, Tom F. "The Review That Was Too True to Be Published." *Critical Essays on James Baldwin.* Ed. Fred L. Standley and Nancy V. Burt. Boston: G.K. Hall & Co., 1988.

Freud, Sigmund. *Totem and Taboo.* Trans. James Strachey. London: Routledge & Kegan Paul, 1950.

Hernton, Calvin C. "A Fiery Baptism." *James Baldwin: A Collection of Critical Essays.* Ed. Keneth Kinnamon. Englewood Cliffs, NJ: Prentice-Hall, Inc., 1974.

Kristeva, Julia. *The Powers of Horror.* Trans. Leon S. Roudiez. New York: Columbia University Press, 1982.

———. *The Sense and Non-Sense of Revolt.* Trans. Jeanine Herman. New York: Columbia University Press, 2000.

Littlejohn, David. *Black on White: A Critical Survey of Writing by American Negroes.* New York: Grossman Publishers, 1966.

Mitchell, Loften. *Black Drama.* New York: Hawthorn Books, 1967.
Molette, Carlton W. "James Baldwin as Playwright." *James Baldwin: A Critical Evaluation.* Ed. Therman B. O'Daniel. Washington, DC: Howard University Press, 1977.
Nelson, Emmanuel S. "James Baldwin's Vision of Otherness and Community." *Critical Essays on James Baldwin.* Ed. Fred L. Standley and Nancy V. Burt. Boston: G.K. Hall & Co., 1988.
Raper, Arthur F. *The Tragedy of Lynching.* Chapel Hill: University of North Carolina Press, 1933.
Roth, Philip. "Blues for Mister Charlie." *Modern Critical Views: James Baldwin.* Ed. Harold Bloom. New York: Chelsea House Publishers, 1986.
Simon, John. *Uneasy Stages: A Chronicle of the New York Theater, 1963–1973.* New York: Random House, 1975.
Sylvander, Carolyn Wedin. *James Baldwin.* New York: Frederick Ungar Publishing Company, 1980.
Turner, Darwin T. "James Baldwin in the Dilemma of the Black Dramatist." *James Baldwin: A Critical Evaluation.* Ed. Therman B. O'Daniel. Washington, DC: Howard University Press, 1977.
Turpin, Waters E. "A Note on *Blues for Mister Charlie.*" *James Baldwin: A Critical Evaluation.* Ed. Therman B. O'Daniel. Washington, DC: Howard University Press, 1977.
"The Untold Story of Emmett Louis Till." 19 April 2006. <http:// www.emmetttillstory.com>

4

African Queens and Messed-Up Chicks

Representations of Identity in Alice Childress's *Wine in the Wilderness*

JOY E. CRANSHAW

Race, class, and gender are hopelessly intertwined in our society, and points of both convergence and conflict have found their way into African American literary representations throughout the history of the United States. But perhaps the relationships between these social concerns had never been so sharp a focus of investigation as in the 1960s, when the cultural climate was shaped by the Civil Rights and feminist movements, the significant growth of the black middle class following World War II (Wilson 126–43), and the rise of the Black Arts Movement. In "Afro-American Literature and Class Struggle," for example, Amiri Baraka divides black writers into two categories in a move that recognizes the tensions between race and class, as perceived by the Black Arts Movement. He calls black writers either "revolutionaries" or "capitulationists" and, not surprisingly, connects them with the working class and the middle class, respectively. Though written more recently, Ishmael Reed's frequent use of the term "gender-first feminist"—as in his essay "Mike Tyson and the White Hope Cult" (69)—reflects long and commonly held perceptions of a similar conflict between race and gender. Of course, not all writers fit easily into one or the other of Baraka's categories, nor do they always feel the need to prioritize the importance of race and gender. The literature of more ambivalent writers offers more complex explorations of the intersections of identities, which rarely coincide neatly.

Alice Childress, by no means the "revolutionary" that Baraka would have desired, but not a capitulationist either, is subtle in her presentation of views concerning social issues, to the point where occasionally it is difficult to determine what exactly her views are. She claims to "concentrate on portraying have-nots in a *have* society" ("Candle" 112)—a description of inequality that could equally refer to race, class, or gender—and *Wine in the Wilderness* (1969) deals with these themes in problematic and even contradictory ways. Through a close reading of this play, I offer an analysis of the potential and actual intersections of race, class, and gender and the ways in which characters navigate these intersections. By considering a writer who was neither inflammatory nor assimilationist, I hope to provide a more balanced portrait than Baraka's of the struggles that African American writers and the African American community in general have encountered. Numerous conflicts arise when attempting a reconciliation of these potentially divisive—yet ideally unifying—categories of identity, and *Wine in the Wilderness* is particularly illustrative of these difficulties.

Most criticism of Childress has focused on race, but many critics have also viewed Childress's work—particularly *Wine in the Wilderness*—through a feminist lens,[1] pointing out the ways in which race is integrally connected to gender oppression. A few critics have also looked at issues of class in the play, recognizing that race cannot be understood in isolation.[2] Indeed, questions about class and gender both complicate and elucidate a consideration of race—besides being fruitful explorations in their own right—as the three are never extricable in Childress's work or in the real world. An exploration of these interconnected systems of difference reveals multiple layers of complexity in Childress's play.

It is surprising that critics have not culled *Wine in the Wilderness* more extensively for its statements about these topics, as it is perhaps one of Childress's most transparent social commentaries. Her ultimate conclusion may not be transparent, as she problematizes all of the assumptions that she initially encourages her readers to adopt, but it is clear that she is attempting to draw attention to these social issues whether or not she offers any definitive statements about them. Because her intended message is so convoluted, it is useful to begin with a superficial reading of the play, one which typically leads to the conclusion that Childress raises class solidarity over middle class aspirations, perhaps even marrying the working class to an idea of authentic blackness, and that she likewise advocates for the autonomy of black women in opposition to the restraints of patriarchy.

Bill Jameson, an African American artist, is working on a triptych of black womanhood, revealing his particular views of women and their role within the race. The first panel on "Black girlhood" (8)[3] is barely mentioned in the play, while the center panel draws the most admiring attention in its portrayal of "'Wine In The Wilderness' [. . .] *a beautiful woman*" with a "*deep mahogany complexion,* [. . .] *cold but utter perfection, draped in startling colors of African material, very 'Vogue' looking* [. . .] *wear*[*ing*] *a gold head-dress sparkling with brilliants and sequins applied over the paint*" (9).[4] Bill is missing only the final panel, which has been reserved for "a poor, dumb chick," the "lost woman" created by the corruptive society that Bill sees embodied in a Harlem riot going on outside his apartment building (9).

Bill's friends Sonny-man and Cynthia—a writer and social worker, respectively—find Tommy, a factory worker, in a bar during the riot and bring her to Bill's apartment to model for him, her lower-class status marking her, in their minds, as a "messed-up chick" (32) appropriate for the role. Tommy thinks that Bill is interested in her romantically, but the morning after they sleep together Tommy discovers the true reason for her presence, and she accuses Bill, Cynthia, and Sonny-man of being "phoney niggers" (35). Bill has altered his opinion of her in the interim, and after her angry denunciation of her treatment he announces his decision to paint her not as the "messed-up chick," but instead as "Mother Africa . . . black womanhood in her noblest form" (9), the original conception for the center panel of "Wine In The Wilderness."

Based on this view of the plot, critics have understandably read the play as one which indicts African American bourgeois culture for denying and suppressing the supposed authenticity of the black masses. Elizabeth Brown-Guillory, for example, argues that the "play pokes fun at bourgeois affectation" by "level[ing] an attack at blacks who scream blackness, brotherhood, and togetherness but who have no love or empathy for poor, uneducated, and unrefined blacks" (*Their Place* 33). Brown-Guillory shows here a sharp distinction between middle-class and working-class African Americans, and implies that the play argues for the healing of class conflicts—or, more precisely, a return to a unified working class culture and values—in order to unite in "blackness, brotherhood, and togetherness."

Even more often, critics claim that the play raises gender equality and respect over misogyny, recognizing the beauty all women possess. La Vinia Delois Jennings associates femininity with whiteness and accuses the black, middle-class culture of *Wine in the Wilderness* of being assimilationist, arguing that "Bill's misguided vision of 'Wine in the Wilderness' is the Madison Avenue paradigm of physical female beauty, only in blackface. . . . With her blackness defamiliarized in a traditional white imaging of beauty, she propagates the ideology of whiteness, not blackness" (69). Indeed, accusations of assimilationist tendencies in Childress's characters are common, and critics point to the use of both class and gender norms as a means of seeking acceptance where racial differences have made complete assimilation impossible.[5] Jennings summarizes by saying that the play "target[s] blacks in need of liberation from the influence of middle-class, white, and sexist values" (57–58).

On first reading, the play has an Aristotelian roundness that encourages definitive interpretations. But these interpretations tend to be overly simplistic: the reader is easily misled by the familiar plot structure of the play to draw premature conclusions about the outcome and the resulting statements about race, class, and gender issues. Misleading clues about the role of class in the play appear right from the beginning, in the list of characters, where each of them is identified not only by age, but also by profession. Class distinctions are clear here—Tommy, as a "woman factory worker" (4), stands as a particular contrast to the others—and they encourage a straightforward interpretation of the play.

The problem with reading the play as a blanket statement about class (or gender) in connection with race is that such a reading accepts unquestioned the characters' own assessments of each other and their positionings within these hierarchies, when in fact the minor details of the play provide a much more complex picture. Class is a particularly troublesome category in the case of Tommy, who occupies the very center of the play. Her working-class status is not what it at first appears to be, and an accurate reading of the play is dependent upon this classification.

Bill's initial description of what he wants for his painting frames the reader's first impression of Tommy as a "back-country chick right outta the wilds of Mississippi" (10), which is apparently the farthest thing Bill can imagine from his bourgeois, urban life.

> She's gonna be the kinda chick that is grass roots, . . . no, not grass roots, . . . I mean she's underneath the grass roots. The lost woman, . . . what the society has made out of our women. She's as far from my African queen as a woman can get without crackin' up . . . she's ignorant, unfeminine, coarse, rude . . . vulgar . . . a poor, dumb chick that's had her behind kicked until it's numb . . . and the sad part is . . . she ain't together, you know, . . . there's no hope for her. [. . .] A Chick that ain' fit for nothin' but to . . . to . . . just pass her by. [. . .] If you had to sum her up in a word it would be nothin'! (9–10)

Indeed, when Tommy enters the scene she is "dressed in a mismatched skirt and sweater, wearing a wig that is not comical, but is wiggy looking. [. . .] She wears sneakers and bobby sox, carries a brown paper sack" (11). This visual impression of sloppiness is then compounded by an aural one, as Tommy's speech clearly marks her as uneducated, and, secondarily, unfeminine. Her grammar is littered with errors, and she uses terms like "nigger" in company that obviously does not approve of such crassness and informality. Childress's representation of Tommy's poor speech even goes beyond anything audible. Tommy's dialogue frequently includes misspelled words that, if spoken phonetically, would sound exactly the same as those same words spelled correctly. "Incense" becomes "In-sense" (23), and "Trip-tick" replaces "triptych" (32). Childress thereby implies that Tommy lacks a solid grasp of literacy and an advanced vocabulary, in addition to possessing poor speaking abilities.

Cynthia and Sonny-man presumably recognize Bill's painting description in Tommy's outward appearance, yet Tommy is hardly a "back-country chick"; she was born in Baltimore and raised in Harlem, and is just as much a part of the civilized culture of New York as Bill himself is. Furthermore, though she is viewed as a woman off the street, she was not involved in the riots, but was instead a victim, driven out of her house when it was burned down. Although Bill has not realized it yet, there is a disjuncture between his idea of Tommy and her actual person.

Bill and his friends are right that Tommy is, in a literal sense, poor and working class, and has been since childhood. As a result, she was forced to leave school and go to work after eighth grade. She explains to Cynthia, "I come from poor people. [. . .] I remember my mother tyin' up her stockin's with strips-a rag 'cause she didn't have no garters. When I get home from school she'd say, . . . 'Nothin' much here to eat.' Nothin' much might be grits, or bread and coffee. I got sick-a all that, got me a job. Later for school" (19). Yet, despite this concession, which acknowledges her place in the working class, it appears that she has had the opportunity of living in the leisure class, and has chosen not to accept it. She claims that a "Woman I use to work for say . . . 'Tommy, any time, any time you want a sleep-in place you come right here to me.' . . . And that's Park Avenue, my own private bath and T.V. set. . . . But I don't want that . . . so I make it on out here to the dress factory" (14).

Tommy's class is therefore more complicated than it at first appears, but it is in the literal measure of her wealth that her class markings are clearest. An analysis limited to investigating the connections between material wealth and the relationships and interactions of the characters facilitates a traditional reading of class in the play. In this reading Bill judges Tommy based on her class, and Tommy teaches him that the working class is more authentically black than the middle class, which is doing nothing more than imitating white culture and acting as Baraka's "capitulationists." But there are many external markers of class, and it is these markers, more than an actual measure of wealth—which is rarely visible in public anyway—that determine the status granted to individuals within the social hierarchy. Tommy's nominal class and her class markers often do not coincide, and while it would be futile to argue that Tommy is a member of the middle class in any literal sense, she displays a number of middle-class markers that alter a traditional reading of the play.

A reevaluation of Tommy's physical appearance is necessary because it is precisely this appearance that has initially marked her—in the minds of Cynthia, Sonny-man, Bill, and the reader—as a poor, masculinized, working-class woman. But, as she relates when she has reached Bill's apartment, the house fire has destroyed all of her possessions, including her clothes (13–14), accounting for her particular outfit that day. There is no arguing that Tommy's taste is eccentric, evidenced particularly in her decision to wear a wig, but her physical appearance and choice of dress cannot be attributed to a "back-country" backwardness, or even to the urban working class. She complains that she feels foolish because "I'm standin' there in a mis-match skirt and top and these sneaker-shoes. I just went to put my dresses in the cleaner" (15). She does not want Bill to paint her in this outfit because she does not "feel proud-a myself in this," and instead wishes she had her white dress, Orlon sweater, and pink linen shoes (25).

Bill thinks that he is looking at a lower-class, "back-country" black woman, but in fact he is viewing a woman who has both willingly and unwillingly put on a variety of disguises at that particular moment. As the play continues, these disguises are slowly peeled away or exchanged for new costumes, and it is the revelation of various middle-class markers that slowly changes Bill's view of Tommy. Brown-Guillory, Jennings, and other critics have viewed Bill's shifting opinion as one that indicates a conversion to respect for the working class, and Tommy as the "catalyst for the growth of Bill Jameson, Cynthia, and Sonny-Man" (Brown-Guillory *Their Place* 33) because she "rescues [the]m from [their] bourgeoisie vapidness and points [the]m in the direction of humanity" (Brown-Guillory *Wines* 108–9). As ideal as this reading may sound, it unfortunately does not quite match the evidence.

In *"Color Struck" Under the Gaze: Ethnicity and the Pathology of Being in the Plays of Johnson, Hurston, Childress, Hansberry, and Kennedy*, Martha Gilman Bower suggests the possibility of a more nuanced understanding of the play, though she does not explore this possibility herself. She credits Tommy with Bill's conversion, but there is a strange, unexplored twist at the very end of Bower's analysis. The final sentence of her article reads, "She [Tommy] rejects her streetwise, bewigged persona, and accepts Bill's intelligence and art to achieve authenticity of self" (75). While her argument to this point has been that Bill bends to Tommy, this final statement seems to reverse the argument, to indicate that, in fact, Tommy implicitly agrees to fulfill the role Bill desires for her. Most readings assume that Childress's bourgeois characters learn in the course of the play how out of touch they are with true blackness in comparison with the working-class masses, but in fact the play to some degree reinscribes the class hierarchy that on the surface it appears to subvert. Bill has not changed significantly after all, and Tommy is not so securely working class as the reader initially is led to believe.

Even her decision to wear a wig reveals an understanding of intraracial conflict and contradictory expectations within African American culture that is more sophisticated than bourgeois Cynthia's, even if it is not uttered in sophisticated speech: "I'm just sick-a hair, hair, hair. Do it this way, don't do it, leave it natural, straighten it, process, no process. I get sick-a hair and talkin' 'bout it and foolin' with it. That's why I wear the wig" (20). She believes that wearing a wig is the only means of obtaining the silky hair that men like Bill desire "without burnin' my mother-grabbin' brains out" (27). These comments reveal Tommy's ability to step outside of the culture and critique it in an advanced manner, and it is this advanced thinking that lies behind her choice to wear a wig, which is presumed to indicate a lack of femininity. Her "unfeminine" choice of hairstyle is therefore an attempt to attain middle class markers of femininity and to attract desirable men, and is not the renunciation of femininity that Bill, Sonny-man, and Cynthia first assume.

Tommy's justification of her hair, and other similar demonstrations of socially aware self-determinism begin to make Cynthia uncomfortable with the role she is playing in Tommy's deception, and when they are left alone for a bit, she tries to discourage Tommy from becoming too interested in Bill. She realizes that Tommy—or at least the Tommy she knows based on her first impression—is not the kind of woman that Bill would find attractive, and she begins "*Feeling sorry for* [*her*]" (18). "Oh, Honey, . . . Tommy, you don't want a poor artist. [. . .] don't be in a rush about the marriage thing. [. . .] About Bill, it's best not to ever count on anything, anything at all, Tommy. [. . .] don't be too quick to put your trust in these men" (17–18). Though Cynthia cannot relate to Tommy in terms of class, she connects with her on questions of gender, and she evinces compassion for her in a form different from that shown by the male characters. She has internalized the black middle-class expectations of femininity prevalent in the late 1960s, as shown in her "*natural style*" hair and her "*tweedy*" clothing (11), and she is therefore sympathetic to Tommy's struggle with feminine presentation.

When Tommy will not be turned away from her pursuit of Bill, Cynthia tries to coach Tommy on ways to increase her chances of success with him, and perhaps with (middle-class) men in general. Her comments reveal that she has connected Tommy's working-class status with a lack of femininity and an ignorance of romantic relationships, and she attempts to enlighten her on these topics. Tommy feels a similar impatience for a change in her love life because she sees her age as a sign of deterioration in her femininity and, by implication, her ability to attract desirable men: "Keep it to yourself, . . . but I was thirty my last birthday and haven't ever been married" (18). She almost begs Cynthia for advice, repeatedly asking, "What's wrong with me?" (18–19). Cynthia finally responds by saying, "You're too brash. You're too used to looking out for yourself. It makes us lose our femininity . . . It makes us hard . . . [. . .] We do for ourselves too much. [. . .] You have to let the black man have his manhood again" (19). Tommy's ability to "do for herself," the self-sufficiency that marks her as working-class, also marks her as hard and unfeminine. It is no accident that Childress names her Tommy, a male name that further masculinizes her, particularly in relation to the "*good, quiet taste*" of Cynthia (11). Cynthia urges Tommy to "Soften up" (21) and concludes her list of instructions with an appeal to passivity and the ultimate importance of physical appearance in attracting a man: "Don't chase him . . . at least don't let it look that way. Let him pursue you. [. . .] Let him do the talking. Learn to listen. Stay in the background a little. [. . .] What we need is a little more sex appeal [. . .] One more thing, . . . do you have to wear that wig?" (20). As is shown later on, Tommy is perfectly capable of fulfilling the role of a beautiful, African American woman. But for now, her appearance marks her as working class and therefore unfeminine.

Tommy's actions, on the other hand, begin to reveal a hint of middle-class awareness and distinction. For example, she recognizes and attempts to manipulate the connotations associated with particular food choices. She requests Chinese food when Bill offers to get her something to eat, and when he returns with excuses, she says, "You bought me a frank-footer? That's what you think a-me, a frank-footer? . . . If a queen sent you out to buy her a bucket-a Foo-yung, you wouldn't come back with no lonely-ass frank-footer" (22). She recognizes that she is being treated as something significantly lower than royalty, and she will not accept it. She is unashamedly vocal about deserving and expecting better. Even once the argument has passed, she comments dryly, "A orange never been near this" as she sips her orange drink (22).

Bill doesn't at first catch on to these clues, however, and the first adjustment of his perception of Tommy doesn't come until she reveals that her full name is Tomorrow, not the Thomasina that Bill expects. He responds, "Crazy! I never met a girl named Tomorrow" (23). Tommy begins to move out of her masculinized position as a working class, everyday woman, "what the society has made out of our women" (9), and is instead exoticized and eroticized, matching more closely with the ideal of feminine beauty presented in the centerpiece of Bill's "Wine In The Wilderness." Bill even connects the name—and, by implication, Tommy herself—to Shakespeare, the quintessential writer of bourgeois pretensions: "That's what Shakespeare said, . . . 'Tomorrow and tomorrow and tomorrow'" (23).

Bill has started to adjust his opinion of Tommy, but he does not seem to realize fully the error in his assumptions until he sees a change in her appearance—the same marker that he initially used to judge her. She changes out of her mismatched clothes into an African wrap and removes her wig. "*Her hair . . . must not be an accurate, well-cut Afro . . . but should be rather attractive natural hair*" (28). Bill is astounded by the change, and he stammers, "Baby, what . . . ? Where . . . where's the wig?" As he begins to take it all in, his approval is evident: "That is very becoming . . . the drape thing. . . . I don't know what to say" (28). He cannot seem to reconcile Tommy's changed appearance with his initial assumptions about her lower-class status.

Bill's perception of Tommy as increasingly feminine and middle class—whether or not she really is middle class—makes her desirable in his eyes, and he becomes flustered. "*He makes a haphazard line or two as he tries to remember the other image,*" and then, apparently giving up, he says to her, "Tell me something about yourself . . . anything" (28). To this she responds with a bit of personal and family history that quickly evolves into a brief history of the black Elks. She similarly educates Bill about the history of the African Methodist Episcopal (A. M. E.) Church, for which she was a Sunday school teacher for two years (29). Bill's first reaction is one of surprise—"I didn't know that" (29)—but the scene quickly moves into a reversal of a previous conversation about African American history, in which Bill tells Tommy about the various historical figures pictured in photographs on the walls of his apartment. Now Bill is the one asking questions, and Tommy is the one educating. She may not be intimately familiar with the image of Frederick Douglass, as Bill is, but she has her own history, more closely linked with the day-to-day, the here-and-now of the working class. Yet Bill still is having trouble matching her knowledge with his previous conception of her, and he asks, "How do you know about it?" It is not long before he is "*Seeing her with new eyes*" (29).

This conversation signals a disconnection between conventional ideas of education—or Bill's ideas of them—and the forms of education that Tommy has received. By presenting both Bill's and Tommy's versions of history in a positive light, where they are eager to learn from each other, Childress endorses a mingling of formal and informal education. Despite not having a high school education, Tommy is apparently qualified to teach the history of the A.M.E. Church, and, as Bill acknowledges, formal schooling is not necessarily useful in learning African American history anyway: "[Y]ou wouldn't a found out too much 'bout black history cause the books full-a nothin' but whitey, . . . all except the white ones who dug us, they not there either" (24).

To the contrary, formal, middle-class education—the kind Bill received—is connected in the play with whiteness. Bill devalues it in a number of instances, and Cynthia discredits her experience with formal education as well. She explains that she has had "the degree and the whole bit. For a time I thought I was about to move into another world, the so-called 'integrated' world, a place where knowledge and know-how could set you free and open all the doors, but that's a lie. I turned away from that idea. The first thing I did was give up dating white fellas" (19). What begins as an account of her educational history turns almost immediately into a statement about the limits of integration. Class—as embodied in an advanced education—is thus equated with race, providing one of many examples of the assumed link between the middle class and whiteness.

Tommy's lack of formal education is therefore not necessarily a problem in terms of building African American solidarity. To the contrary, the education that Tommy has received as a member of the uneducated, working classes places her, in some cases, in a position superior to that of the middle-class characters. In addition to telling Bill about the black Elks and the A.M.E. Church, she also teaches him and his friends the true meaning and social significance of the word "nigger," which none of them has previously understood. As in earlier instances, Tommy's understanding of social workings is much more sophisticated than what would be expected based on her unpolished exterior: "When they say 'nigger,' just dry-long-so, they mean educated you and uneducated me. They hate you and call you 'nigger,' I called you 'nigger' but I love you" (36).

But once again, Childress's representation of the relative values of lower and middle-class forms of education is not entirely consistent. Tommy continues to yearn for a formal education, and she comments as she tours Bill's apartment, "Books, books, books everywhere. 'Afro-American History.' I like that" (18). In fact, as Bill's perception of her slowly changes, Tommy adapts her appearance to match this perception and performs the part of his girlfriend, of the ideal bourgeois woman. This is not to imply that her performance is inauthentic. To the contrary, as shown earlier, in many ways this role appears to be more "natural" to her than the working class identity Cynthia and Sonny-man place upon her. But all identity, no matter how natural it may feel, involves a degree of performativity, and Tommy is playing middle class (and attractive woman) in all the right places.

This performance is made most explicit when Tommy overhears a telephone conversation in which Bill is heaping lavish praise on the beautiful woman depicted in the centerpiece of his triptych, "Wine In The Wilderness." Tommy mistakenly believes he is describing her, and her resulting growth of self-confidence manifests itself both internally and externally. "*She is suddenly awakened to the feeling of being loved and admired. She removes the wig and fluffs her hair* [. . .] *studies herself in a mirror. We see her taller, more relaxed and sure of herself*" (28). The changes to her physical appearance mirror an internal shift, but it is the external changes that create in the reader's mind the image of a more relaxed and self-confident Tommy. The performance, on one level, actually creates the change in her internal state.

Tommy's willingness to change reveals the conflation of her attraction to Bill with her middle-class aspirations, and in the course of the play it is difficult to separate the two. She wants to learn about Shakespeare, Frederick Douglass, and whatever else Bill will teach her. She sheds her own clothes and wears those that Bill provides for her. She attempts to impress him with her knowledge of black history. It is not long before she seems ready to leave her past life entirely behind, and again, she equates the internal with the physical, saying, "I'm gonna take a bath and let the riot and the hell of living go down the drain with the bath water" (30). The "hell of living" has seemingly been replaced, to her satisfaction, with Bill's middle-class life, which she hopes to enter as his girlfriend.

Of course, in order to be his girlfriend, she feels that she must please him by playing the role of the subservient female, following his lead and giving him exactly what he wants, and the middle of the play is an extended series of attempts to do just that. When Bill tries to paint her, he asks her to put her wig back on, but she responds, "You don't really like wigs, do you?" He confirms her suspicion, and she says, "Then let's have things the way you like" (28). When Bill gives her a crash course on Frederick Douglass, Monroe Trotter, and Harriet Tubman, Tommy drops the names of Martin Luther King and Malcolm X; as Childress notes, she is "*Eager to impress him*" (24). And after telling him about the A.M.E. Church, she confesses, "Oh, I'm just showin' off" (29).

At this point in the play, Tommy appears to associate middle-class markers with Bill alone—a black man—and not with white people. She says of "White folks, nothin' happens when I look at 'em. I don't hate 'em, don't love 'em, . . . just nothin' shakes a-tall. The dullest people in the world. The way they talk . . . 'Oh, hooty, hooty, hoo'. . . ." She then says that she likes Bill "with his black, uppity, high-handed ways" (20). In a single sentence she appears to present Bill as an alternative to whiteness, but simultaneously indicates that he shares many of the markers of the white folks that do nothing for her. These presumed similarities are confirmed a few lines later when Tommy imagines a conversation with Bill in which he says: "Mmmmm, 'Oh, hooty, hooty, hoo'" (20). This is precisely the language she has just placed in the mouths of white people. On the one hand, she distinguishes herself from everything that she associates with the white middle class; on the other hand, she aspires to these same middle class values when they are embodied in Bill.

It is only when she is rejected from Bill's group that she condemns the middle class and drops her subservient demeanor. She discovers that she was intended as the model for the "messed-up chick" and attacks Bill and his friends for their place within the class system and their disconnectedness from "real blackness." Perhaps because of the equation of the middle class with whiteness, she strikes back at the very middle-class values that she has just been revering and aspiring to by accusing them of whiteness and denying Bill the blackness that he so clearly wants to embody. Through this tirade she must therefore drop the performance of middle-class identity that she has adopted in Bill's apartment; she reverts to her former self, a change symbolized first and foremost—as at earlier points in the play—by her appearance. Almost the first thing she does is change back into her original mismatched outfit.

Tommy even admits to her earlier performance and hope of inclusion: "Trouble is I was Tommin' to you, to all of you, . . . 'Oh, maybe they gon' like me.' . . . I was your fool, thinkin' writers and painters know moren' me, that maybe a little bit of you would rub off on me" (34). Though her true name is Tomorrow, she admits to being an Aunt Thomasina as well; ironically, Bill is attracted to both the middle-class "Tommin'" of Aunt Thomasina and the femininity and exoticness of Tomorrow. But at this stage Tommy has abandoned her aspirations of upward mobility, and she viciously attacks the other characters' middle-class pretensions:

> The "black people" this and the "Afro-American" . . . that . . . You ain' got no use for none-a us. [. . .] Ain't a-one-a us you like that's alive and walkin' by you on the street

> . . . you don't like flesh and blood niggers. [. . .] If a black somebody is in a history book, or printed on a pitcher, or drawed on a paintin', . . . or if they're a statue, . . . dead, and outta the way, and can't talk back, then you dig 'em and full-a so much-a damn admiration and talk 'bout "our" history. But when you run into us livin' and breathin' ones, with the life's blood still pumpin' through us, . . . then you comin' on 'bout how we ain' never together. You hate us, that's what! You hate black me! (35)

Tommy's final statement, the culminating moment in her diatribe, gestures toward a belief in an essential identity, an essential blackness, the spirit of the African American woman that Bill imagined for the centerpiece of "Wine In The Wilderness." Though it is questionable whether this stable, internal self truly exists, Tommy continues to refer to it as she begins to calm down.

> Somewhere, in the middle of last night, I thought the old me was gone, . . . lost forever, and gladly. But today was flippin' time, so back I flipped. [. . .] I'm goin' back to the nitty-gritty crowd, where the talk is we-ness and us-ness. [. . .] Tomorrow-Marie, cussin' and fightin' and lookin' out for my damn self cause ain' nobody else 'round to do it, dontcha know. [. . .] if my hair is straight, or if it's natural, or if I wear a wig, or take it off, . . . that's all right; because wigs . . . shoes . . . hats . . . bags . . . and even this . . . (*She picks up the African throw she wore a few moments before . . . fingers it.*) They're just what you call . . . [. . .] Accessories. Somethin' you add on or take off. The real thing is takin' place on the inside . . . that's where the action is. That's 'Wine In The Wilderness,' . . . a woman that's a real one and a good one. And yall just better believe I'm it. (37)

But strangely, just as she is claiming the "real thing," everything that precedes the speech refutes such essentialism; it is Tommy's very mutability that allows her to fit herself to her surroundings. Even within this monologue, contradictions are visible: she talks about an unchanging, stable self, onto which she may place accessories, but she also refers to an "old me," indicating the possibility of a "new" self, of a recreation of identity.

What makes this discontinuity even more striking is Tommy's articulateness in these final speeches. Just when she is denouncing the middle class and heading back to the "nitty-gritty crowd," she slips into a highly nuanced assessment of societal structures and is even able to critique the fine points of language. For example, she warns Sonny-Man to "stop callin' me 'the' sister, . . . if you feelin' so brotherly why don't you say 'my' sister? Ain't no we-ness in your talk. 'The' Afro-American, 'the' black man, there's no we-ness in you. Who you think you are?" (35). This awareness of and facility with language analysis again is more indicative of formal, middle-class education than of the knowledge acquired by a high school drop-out. But it should be no surprise by now that Tommy draws from both.

While most readings of *Wine in the Wilderness* assume that the conclusion of the play indicates Bill's bending to Tommy, his recognition of her feminine beauty and her essential blackness, and her equal, if not superior claim to respect as a member of the working class, there in fact appears to be abundant evidence that Tommy bends to Bill, aspiring to, and attaining to some degree, the various markers of the middle class for the sake of gaining his approval. She has done the same in molding herself into a particular kind of woman: she has not convinced Bill that there are alternatives to his ideal woman, and she does not win him over with her unusual dress and her spunkiness. Rather, he discovers that Tommy has the ability to change herself into the feminine beauty that he has desired all along. Her performance throughout the play has convinced him of her ability to fill that role, and when he assures her that she has earned his love and respect, she chooses to stay, now posing for the centerpiece of the triptych. She is right; she is "Wine In The Wilderness." But Bill does not grant her this position because of her "cussin' and fightin'," as she may hope. Instead, she has earned her place by demonstrating her feminine beauty, her knowledge of class and race issues, and her quirky, yet sophisticated taste. Most importantly, she has shown her willingness to be the bourgeois woman that Bill wants her to be, and she has followed Cynthia's advice to "let the black man have his manhood again" (19).

Because Tommy is the main character in the play, she is typically read as the representative of the working classes and the primary character effecting change in Bill, but in fact the only character who is unequivocally marked as lower class is Bill's friend Oldtimer. He is described merely as an "old man," and he first appears in the play when he bursts into Bill's apartment, searching for a place to hide his loot—"*two or three bottles of liquor, a ham, a salami and a suit with price tags attached*" (6)—that he has picked up off the streets during the riot. His initial portrayal therefore lines up with that of Tommy, whom Sonny-man found "runnin' round in the middle-a this riot" (10). Unlike Tommy, however, who later reveals that she was an innocent bystander, Oldtimer has been a participant. He has not smashed any windows, instead grabbing looted items discarded by others, but he has nevertheless partaken in and contributed to the general lawlessness. He is thereby identified with the working class masses carrying out the riots in a way that Tommy is not.

Oldtimer is also, from this early stage, portrayed as crass and uneducated. His speaking skills are as poor as Tommy's and he is similarly given words like "trip-tick" (8) and "Likker" (32) to pronounce. But unlike Tommy, Oldtimer's speech content is also lacking. In many instances, Oldtimer echoes whatever Bill says, as though he cannot come up with anything to say on his own, or worse, he does not quite understand what Bill is talking about. As Bill describes his triptych, Oldtimer responds with parroted phrases like, "To our Abyssinian maiden," while pouring a drink (9); "Trip-tick will be finish . . . trip-tick will be finish . . ." (10); and "Wine in the wilderness . . . up against the wall . . . wine in the wilderness . . . up against the wall . . ." (10). When Bill compares "Wine In The Wilderness" to Victoria Falls, Oldtimer thinks that the woman's name is Victoria Falls, and when Bill uncovers the bare canvas intended for the "messed-up chick," Oldtimer gasps, "Your . . . your pitcher is gone" (9).

Perhaps some of this lack of mental acuity can be attributed to the looted liquor that he and Bill are drinking, but even this explanation is problematic. Bill does not appear to be having such a difficult time handling the alcohol, and Oldtimer comes off looking like a drunk. This is not inconsistent with his later appearance in the play, when he enters "*soaking wet*" after "*a hard night of drinking and sleeplessness*" (31). He explains that he was "Drinkin' with the boys. Likker was everywhere all night long" (32). He is seen drinking throughout the play and is out cavorting the whole night, and there is never any mention of a job, a home, or a family. He is presented as the quintessential, lower-class drifter, following like a puppy dog at Bill's heels.

In the end, it is not Tommy but Oldtimer that most closely matches Bill's vision for the final panel in his triptych. When Bill describes the woman for this panel, Oldtimer responds, "Oh, man, you talkin' 'bout my first wife" (9). He has openly acknowledged, in this way, his connection with people who are "ignorant [. . .] coarse, rude . . . vulgar . . . [. . .] poor, dumb." By implication, Oldtimer can also be viewed as someone who has had his "behind kicked until it's numb," until "there's no hope for [him]" (9). In the minds of Bill and his friends, he truly is "nothin'" (10), as shown by the fact that they do not even know his real name until Tommy arrives and asks him. It appears that Bill is not offended by him, as he is by the "messed-up chick" because, for one thing, Oldtimer is not a woman. Whereas Tommy's working-class status marks her as unfeminine and unattractive, these characteristics are not negative for Oldtimer, particularly from Bill's point of view. But perhaps more importantly, Bill allows Oldtimer to hang around because he is unobtrusive. Oldtimer's portrayal as stupid and unconcerned with class issues means that there is no conflict between him and Bill. Instead, he seems to idolize Bill, questioning nothing, and agreeing with everything he says and does. He is therefore portrayed not only as lower class, but also as being unaware of his lower-class status and of any possibility of change. He is perhaps even devoid of the desire for change, as he seems too stupid even to be unhappy. At the very least, he is incapable of voicing any frustration or call for equity. He lacks Tommy's sophisticated thought and action and is therefore completely unthreatening.

Oldtimer is a strange character, especially when placed side by side with Tommy, who seems to promote the potential for intelligence and race consciousness within the working class. But Tommy, as shown earlier, crosses these particular boundaries in places where Oldtimer does not. Childress cannot seem to imagine the lower class possessing intelligence or the inclination for social organization, and it is only a character like Tommy, who has begun to bridge the gap between the working and middle classes, who is capable of such things.

Writing that addresses lower-class issues is often paradoxical, because it is typically written by middle-class writers. *Wine in the Wilderness* is no exception. Childress is arguing on some level for race solidarity across class lines, but she is also attempting to create representations of the lower classes in Oldtimer and Tommy. Tommy is a believable character, largely because she has adopted middle-class characteristics, remaining lower class only on the most superficial levels: in her speech, her dress (at times), and her profession. But her inner self, her thoughts and feelings, mark her thoroughly as middle class. Childress needs Tommy to be able to speak for the working class, and she does not know how to do this other than to give her at least honorary middle-class status. On the other hand, Childress portrays Oldtimer as offensively, stereotypically lower class on all levels. There is no way that his character, as presented, would ever be able to speak for himself and his class like Tommy does.

Tommy therefore serves not as a character solely from one class or the other, but instead as a mediator between the lower and middle classes, between Oldtimer and Bill. Her interactions with Oldtimer are much more intimate than those he has with any of the other characters, and her relationship with him can be read as a friendship formed through a common class, mirroring the gender-based connection that she has with Cynthia. When Oldtimer arrives wet at Bill's apartment in the morning, she first helps him try to find his loot, then "*Leads him to a chair, dries his head with a towel*" (32). Almost like a mother, she says to him, "Get outta the wet things. You smell just like a whiskey still. Why don't you take care of yourself." Unmistakably—yet compassionately—placing herself above him, she scolds, "You got to be better than this." She has distanced herself from him and his behavior, separating herself from the lower class, but at the same time, she has an interest in returning to it, encouraging him and helping him to escape from it. Oldtimer cries, "I don' know nothin'. I'm ignorant," and she replies, "Hush that talk . . . You know lotsa things, everybody does" (32).

This intimate connection seems to flow in the other direction as well. When Oldtimer first hears about Tommy as Bill anticipates her arrival and describes his plan for the painting, he suggests that, "when she get here let's us stomp her to death" (10). But he is doing little more than following Bill's lead, attempting to predict Bill's train of thought and what he would like to hear. For, as soon as he meets Tommy, his attitude toward her changes. She inquires after his real name—Edmond Lorenzo Matthews—shaming the rest of the party for never even having wondered, let alone asked. Oldtimer responds by giving her a chair, saying, "Nobody call me that in a long, long time" (12), and soon he is "*Admiring Tommy*" and saying things like,

"Oh, Lord, I wish, I wish, I wish I was young again" (13). She has no problem reciprocating the flirtation.

As the scene continues, Tommy is fully engaged with the other characters in a lively conversation, with much joking and playful sparring. Oldtimer, however—presumably not quite sharp enough to contribute to the conversation—is focused on Tommy and is carefully attending to her story with a degree of interest and understanding unmatched by the others. As she describes her experiences in the riots, Oldtimer cuts in periodically with comments like "Oh, no they didn't!" (13), "Shame, what a shame," and "Child, when hard luck fall it just keep fallin'" (14). He empathizes with her and her situation in a way that the other characters do not.

At the end of the play, though it is Oldtimer who enlightens her to her role in the triptych, Tommy is nevertheless willing to forgive him, implicating Bill, Cynthia, and Sonny-man in the deception, but not him. He is the only one in the room that is spared her wrath. Bill starts to get upset when he finds out that Oldtimer has leaked the information, but Tommy jumps in with, "Leave him the hell alone. He ain't said nothin' that ain' so!" (33). Her sole criticism of him is that he lets the others take advantage of him. "Oldtimer, you their fool too. 'Til I got here they didn't even know your damn name. There's something inside-a me that says I ain' suppose to let nobody play me cheap. Don't care how much they know!" (34). She has a connection with Oldtimer through a shared class that the others do not, and she sides with him on a number of issues. But she has also made the move toward a more middle-class standing, and she is doing her best to pull him along with her to that more privileged position as well as to protect him from the harshness of it.

Tommy's final place in the triptych is representative of this intermediary position, as she does not simply replace the first "Wine In The Wilderness." While the original triptych is intended as a reflection on "black womanhood," composed of "Black girlhood," "Wine In The Wilderness," and the "messed-up chick," the final version of the triptych represents blackness through history. It begins not with the young girl, but with Oldtimer, whom Bill describes as "the guy who was here before there were scholarships and grants and stuff like that, the guy they kept outta the schools, the man the factories wouldn't hire, the union wouldn't let him join . . ." On the far side are "Young Man and Woman [Cynthia and Sonny-man], workin' together to do our thing." And, finally, in the middle, is Tommy as "Wine In The Wilderness," though Bill refers to her as Tomorrow, granting her the increased femininity necessary for her role in the centerpiece. "Look at Tomorrow. She came through the biggest riot of all, . . . somethin' called 'Slavery,' and she's even comin' through the 'now' scene, . . . folks laughin' at her, even her own folks laughin' at her. And look *how* . . . with her head high like she's poppin' her fingers at the world" (38).

Bill does not explicitly lay out its trajectory, but the implications of the triptych are striking. The references to Oldtimer's place in the past, when all was not good with the race, combined with the "now" of Tommy's panel, implies that Cynthia and Sonny-man's panel represents the possibility for the future. This is perhaps the clearest proof that Bill has not substantially adjusted his view on class, instead seeing the progression of the race as a movement upward from the meager working class opportunities afforded Oldtimer to the lives of bourgeois social workers and writers. Tommy is left in the middle. She is the "now," but she is also connected with the past of slavery, and her name, "Tomorrow," connects her with the future as well. She is the bridge between Oldtimer and Cynthia and Sonny-man, connecting the past and the future, the lower and the middle class. Tommy's movement between classes in the play is thereby mirrored in the triptych, as she represents the race's "progress" through the generations.

In the end, *Wine in the Wilderness* offers a confused vision of the relationships among race, class, and gender. Readers are clearly meant to scorn Bill's middle-class character for belittling Tommy and Oldtimer, but the working class is simultaneously criticized for its riotous behavior through the voice of Tommy: "They hollerin' whitey, whitey . . . but who they burn out? Me" (14). The working class is thereby beaten down just as it is being elevated. Meanwhile, Tommy is successful in attaining a degree of self-respect and autonomy by the end of the play, not allowing Bill and his friends to judge her prematurely, despite their apparent sexism, but she then uses the autonomy she has earned to pursue and acquire a stereotypically feminine and subservient role. Childress successfully demonstrates that the working class and femininity are not mutually exclusive, but she also adheres to the limiting notion that femininity and passivity are necessary components of middle-class womanhood and female attractiveness.

As a result, race subjugates both class and gender in *Wine in the Wilderness*. In attempting to juggle all of these issues, Childress cannot come up with a successful, consistent pattern of beliefs and practices. The one undisputed location of social and cultural value in the play is in "true" blackness, in "flesh and blood niggers," but there is no clear indication of who qualifies for this title. As much as Childress would like to proclaim the importance of working-class or feminist solidarity, she cannot find a way to reconcile these goals fully with the fundamental objective of maintaining race solidarity.

Given the inherent messiness of the categories, Childress's representation of the workings of class and gender within the context of race is a realistic one (though not, I hope, a final one), even as it proves to be problematic and to raise more questions than it answers. There has been a reluctance to take a close look at these issues within the African American community, perhaps because of the fear that "they might . . . lose valuable and hardworking allies in their struggles" against racism (Combahee River Collective 279). It is this fear that accounts for much of the pronounced backlash in response to the publication in 1978 of William Julius Wilson's

The Declining Significance of Race: Blacks and Changing American Institutions, but scholars have nevertheless continued to attempt an investigation of these controversial topics. Angela Y. Davis undertook the challenge in *Women, Race and Class* in 1981, and bell hooks has offered her perspective more recently in *Where We Stand: Class Matters* (2000). On the literary front, Nicole King has begun to consider the implications of class within African American literature, but there is still a disturbing lack of criticism that engages with these concerns. *Wine in the Wilderness* provides a fertile ground for the discussion and analysis of these issues, because Childress, whether intentionally or not, avoids the perpetually flawed generalizations of writers like Baraka and Reed, and instead offers a realism that leaves her audience with the burden of pondering the questions raised by the convoluted intersections of race, class, and gender.

Notes

1. For feminist considerations of *Wine in the Wilderness*, see Gayle Austin, "Alice Childress: Black Woman Playwright as Feminist Critic," *The Southern Quarterly: A Journal of the Arts in the South* 25:3 (1987): 53–62 and *Feminist Theories for Dramatic Criticism* (Ann Arbor: University of Michigan Press, 1990) 88–92; Martha Gilman Bower, *"Color Struck" Under the Gaze: Ethnicity and the Pathology of Being in the Plays of Johnson, Hurston, Childress, Hansberry, and Kennedy* (Westport, CT: Praeger, 2003); and Janet Brown, *Feminist Drama: Definition and Critical Analysis* (Metuchen, NJ: Scarecrow Press, 1979) 56–70.
2. Elizabeth Brown-Guillory argues that "sexism, racism, and classism are immutably connected to black women's oppression" (106) in her brief "Synopsis and Analysis" introducing *Wine in the Wilderness* in her collection *Wines in the Wilderness: Plays by African American Women from the Harlem Renaissance to the Present* (New York: Greenwood Press, 1990) 104–9. For further investigations of these interrelated issues in the play, see La Vinia Delois Jennings, *Alice Childress* (New York: Twayne, 1995) 65–75 and Patricia R. Schroeder, "Re-Reading Alice Childress," *Staging Difference: Cultural Pluralism in American Theatre and Drama*, ed. Marc Maufort (New York: Peter Lang, 1995) 323–37.
3. *Wine in the Wilderness* by Alice Childress. Copyright, 1969. Used by permission of Flora Roberts, Inc.
4. Childress is liberal in her use of ellipses, and I have left them intact in my quotations. Where they are mine, I have enclosed them in brackets [. . .]. Italics are taken from the original and indicate stage directions.
5. See Brown 67 and Jennings 58–59, 65–66.

Works Cited

Baraka, Amiri. "Afro-American Literature and Class Struggle." *Black American Literature Forum* 14.1 (1980): 5–14.

Bower, Martha Gilman. *"Color Struck" Under the Gaze: Ethnicity and the Pathology of Being in the Plays of Johnson, Hurston, Childress, Hansberry, and Kennedy.* Westport, CT: Praeger, 2003.
Brown-Guillory, Elizabeth. *Their Place on the Stage: Black Women Playwrights in America.* New York: Greenwood Press, 1988.
———. *Wines in the Wilderness: Plays by African American Women from the Harlem Renaissance to the Present.* New York: Greenwood Press, 1990.
Childress, Alice. *Wine in the Wilderness: A Comedy-Drama.* New York: Dramatists Play Service, 1969.
———. "A Candle in a Gale Wind." *Black Women Writers (1950–1980): A Critical Evaluation.* Ed. Mari Evans. Garden City, NY: Anchor-Doubleday, 1984. 111–16.
Combahee River Collective. "The Combahee River Collective Statement." *Home Girls: A Black Feminist Anthology.* New York: Kitchen Table/Women of Color Press, 1983. 272–82.
Davis, Angela Y. *Women, Race and Class.* New York: Random House, 1981.
hooks, bell. *Where We Stand: Class Matters.* New York: Routledge, 2000.
Jennings, La Vinia Delois. *Alice Childress.* New York: Twayne, 1995.
King, Nicole. "'You think like you white': Questioning Race and Racial Community through the Lens of Middle-Class Desire(s)." *Novel: A Forum on Fiction* 35:2–3 (2002): 211–30.
Reed, Ishmael. "Mike Tyson and the White Hope Cult." *Airing Dirty Laundry.* Ed. Ishmael Reed. 1993. New York: Addison-Wesley, 1994. 68–74.
Wilson, William Julius. *The Declining Significance of Race: Blacks and Changing American Institutions.* 1978. 2nd ed. Chicago: University of Chicago Press, 1980.

5

Child's play

Ntozake Shange's Audience of Colored Girls

PAMELA HAMILTON

With its head-on tackling of rape, feminine sexuality, sisterhood, and domestic abuse, Ntozake Shange's *for colored girls who have considered suicide when the rainbow is enuf* is doubtless a feminist play, lauded and disparaged as such since it first found its way to America's most prominent stage, Broadway, in 1976. But critics' focus on issues of black womanhood obscure the play's deliberately chosen title. Interpreted literally, the title addresses not adult women but their daughters, and Shange, in her introductory comments, characterizes her poems as words of "a young black *girl's* (emphasis added) growing up" (xv).[1] With a title explicitly targeting girls, an author's characterization of her work as a charting of girlhood, and significant portions of the choreopoem that seem to speak directly to youth, it is surprising that critics primarily consider what women of color find in the piece. *for colored girls* likely becomes a woman's, rather than a girl's, play because of its explicit treatment of life experiences from which most parents strive to shield youth: sex, unwanted pregnancy, disappointment, death. This group of poems, which detail the danger and distress of being a woman of color, does not seem at first the type of text unreservedly handed a child. Yet, for Shange, it is exactly this withholding of vital information by generations of women that does more harm than good to the young, and she hopes to interrupt this silence with *for colored girls*:

> The reason that *For Colored Girls* is entitled *For Colored Girls* is that that's who it was for. . . . I want a twelve-year-old girl to reach out for and get some information that

> isn't just contraceptive information but emotional information. . . . If there is an audience for whom I write, it's the little girls who are coming of age. I want them to know that they are not alone and that we adult women thought and continue to think about them. (Tate 161–162)[2]

Shange's claim that her text is for girls need not be accepted at face value or dismissed completely. Her audience is likely a combination of girls and women.

Critics have observed that certain poems in Shange's text seem to appeal directly to a younger audience. Frances Smith Foster comments that portions of the play "imply that the work is for young people as well as adults" (201). Neal A. Lester notes Shange's text addresses an audience of both children and adults. Jean Young describes *for colored girls* as a ritualistic piece in which women undergo rites of passage on their way to self-fulfillment and notes that some poems seem to serve as warnings for young girls.[3] What is missing from this critical commentary is an extended meditation on strategies Shange uses to address this dual audience. This chapter seeks first to enrich what has been passing commentary on the text's child audience by using the concept of cross-writing (which succeeds Foster's and Lester's commentary) to establish a framework for considering *for colored girls* as a text that speaks to the young and the old. This framework allows for acknowledgment of an older audience and Shange's feminist project. But, as critical works have meditated extensively on that topic, the chapter will not focus on what women (and men) may find in the piece. Instead, it focuses on what the text offers youth. In addition to exploring the play's usefulness for a youthful audience, a second, related goal is establishing a foundation for considering where and how the piece might fit within the tradition of children's theatre, as well as African American children's literature.

Applying concepts of children's literature to a feminist text is appropriate, considering the mergers between the projects of feminist and children's literature critics. Lissa Paul points out the usefulness of "appropriating feminist theory to children's literature" (149) in exposing commonalities between women's literature and children's literature, one of them being the language of otherness. Appropriating children's literature theory to a feminist text also proves useful in illuminating such mergers.

In their attempt to gain for children's literature the same sort of increased critical recognition accorded once-ignored fields such as women's and African American literature, children's literature theorists have advanced the concept of cross-writing as a means to rescue children's books (and their critics) from the periphery of literary studies. "It will help us relocate children's literature at the center of the curricula at our schools and universities," U. C. Knoepflmacher and Mitzi Myers write in an introduction to a special issue of *Children's Literature* on the topic (xiv). The authors define cross-writing texts as those that transcend culturally imposed binaries by employing a "dialogic mix of older and younger voices" and activating "traffic between phases of life we persist in regarding as opposites" (vii–viii). Shange's text reflects both features.

The seven female characters in the text are at a variety of life stages. Among the voices that emerge from *for colored girls* are those of an excited eight-year-old courting a childhood hero, a curious teen pondering shedding her virginity, and a world-weary woman who has suffered through physical abuse and the loss of her children to emerge self-fulfilled. These voices often complement and parallel each other. Ideas about sexuality, relationships, and identity that younger characters express emerge altered by experience in the words of older characters.

Such parallels may be drawn between the poems "toussaint" and "i used to live in the world." The voices of speakers of these two poems clearly reflect female characters of markedly different ages. The speaker in "toussaint" identifies herself repeatedly as a girl or child and refers to her male counterpart as a boy. The poem is filled with images of childhood—hopscotch games, children's books, and a Raggedy Ann doll. In contrast, the speaker in "i used to live in the world" refers to herself as a woman and her male counterparts as men. Her life experiences have forced her to shutter herself against potential peril. The girl in "toussaint" can engage with a boy she encounters on the riverbank, even if she must overcome initial hesitation. The woman in "i used to live in the world" cannot; like her universe, the lady in blue, at this stage of life, is a "tunnel closin" (39). Unlike the girl, who traipses clear across the city of St. Louis from the library to her home to the river, the woman's once-expansive world has been constricted to a six-block radius in Harlem.

And yet, though these characters are at different stages of life, there are parallels between their worlds. As the girl skips beside the river imagining eating bananas with Toussaint L'Ouverture, she actually is skipping past drunken men, a perilous position for any woman, much less a little girl alone. Her exposure to danger parallels that of the woman, who notes the presence of "shit & broken lil whiskey bottles" (36) as she describes life in Harlem. The girl's acknowledgment of "skipping past ol drunk men" (28) lacks the conscious awareness of the woman. Though she recognizes their presence, she does not understand the threat posed. The woman, however, interprets the presence of whiskey bottles "left to make me bleed" and aggressive men as a direct threat to her life.

The girl's casual observation about her surroundings makes her encounter with Toussaint Jones, whom she accepts as a replacement for Toussaint L'Ouverture, somewhat startling. Immediately, after she skips past drunkards, Toussaint Jones seems to "jump out" of nowhere. His calling to her, "HEY GIRL YA BETTAH COME OVAH HEAH N TALK TO ME" (28) is hauntingly similar to the threatening language of men who accost the woman, saying "COME OVER HERE BITCH/CANT YA SEE THIS IS $5" (38). Perhaps even Toussaint Jones could pose the same latent threat as the drunken men or the friend-rapist. The disturbing alignment of young Toussaint with dangerous men does not negate the positive aspects of the girl's encounter with him. Threats to life are mostly muted in "toussaint" and the overall tone of the poem is buoyant.[4] Shange's choice to locate positive relationships in childhood suggests that camaraderie between men and women is possible only when relationships are nonsexual. Sexual activity with men has the potential to sever otherwise positive relationships with them.

One of Shange's projects in the text is to warn young women about the dangers of sexual intercourse. In her interview with Tate, Shange claims that a purpose of the play is to provide "emotional information" to young girls as an alternative to contraceptive information. Her teachings, then, are limited primarily to relationships between men and women, and many of the poems detail the potential danger of heterosexual relationships—a woman becomes pregnant and must abort her fetus; a woman spurns male lovers revengefully but is left empty; women sever their bond of sisterhood for the love of a man and are left wanting. Even the joyous celebration of the lady in yellow's loss of virginity in "graduation nite" and the lady in blue's devotion to music and dance in "now i love somebody more than" are fast undercut—first slightly, by an angry poem of disappointed love and, then severely, by ominous passages introducing the threat of rape. Sexual awakening for women in patriarchal societies "becomes a social liability" putting women at risk for "emotional and psychological vulnerability and abuse" (Lester, *Critical Study* 38–39).

"abortion cycle #1" sounds a similar warning and also illustrates the difficulty of clearly categorizing Shange's characters as fully grown adults or infantile children. The lady in blue's description of the abortion is very much in the voice of a young, perhaps teenage, mother-to-be. The character expresses naiveté at learning of her pregnancy: "i really didnt mean to/i really didnt think i cd" (22). These statements make the character seem more like a girl, only beginning to learn the workings of her body and the consequences of sex, than a grown woman. The speaker is also especially concerned with the reaction of her peer group and others: "i cdnt have my friends see this/dyin danglin tween my legs" (22).

The characters in "graduation nite," and "now i love somebody more than" are also not quite "grown." The lady in yellow, in "graduation nite," celebrates her high school graduation and speaks of seventh-grade crushes as if they still have relevance in her life. Though she proclaims "WE WAZ GROWN," even she knows that she is only partly adult (9). She admits her lover looks at her "*like* I waz a woman or something" (emphasis added, 10). The lady in yellow recognizes that she is not quite a woman but expects the experience of sex to bring her closer to it.

This poem, along with "now i love somebody more than," are among the few poems in which Shange's characters still speak of parents. The lady in yellow speaks of their high school training preparing to move them "from mama to what ever waz out there" (7). The lady in blue mentions the Spanish heritage of her "papa" before claiming a new heritage that mixes her father's Spanish heritage with American blackness. The speaker in the poem "toussaint" also comments on the presence of parents when she notes the generational shift that causes her to refer to toussaint as a black man, rather than a Negro. In these poems, the specter of guardians hovers over these teenagers, making them seem quite young in comparison with other women in the text, who have long ago stopped referencing parents and the protection they provide. The characters in these poems are thus more like children than adults. But, they are children on the precipice of adulthood, about to break free of parental protection and into their own worlds. Once they escape parental protection, these women are free to enter into a new familial structure, formed through relationships with men.

These meeting grounds between child and adult characters do not diminish the text's establishment of a buffer—temporal though it may be—between the worlds of the child and the adult. The title addresses "colored girls," but Shange's characters are described as ladies, creating distance between youth and adulthood. Still, the buffer is easily breached. Repeatedly, the experiences of child and adult meet on the grounds of commonly experienced trauma. These common traumas establish the second basis for considering *for colored girls* a cross-writing text—it activates traffic between life phases. Trauma is the copula between child and adult in Shange's text.

The play's structure emphasizes this contact between life stages. *for colored girls* lacks the rigidity that divisions into acts or scenes might provide, suggesting fluidity between the life stages of the lives staged. Instead, poems meet seamlessly. Music, lighting, and quiet entrances and exits of characters subtly mark shifts from one voice to another. "dark phrases" slides silently into "graduation nite" with a switch from the children's play songs "Shortenin' Bread" and "Little Sally Walker" to a playing of a then-popular record, "Dancing in the Street." A "sudden light change," accompanied by hurried exits offstage ushers in the poem "latent rapists." Even characters slip in and out of different personas: The lady in purple's narration of the story of Sechita conjures her image in the form of the lady in green; stage directions indicate that the lady in blue "becomes" a man hounding a woman in "i used to live in the world." In its structure and its characters' experiences of trauma, the text rejects conventional wisdoms that treat childhood and adulthood as two separate life periods, allowing Shange to address literal (adolescents) and figurative (grown women) "colored girls." In *for colored girls*, except at the play's end, a child is never completely a child and an adult never a full adult.

Both children and adults experience extreme forms of trauma—whether they are children dropped from a fifth-story window, the physically and emotionally abused mother of those children unable to save them, or the father of those children made crazier by war. Traumatic experiences of child characters in the text shatter the myth of an idyllic childhood in which the protection of parents and other guardians spares the child pain. The girl speaker of "toussaint" suffers the traumatic effects of racism; the doomed children of Crystal and Beau Willie Brown are abused by their father and unaided by their mother; the unnamed "black girl" who is the subject of "dark phrases" struggles to locate herself in the world, to find her own song.

"dark phrases" introduces the original trauma that will incarnate itself again and again through the lives and experiences of Shange's seven different characters. The lady in brown introduces the original traumatic event of the black girl: she inhabits the space where gender and race intersect. Being born black and female is not in itself a traumatic event, but, American black femininity has historically faced a multipronged attack. The Combahee River Collective asserts that the origins of the black feminist project—*for colored girls* is one of the earliest artistic representations of its ideology—lie in the "historical reality of Afro-American women's continuous life-and-death struggle for survival and liberation" ("Black Feminist Statement" 210). The black girl's inability to discover her own song is not due to an innate lack of rhythm or voicelessness. Instead this girl's fledging voice is silenced early in life by an oppressive patriarchy.

Like a textbook victim of early trauma, this girl's childhood has been stolen. The lady in brown narrates her dilemma:

dark phrases of womanhood
of never havin been a girl
half-notes scattered
without rhythm/no tune
distraught laughter fallin
over a black girl's shoulder
it's funny/ it's hysterical
the melody-less-ness of her dance
don't tell nobody don't tell a soul
she's dancing on beer cans & shingles (3)

The girl is forced into early womanhood and is never a girl because she remains fixated on the original trauma and is thus unable to move into a healthy adulthood. "Trauma arrests the course of normal development by its repetitive intrusion into the survivor's life," according to psychiatrist Judith Herman (37). The early traumatic experiences of childhood steal the innocence of girlhood and plunge her into dark phrases of womanhood. The distraught laughter surrounding the girl indicates the sort of mockery she faces by the doubly oppressive white patriarchal society.

Interestingly, Shange chooses the word "hysterical" to describe the girl's physical movements. Hysteria—what Herman calls the "archetypal psychological disorder of women" (9)—gave rise to the first serious investigations of psychological trauma. Study of hysteria by Jean-Martin Charcot and his successors Sigmund Freud and Pierre Janet laid the groundwork for modern psychological trauma theory. In *The Aetiology of Hysteria*, Freud claimed that every case of hysteria was rooted in premature sexual experience. Freud later came to doubt his patients' stories of early childhood abuse and abandoned the traumatic theory of hysteria for psychoanalysis. "Freud's recantation signified the end of the heroic age of hysteria" (Herman 14). Eventually, the word hysteria was abandoned for its burdensomely negative connotation. Shange's reference to hysteria recalls the long-discarded term for the trauma-induced disorder. The word serves doubly to indicate the girl's trauma and as authorial criticism of society's mockery of this young black girl, its denial of her voice and song. Like Freud's denial of early sexual abuse in women precipitated by a rise in anti-feminism at the twilight of the nineteenth century silenced those women once given voice through the work of their investigators, the black girl, too, has been shut up. The lady in brown demands this silence end:

sing a black girl's song
bring her out
to know herself
to know you
but sing her rhythms
carin/ struggle/ hard times
sing her a song of life
she's been dead so long
closed in silence so long
she doesn't know the sound
of her own voice
her infinite beauty
she's half-notes scattered
without rhythm/no tune
sing her sighs
sing the song of her possibilities
sing a righteous gospel
let her be born
let her be born
& handled warmly. (4–5)

This black girl's song must stimulate recognition, of both herself and her sisters, and of the "struggle" and "hard times" inherited because she inhabits the space where color and gender intersect. The black girl's song breaks deadening silence, requires admission of one's own beauty, and citation of one's own potential. Most importantly, it is a song that stimulates rebirth, necessary for the survival of the black woman. Black women in the text lack direction in adult life because of lost childhood; the poem "dark phrases" foregrounds the cacophony of the women in the text, who do not achieve harmony until the final song of the play.

The trauma of the girl's childhood not only holds destructive potential for the black woman she will become but also provides the basis for her survival. Cathy Caruth argues that modern trauma theory too often neglects trauma's role in sustaining the lives of its victims. Instead, theory tends to focus on the destructive repetition of trauma. Caruth suggests a more complex understanding of the traumatic effect; it becomes a way of surviving:

> Repetition, in other words, is not simply the attempt to grasp that one has almost died but, more fundamentally and enigmatically, the very attempt *to claim one's own survival.* If history is to be understood as the history of a trauma, it is a history that is experienced as the endless attempt to assume one's survival as one's own. (64)

Throughout the text, the experiences of women in the play represent repeated incarnations of the original trauma of black femaleness. It is difficult to pinpoint exactly what type of trauma the black girl in "dark phrases" has experienced, but this nebulousness is appropriate. Repetitive episodes of trauma, typically revisited through memory, are the means by which the circumstance of the original traumatic event is clarified. Thus, when women throughout the text experience the trauma of racism and the trauma of physical abuse, they are moving steadily toward reclamation of their own lives; they are learning to survive.

The lady in brown revisits a traumatic childhood in "toussaint." The poem, clearly in the voice of a child, transforms the lady in brown on stage and in the text from an adult woman to a youngster finding her way to a public library in 1955. In her recollection of the discovery of Toussaint L'Ouverture, the lady in brown creates the closest thing to an idyllic childhood in the text, and yet, as her choice of childhood hero suggests, this child, too, experiences trauma.

Toussaint L'Ouverture becomes a shield to protect her from the brutality of being a colored girl in America in 1955. She chooses a warrior for a protector because she is constantly under assault. She imagines removing white girls from her hopscotch games and running away from integrated homes, streets, and schools. As she puts it: "1955 waz not a good year for lil black girls" (27). In 1955, many schools in America in fact were not integrated, but a Supreme Court ruling ordering the desegregation of the nation's schools had laid groundwork a year earlier for the conditions the child describes. It was also the year in which Rosa Parks refused her seat to a white rider and sparked an 11-month bus boycott that forced desegregation of buses in Montgomery, Alabama. The colored child's world is one of violence, and she chooses a figure of resistance and violence as "the beginning uv reality for me" (26).

This mostly positive girlhood remembered by the lady in brown exists only in memory and may well be fictitious, but the recreation through memory or other means of such a childhood is necessary to the woman's survival. It is impossible for the victim of childhood trauma to recover belief in protective parents or guardians—or of a protective society—foundational to building relationships with others. What the trauma survivor victim must do is remember and mourn the loss of such protection in childhood. A positive memory of a caring, comforting guardian "salvaged from the wreckage" of trauma may help sustain the survivor of childhood trauma during the period of remembrance and mourning (Herman 194). Toussaint represents such a positive memory not only for the lady in brown, but for all the women in the text.

Because the girl's existence is literally codified by her skin color—to the point where she can only compete against other "colored" children in the summer reading contest—the girl is unable to find self-identification in popular books for (white) children. First, there are no black characters represented in the books she describes as the typical fare in the children's room. But, perhaps more importantly, books filled with "magic rabbits" or "a pooh bear" cannot adequately address the unimagined dilemmas this child faces.[5] Her inability to relate to the books in the children's reading room forces the child version of the lady in brown into the ADULT READING ROOM to search for books. Upon entering the forbidden ADULT READING ROOM, the child transgresses a boundary between adulthood and childhood and is punished by the adult world for doing so. When she wins a reading contest for the most books read by a "colored" child, she is disqualified for reading an "adult" book. But the experiences of the child underscore the artificial nature of the boundary between childhood and adulthood. As a "colored" person, this child is subject to the same Jim Crow laws as an adult, and the psychological and emotional effects cannot be assumed to be different. They may even be more devastating because a youth has not had time to develop coping strategies.[6]

In *for colored girls*, children are typically at peril. Crystal's children, Naomi and Kwame, are not safe even in their own home; their father dangles them from an apartment window in an attempt to elicit a marriage agreement from their mother. Beau Willie's killing his children is the climax of a series of abusive conflicts. Before they are born, he rejects them as bastards, and at one point, he uses Kwame in his high chair as a weapon against Crystal. Naomi and Kwame lack adequate guardians and the protection those guardians would seek to provide. Crystal seeks repeatedly to protect her children from Beau Willie by kicking him out of her home, getting the courts to bar his access to the children, and even threatening to kill Beau Willie if he touches her children. But her desire for love and kindness and dependence on the abusive Beau Willie for them leave her vulnerable and nullify her attempt at guardianship.

Beau Willie and Crystal are inadequate guardians precisely because they are not quite grown-ups. They are not quite grown-ups because their experience of trauma stymies their development. Crystal's sexual initiation occurs when she is only 13, after Beau Willie "caught her on the stairway" (55). His catching her insinuates that Crystal, unlike the lady in yellow, does not choose the timing of her sexual initiation; instead, Beau Willie does. A 13-year-old may be undergoing physical changes that indicate the onset of puberty, but she lacks emotional maturity that would allow her to enter a sexual relationship as an equal rather than a subordinate. Thus, though Shange never identifies Beau Willie by age, his taking of Crystal aligns him with the rapists imagined earlier in the choreopoem. Crystal's experience of the trauma of sexual assault in childhood arrests her, preventing development into adulthood. From her sexual initiation on, she struggles to see herself as more than an extension of Beau Willie Brown. By the time she is 14, according to Beau Willie's account, she wants him to marry her. And, even as she ridicules and rejects him after his return from war, she is unable to resist his "kindness" at the crucial moment when he seizes the children.

Crystal's inability to become a functional adult is typical of victims of childhood abuse. Abuse forces children to relinquish their childhood and prevents the grown adult from ever fully escaping the trauma imposed in youth. Psychiatrist Judith Herman notes that reverberations of childhood trauma continue well into adulthood. The survivor of childhood abuse, according to Herman, is a "prisoner of her childhood" (110) who reencounters the trauma in her attempts to create a new life. Consequently, the survivor of child abuse may find it difficult to mature into adulthood because of her difficulties to form stable relationships.

Where Crystal's assault is a manifestation of systematic, patriarchal oppression of black women, Beau Willie's assault is a manifestation of the oppression of black men. Sadly, too many critics have ignored the sympathetic portrayal of Beau Willie and have instead attacked the play for its allegedly negative treatment of black men. Shange's play attacks both sexism and racism, but does not advocate separatism from black men as a means of resisting sexism. Instead, Shange's characters long for understanding between black men and black women. This is consistent with the ideology of black feminism laid out in the Combahee River Collective statement. In a 1977 manifesto often regarded as a seminal document in the creation of a black feminist movement, this group advocates coalition building based on commonalities. Thus, they seek to build bridges on the basis of gender with white women and on the basis of race with black men.[7]

Besides sharing the burden of racism, Beau Willie and Crystal also share the experience of psychological trauma. As sexual assault represents the feminist experience of trauma, going to war is its masculinist counterpart, Herman argues in her feminist revision of the history of trauma: "Rape and combat might thus be considered complementary social rites of initiation into the coercive violence at the foundation of adult society. They are the paradigmatic forms of trauma for women and men respectively" (61). Herman integrates these male and female versions of trauma in charting its genealogy. Hysteria gives rise to the study of trauma but is abandoned. Traumatic episodes again attract attention at the start of the twentieth century in the experiences of World War I veterans. The women's movement in the 1970s draws attention to rape, but because women (and children) are devalued members of society, their traumatic experiences are not validated until similar episodes are documented in the men returning from the Vietnam War (1–21).

Shange's text, while recognizing the disconnect between Beau Willie and Crystal brought about by Beau Willie's attempt to reinscribe an oppressive patriarchy in Crystal's home, nevertheless stresses commonalities between these male and female characters. Shange neither blames Beau Willie entirely for his predicament nor absolves him. Clearly, Beau Willie is not wholly innocent before Vietnam. He has raped Crystal, who observes that Beau Willie has always been a "fool niggah," but she also says "he came home crazy as hell" (55). Beau Willie contributes to his own demise by spending his money on alcohol and other drugs, but it is unclear whether Beau Willie's substance abuse began before or after his service in the war. Veterans returning from Vietnam often turned to drugs and alcohol as a means of coping with the psychological effects of war. If the Vietnam War has not created Beau Willie's destructive impulses, it has certainly nurtured them. One might even read Beau Willie's post-War attacks on Crystal as a reenactment of violent episodes in Vietnam. Yet, the federal government refuses to acknowledge its role in feeding Beau Willie's neurosis, failing to supply him with adequate financial benefits that would help him survive.

Like Crystal, Beau Willie is needy for kindness and stymied in his personal development. Shange likens him to a "huge baby wit stubble & nuts" (56) before describing his first abusive encounter with Crystal and the children. This image of Beau Willie as an overgrown child is echoed before his second, fatal encounter with the children. Beau Willie sits in hotel room in the middle of the day, doing nothing:

> . . . beau willie
> waz sittin in this hotel in his drawers drinkin
> coffee & wine in the heat of the day spillin shit all
> over hisself/ laughin/ bout how he waz gonna get crystal
> to take him back/ & let him be a man in the house/ & she
> wdnt even have to go to work no more / he got dressed
> all up in his ivory shirt & checkered pants to go see
> crystal & get this mess all cleared up/ (57–58)

As he sits in the hotel room dreaming up a scheme to get a bigger government paycheck, Beau Willie seems more like a boy than a man. His naked body clothed only in underwear and his inability to imbibe without making a mess recall Shange's earlier characterization of him as a huge baby. Like an eager boy, he puts on his Sunday best, hoping it will win Crystal's approval, for she must permit even his desire to "be a man in the house."

Beau Willie's attempt to reinscribe patriarchal oppression in his own house—to be a man in the house and force Crystal into a marriage she does not want—precipitates the destruction of his family. Once he seizes the children, Beau Willie insists on Crystal's acquiescence to marriage. He repeats his demand for marriage four times after grabbing Naomi and Kwame from their mother's arms:

> awright bitch/ awright bitch/you gonna marry me/
> you gonna marry me . . .
> . . . he kicked the screen outta the window/ & held the kids
> offa the sill/ you gonna marry me/
> . . . fifth story/ at alla the people screamin at him/ &
> he started sweatin again/ say to alla the neighbors/
> you gonna marry me/ (59–60)

He is so fixated on reenacting the violence inflicted upon him that even Crystal's eventual agreement to marriage cannot quell his maniacal demands, and he drops his children from the apartment window.

After this final traumatic episode, the women in the play initiate a ritual of self-healing. Two primary features of recovery from trauma, according to Herman, are self-empowerment and the reestablishment of connections with others (133). In the final poem of the play, "a laying on of hands," the women are both empowered and reconnected. The women's self-empowerment is demonstrated by the women's declaration that what they were missing did not lie outside themselves—in the love of a man or mother—but within:

> i know bout/ laying on bodies/ layin outta man
> bringing him alla my fleshy self & some of my pleasure
> bein taken full eager wet like i get sometimes
> i waz missin somethin . . .
> . . . not my mama/ holdin me tight/ sayin
> i'm always gonna be her girl
> not a layin on of bosom & womb
> a layin on of hands
> the holiness of myself released (62)

The women's reconnection with each other is manifested in the communal delivery of the poem. Though the lady in red narrates much of the poem, the other women's participation demonstrates the universality of experiences of the women of color in the text. The lady in red's experiences as Crystal with Beau Willie

Brown could as easily be the experiences of another character in the play. Individual narration particularizes experience, but the sharing of common experiences universalizes them. Thus, a trauma one character experiences is representative of the common traumatic experience of all the play's black female characters. Perhaps nothing illustrates the intersection of the particular and the universal better than the poem "sechita": one character gives a third-person narrative of the dancer, Sechita, while another character acts out Sechita's life on stage. The lady in green's becoming of Sechita indicates that any woman, past or present, might live her life.

In addition to requiring reconnection with others, the women's recovery of the "missing somethin" also relies on a metaphorical return to childhood:

> i waz cold/ i was burnin up/ a child
> & endlessly weavin garments for the moon
> wit my tears
> i found god in myself
> & i loved her/ i loved her fiercely (63)

The reversion to a childlike state is a prerequisite to the completion of spiritual transformation. Becoming childlike allows the lady in red, along with her sisters, to be born again through song. As the ladies come to recognize their lack of a crucial element, they recognize the inadequacies of various stages of development. This final poem reverses the structure of the play, where development of the colored girl proceeds from youth to adulthood. In this poem, the ladies recognize inadequacy first in adulthood, then in childhood. The lady in blue first asserts that she was not missing a man. Next, the lady in purple asserts that she was not missing the protection of her mother. Reclamation of childhood is necessary for the survival of the black women in the text, but they simply cannot return to a state where they have the protection of guardians. Becoming functional adults requires that they become self-sufficient.

Significantly, the final song of redemption and the childhood play song that begins the choreopoem are communal. Stage directions do not indicate that the women are standing in a circle while singing "Mama's Little Baby Loves Shortenin' Bread" or "Little Sally Walker." But, "Little Sally Walker" is traditionally sung by a group of children who join hands and circle around a child sitting in the center. The essentiality of this circle and community of womanhood to the survival of the black woman is again highlighted in the choreopoem's final song, when the women form a tight, inclusive circle. The black girl's song has matured markedly, from scripted, traditional songs like "Little Sally Walker" to one that is improvised.[8] In this shift, Shange signals growing strength and innovation of her characters. The physical birth of the black girl inserts her into an already written story of struggle, chaos, and hard times. Her figurative rebirth requires that she right it.

At the end of the text, the lady in brown, as she did at the beginning, identifies the choreopoem's audience: "this is for colored *girls* who have considered suicide but are movin to the ends of their own rainbows" (emphasis added, 64). Throughout the play, the lady in brown acts as the guardian of black girlhood. It is she who speaks of the perils of being young and black, both in "dark phrases" and "toussaint." In both poems, the lady in brown seeks to protect these young women. In the first poem, the lady in brown, as a grown woman, possesses hindsight that the girl she describes lacks; thus, she is able to identify the girl's missing part and provide her a harmonious song. In "toussaint" the lady in brown seeks to preserve a space of girlhood for adult women. In this way, the lady in brown acts as a spiritual mother, identifying the needs of her children and seeking to meet them.

Much like the lady in brown acts as a guardian for young black girls in the play, Shange appoints herself a "black literary mother-figure" by seeking to provide guidance to black girls through her choreopoem (Lester, *Critical Study* 28). In her assumption of this role, Shange places herself in the tradition of African American children's literature, long before she begins writing children's and young adult books such as *I Live in Music* (1994), *Whitewash* (1997), *Float Like a Butterfly* (2002), *Daddy Says* (2003), or *Ellington Was Not a Street* (2004). Critic Dianne Johnson asserts that literature for black children by black authors, perhaps more so than outside this tradition, is "instructive and pedagogical at its foundations . . . in response to stereotyping and misrepresentation" (2). Shange, in her interview with Tate, claims that her text is meant to correct the "mythology and lies" about womanhood that were handed down to her:

> It's the silence of mothers that is so shattering. The mothers know that it's a dreadful proposition to give up one's life for one's family and one's mate and, therefore, lose oneself in the process of caring and tending for others. To send one's daughter off to that kind of self-sacrifice in silence with no preparation is a mortal sin to me. . . . To break this silence is my responsibility, and I'm absolutely committed to it. (Tate 162)

The overt celebration of blackness, specifically black femininity, also places Shange's text in the tradition of African American children's literature, whose authors seeks to create positive images of black life. While the women—or girls—in *for colored girls* experience sometimes harrowing life events, they find peace by the end of the play. *for colored girls* provides a sense of hope that black women can find their own songs and situate themselves for survival in the world.

The play also fits well in the paradigm of children's theatre, which seeks to expose children to nasty truths on stage rather than in real life. In the text, characters—adults and children alike—are exposed to various traumatic episodes, helping adolescents to see that the protection of parents is only temporary, and, indeed, some children do not even start with it. The text also reveals for young girls the pleasures and perils of sex and relationships with men. Through writing about and staging the bitter experiences of the women in *for colored girls*, Shange hopes to prevent young women from replicating these very experiences. While acquainting girls with risk, the text also shields them from it by confining "reality" to the stage. In this way, *for colored girls* becomes what *Children's Theatre Press* editor Sara Spencer defines in 1964, a decade before Shange's text bursts with fanfare onto the Broadway stage, as a better type of children's theatre, not fairy tales that continued to form typical fare, but the stuff of real life:

> Outside the theatre, hard lessons are waiting for our children. Life is going to teach them that good and bad take many forms, and that good never really wins. . . . Nobody likes to put an end to innocence. There will be time enough, we say. But actually, what better way is there to bring children to a true understanding of good and evil, than through the unfolding of a play? What better place is there than the theatre to speak the truth to children? Is it not better they should learn some of the bitter things from the experience of actors on a stage, than at first hand? (qtd. in Jennings: 2) [9]

In an interview, Shange defines her audience as girls around the age of 12. Children of this age group are often neglected by playwrights of children's theatre, where the most popular scripts are adaptations of fairy tales. Fairy tales might well appease the youngest children, but are rarely entertaining or instructive for older children. "After age twelve, the young person, entering a period of important discoveries about life, rejected most material that was intended to keep him or her interested in theatrical fare," according to children's theatre scholar Jed H. Davis (Jennings vii). Adolescents want acquaintance with more mature themes, such as "death and dying, adolescence, maturation, sexuality, and divorce" (Jennings 1), exactly the types of situations Shange stages in *for colored girls*. Raw subject matter of Shange's text, then, need not put it out of reach for children. Indeed, it is exactly the type of youth theatre critics sanction.

Shange has not shied away from presenting disturbing topics, even in books marketed explicitly for children. In *Whitewash*, for example, a young black girl and her brothers are the targets of a racially motivated physical attack. The young protagonist, Helene-Angel, gives a first-person account of her face being painted white by a group of predators, who want to make her "white" and "American" and ends with her declaration that she and her brother, as people of color and perhaps also as immigrants, have "a right to be here, too!" Race, like issues of sexuality, may at first seem too mature for audiences of youth. But Shange seems to insist on presenting real-life issues to young audiences.

The choreopoem has not traditionally been performed for audiences of youth. The play was originally performed in women's bars before moving to Broadway, where the typical audience member is closer to 40 than 12. This fact does not however eliminate the possibility that young girls attended Broadway performances with their mothers or other adults or attend reincarnations of the play at colleges and universities or versions staged by local troupes. Even if original performance venues place the play out of reach of much of Shange's imagined audience of adolescents, the written text is accessible to anyone—adult or child—able to afford the cost of the book or with access to public libraries. Shange imagines the book becoming an heirloom of black womanhood, handed down from generation to generation: "I'd like to be part of a collection of books by a woman that someone might give a female child" (Lester, *Critical Study* 28).

Finally, Shange's abstruse poetics need not put the text out of the reach of adolescents. Critics have suggested that poetry may indeed be more accessible to youth than prose.[10] Children and adolescents, who are only beginning to learn language, may be more comfortable than adults playing along the boundaries of language and experimenting with new forms. *Ellington was Not a Street* (2004) illustrates that Shange's inscrutable language can be rendered simple enough to be understood by the youngest children. Illustrator Kadir Nelson's colorful drawings of a tiny black girl peeping around kitchen walls to peer at the great men Shange remembers in "Mood Indigo" make the poem easily accessible to children, and the book's final pages are filled with factoids about the men mentioned in the poem. While there are no illustrations or fact sheets in *for colored girls*, there are guides. Shange's poetry in *for colored girls* is accessible because of its storytelling and its mix of esoteric speech and the black vernacular, close-to-the-ground language reflective of a natural speech. The close juxtaposition of the familiar and the figurative allows a hearer (or reader) to skip over enigmatic phrases to those that are easily accessible. A good example is the poem, "abortion cycle #1." The poem begins with figurative descriptions of the room and the feelings of the speaker. The language is indirect; for example, the lady in blue never states that she is in the procedure room of an abortion clinic, requiring listeners and readers to deduce her location from cryptic descriptions:

tubes tables white washed windows
grime from age wiped over once
legs spread
anxious
eyes crawling up on me
eyes rollin in my thighs
metal horses gnawin my womb
dead mice fall from my mouth (22)

Descriptions of a doctor's exam and his insertion of surgical instruments into the body of the young woman on the table are veiled by metaphor, but Shange follows up these descriptions with direct language clearly stating the lady in blue's source of distress and directly stating the feelings, emotional and physical, produced by the procedure:

get them steel rods outta me
this hurts
this hurts me
& nobody came
cuz nobody knew
once i waz pregnant & shamed of myself (22–23)

With its inventive mixture of drama, poetry, song, and choreographed dance, *for colored girls* inherently resists easy labeling or categorization. Studying *for colored girls* as a textbook adds dimension to the seven female characters; they become practical models. It also adds dimension to the choreopoem; it may be appropriately described as a child's play or child's text. *for colored girls* becomes a theatrical bildungsroman, with characters progressing onstage through life stages.[11] As the piece progresses, the characters in the play undergo rites of passage that illustrate the growing psychological and, importantly, spiritual development of seven girls who are coming of age. The choreopoem begins in a black girl's childhood, charts first and successive sexual experiences, and ultimately ends as the girl crosses the threshold of adulthood with improved awareness.

Notes

1. Ntozake Shange, *for colored girls who have considered suicide when the rainbow is enuf*. New York: Scribner Poetry, Copyright, 1975. Reprinted by permission of Scribner, an imprint of Simon and Schuster Adult Publishing Group, from *for colored girls who have considered suicide when the rainbow is enuf* by Ntozake Shange. Copyright 1975, 1976, 1977 by Ntozake Shange. All rights reserved.
2. In a more recent interview, Shange continues to insist her audience is composed of young girls of color. "I write for young girls of color," she says, "for girls who don't even exist yet, so that there is something there for them when they arrive." See Ntozake Shange, "Back At You." Interview with Rebecca Carroll. *Mother Jones* January–February 1995: 69. Shange authored a foreword in Carroll's *Sugar in the Raw: Voices of Young Black Girls in America,* a collection of 15 interviews with black adolescents and teenagers. See Rebecca Carroll, *Sugar in the Raw: Voices of Young Black Girls in America*. New York: Random House, 1997.
3. See Frances Smith Foster, Rev. edition of *The Black American in Books for Children: Readings in Racism*, by Donnarae MacCann and Gloria Woodard. *Black American Literature Forum* 21.1–2 (1987): 199–204. Neal A. Lester, *Ntozake Shange: A Critical Study of the Plays*. New York: Garland Publishing Inc., 1995. See also Jean Young, "Ritual Poetics and Rites of Passage in Ntozake Shange's *for colored girls who have considered suicide/when the rainbow is*

enuf." *Black Theatre: Ritual Performance in the African Diaspora*. Ed. Paul Carter Harrison, Victor Leo Walker II, and Gus Edwards. Philadelphia: Temple University Press. 2002.

4. Neal A. Lester suggests that the relationship between the child the lady in brown imagines and Toussaint Jones may indicate the potential for productive relationships between black men and women. "Shange's Men: *for colored girls* Revisited, and Movement Beyond." *African American Review* 26 (1992): 319–28.
5. This commentary by the lady in brown is clearly a statement about the nature of children's literature. Many of the images of blacks in children's stories, particularly at the turn of the twentieth century, tended to be those put forth by white authors in stories such as *Little Black Sambo* (1899) or the Uncle Remus tales of Joel Chandler Harris. The dearth of published books aimed at black children is due mostly to the difficulties children's book authors and illustrators face at the publishing house door, according to African American children's literature scholar Dianne Johnson.
6. Herman notes that children and adolescents are powerless in comparison to adults and thus particularly susceptible to abuse.
7. For a linking of Shange's text to black feminist theory, see Tobe Levin and Gwendolyn Flowers, "Black Feminism in *for colored girls who have considered suicide when the rainbow is enuf.*" *History and Tradition in Afro-American Culture.* Frankfurt: Campus Verlag, 1984. 181–92. See also "A Black Feminist Statement," *This Bridge Called My Back: Writings by Radical Women of Color*. Ed. Cherríe Moraga and Gloria Anzaldúa. 2nd ed. New York: Kitchen Table: Women of Color Press, 1983, 210–218.
8. The song that follows the series of "no more love poems" also is an improvised song and foreshadows the play's final communal song. The lady in yellow begins, "My love is too delicate to have thrown back on my face." She is answered by each of the other characters, who assign qualitative value to their love. The women describe their love as "beautiful, sanctified, magic, saturday nite, complicated, and music" (46–47).
9. Spencer advanced the argument that theatre is a better place than the real world for children to experience some of the bitterness of life as the Children's Theater Press published *Reynard the Fox*, a satirical play meant to expose the hypocrisy of Belgian political leaders, but written for an audience of children. See Sara Spencer, "Does Good Always Win?" *Children's Theatre Press* (now Anchorage Press) *Catalogue*, 1964.
10. Kay E. Vandergrift, "And Bid Her Sing: A White Feminist Reads African-American Female Poets." *African-American Voices in Young Adult Literature*. Ed. Karen Patricia Smith. Metuchen, N.J. and London: The Scarecrow Press, 1994.
11. Tobe Levin observes the text's resemblance to the female Bildungsroman in her essay with Flowers.

Works Cited

"A Black Feminist Statement," *This Bridge Called My Back: Writings by Radical Women of Color*. Ed. Cherríe Moraga and Gloria Anzaldúa. 2nd ed. New York: Kitchen Table: Women of Color Press, 1983. 210–218.

Caruth, Cathy. *Unclaimed Experience: Trauma, Narrative, and History*. Baltimore, MD: Johns Hopkins University Press, 1996.

Foster, Frances Smith. Rev. of *The Black American in Books for Children: Readings in Racism*. Ed. Donnarae MacCann and Gloria Woodward. *Black American Literature Forum* 21.1–2 (1987): 199–204.

Herman, Judith. *Trauma and Recovery*. New York: Basic Books, 1992.

Jennings, Coleman A. and Gretta Berghammer, ed. *Theatre for Youth: Twelve Plays with Mature Themes*. Austin: University of Texas Press, 1986.

Johnson, Dianne. *Telling Tales: The Pedagogy and Promise of African American Literature for Youth*. New York: Greenwood Press, 1990.

Knoepflmacher, U. C. and Mitzi Myers. " 'Cross-Writing' and the Reconceptualizing of Children's Literary Studies." *Children's Literature* 25 (1997): vii–xvii.

Lester, Neal A. "Shange's Men: *for colored girls* Revisited, and Movement Beyond." *African American Review* 26 (1992): 319–28.

———. *Ntozake Shange: A Critical Study of the Plays*. New York: Garland, 1995.

Levin, Tobe, and Gwendolyn Flowers. "Black Feminism in *for colored girls who have considered suicide when the rainbow is enuf*." *History and Tradition in Afro-American Culture*. Frankfurt: Campus Verlag, 1984. 181–92.

McCaslin, Nellie. *Theatre for Children in the United States: A History*. Norman: University of Oklahoma Press, 1971.

Paul, Lissa. "Enigma Variations: What Feminist Theory Knows about Children's Literature." *Children's Literature: The Development Of Criticism*. Ed. Peter Hunt. London: Routledge, 1990.

Shange, Ntozake. *for colored girls who have considered suicide when the rainbow is enuf*. New York: Scribner Poetry, 1975.

———. *Whitewash*. New York: Walker and Co. 1997.

———. *Ellington Was Not a Street*. New York: Simon & Schuster Books for Young Readers, 2004.

Smith, Karen Patricia, ed. *African-American Voices in Young Adult Literature*. Metuchen, NJ.: The Scarecrow Press, 1994.

Tate, Claudia, ed. *Black Women Writers at Work*. New York: Continnuum, 1983.

Young, Jean. "Ritual Poetics and Rites of Passage in Ntozake Shange's *for colored girls who have considered suicide/when the rainbow is enuf*." *Black Theatre: Ritual Performance in the African Diaspora*. Ed. Paul Carter Harrison, Victor Leo Walker II, and Gus Edwards. Philadelphia: Temple University Press, 2002. 296–310.

6

Flyin' "Anyplace Else"

(Dis)Engaging Traumatic Memory in Three Plays by Pearl Cleage

BENJAMIN SAMMONS

A contemporary African American novelist, essayist, playwright, and political activist, Pearl Cleage writes of her youth in the Black Liberation Movement, "I grew up in a context of people who were writing to free themselves" (Carroll 50). Three of Cleage's plays—*Flyin' West* (1992), *Blues for an Alabama Sky* (1995), and *Bourbon at the Border* (1997)—find the author writing for freedom, too, seeking to free herself from the political commonplaces of her dramatic medium as much as to liberate her characters from the violence of American racism. Though neither packaged nor produced as such, these plays constitute a trilogy, as they employ the same formal structure to explore a common subject matter, namely the nexus of violence, freedom, and traumatic memory in African American experience. Set in disparate geographical regions and historical eras, the plays each address the problem of constructing and maintaining a space in which black men and women can pursue personal liberation by escaping the grip of a traumatic past. Moreover, these works assign a specific geography to this repeated thematic study: in all three productions, the flight narrative suggested by the title, *Flyin' West*, constructs a textual landscape in which the migratory movements of the characters mirror their changing positions in relation to oppression and freedom. This spatial metaphor achieves for each play a unity of content and form and marks the plays collectively as a coherent intertextual unit. Hence, the trilogy corroborates Page duBois' suggestion that "seeking the truth may involve a journey, a passage through a spatial narrative of some sort, [. . .] a sinking down into the past, into the interiority of memory" (105).

The work of memory, in fact, claims so prominent a position in these plays as to require a theory of its own. Even as Cleage's trilogy posits the distinctiveness of each victim's experience of violence, these plays also frame violence as a theme in African American history. Accordingly, this chapter applies to all three productions a critical framework borrowed from the field of trauma theory, in hopes that a consistent parlance may accentuate the linkages and disparities among Cleage's dramatic explorations of traumatic memory. If the plays' common subject matter invites the application of one critical perspective, though, Cleage's progressively pessimistic vision repeatedly undermines her audiences' assumptions about the nature of trauma and traumatic witnessing. The playwright's shifting position in relation to audiences constitutes a flight narrative unto itself, and a study of the three plays in order of their production clarifies the trajectory of her authorial movement.

Flyin' West

As yet Cleage's plays remain largely unattended by literary critics; to date, only *Flyin' West* has garnered any attention in scholarly publications. It comes as little surprise that critics have addressed this work alone because the play dates to the beginning of Cleage's dramatic career; being produced three years prior to *Blues for an Alabama Sky* and five years before *Bourbon at the Border*, scholars have quite simply had more time to consider *Flyin' West*. I posit, however, that this early play attracts more critical attention than *Blues* or *Bourbon* primarily because it treats the trilogy's shared subject matter more optimistically than either of the later works. The themes remain consistent in all three plays, but with each new production Cleage's modification of her basic formal structure, the spatial-thematic landscape introduced above, renders her dramatic vision more foreboding and less palatable to audiences. *Flyin' West* owes its mostly sunny tone to the landscape where its action transpires.

The play derives its geographical structure, predictably, from the westward flight of its four female characters, beginning in the postbellum American South and terminating in the all-black town of Nicodemus, Kansas. The Homestead Act of 1860 made such a movement financially viable for thousands of emancipated African Americans by offering "three hundred and twenty acres of 'free' land, stolen from the dwindling populations of Native Americans, to U.S. citizens who were willing to settle the Western states" (Cleage 6). The South, then—Memphis, in fact, for all but one of Cleage's four women—represents the past in *Flyin' West*, while the female protagonists' acreage in Kansas constitutes their present and symbolizes their future. Having acquired land around the all-black town of Nicodemus, three sisters—Sophie, Fannie, and Minnie—and the matriarchal Miss Leah consider this physical space a representation and a seal of their independence and security, a refuge from the racially motivated violence they experienced in the South.[1] Sophie, in particular, conceives of Nicodemus as a social and political project, an opportunity to establish for black settlers "something free and fine and all our own" (Cleage 13). However, the arrival of white speculators in Nicodemus threatens this ideal because, as Sophie recognizes, for black citizens to sell their land would jeopardize the racial homogeneity of the town. Minnie differs on this matter with her husband Frank, a dandyish mulatto who disdains his black heritage and hopes to profit from selling Minnie's share of the land, and like Sophie she contends that it is "the land that makes us free women" (Cleage 65). Cleage's plot thus takes its shape from the contours and borders of a physical space; the very hope of the play lies in the retention of Nicodemus citizens' land for black people only.

In *Flyin' West*, the alignment of a community's success with the status of its land points to parallel relationships operating at an interpersonal level. Here, geography derives significance from its symbolic linkage to the human body. Sophie explains this relationship when she returns from making a speech at church on the inviolability of Nicodemus land only to find that Frank has physically abused his pregnant wife, Minnie:

> This morning, while I was standing in that church painting a picture of the future of this town, he beat her and did God knows what else to her in this house. Where she's always been safe. We can't let him do that, Fan. All the dreams we have for Nicodemus, all the churches and schools and libraries we can build don't mean a thing if a colored woman isn't safe in her own house. (Cleage 76)

Sophie's argument confirms that the acquisition and retention of land, the dual engines of Cleage's plot, claim importance only in as much as they ensure the bodily safety of black women. In this instance of physical violence against Minnie, Sophie perceives the imperfect correspondence between geographical space and corporeal space, for she may defend the sanctity of the former even as the latter undergoes violation. *Flyin' West* finally recoups this correspondence only by driving away the white speculators (violators of geographical space) and by killing Frank (a violator of corporeal space).

The play's culmination in the negation of these two threats commends a reading of *Flyin' West* as a narrative of survival. From their original flights westward to the defensive posture they collectively assume toward Frank, protecting both Minnie and their land from him, the female characters consistently position themselves for self-preservation. The habit of fending off hazards to their well-being—whether cold, age, speculators, violence, or forgetfulness—appears as their most familiar and, perhaps, representative activity. Victims of racialized violence in the South, these women corroborate Cathy Caruth's description of trauma as something that entails not only "an effect of destruction but also, fundamentally, an enigma of survival" (58). In her landmark work entitled *Unclaimed Experience* (1996), Caruth argues that to process and endure trauma involves "the endless attempt to assume one's survival as one's own" (64), and this language captures the substance of the women's lives in *Flyin' West*. Rather than transcending the memory of past violence, Cleage's protagonists pursue ownership—and, hence, control—of their traumatic experiences.

To this end, *Flyin' West* sets the women about the work of strategically positioning those memories in a psychical context, a process of narrativization that renders the memories less intrusive and potentially useful. Pierre Janet, a nineteenth-century physician and theorist of trauma, finds this process foundational in the work of memory, claiming that "essentially [memory] *is the action of telling a story*" (qtd. in Young 35). Allan Young distills Janet's work on trauma and therapy in language that accentuates its significance for a reading of *Flyin' West*:

> The role of therapy is to help the patient discover his fixed idea [a sort of traumatic memory] and bring it into consciousness. Then he must recite it and re-recite it, until the recital and its memory are independent of the event and the emotions that they memorialize. Once this point has been reached, patient and therapist move to the final step: they find a resting place for the memory—in Janet's words, as a chapter in the patient's life history. (35)

This therapeutic regimen calls to mind Fannie's story-collecting project in *Flyin' West*, a project intended to culminate in a book where Miss Leah's function as communal keeper of history will surely earn her more than a chapter. Miss Leah's occasional reticence to tell Fannie her stories, though, bespeaks the older woman's ambivalence concerning the narrativization of her memories, or the process of situating them individually in relation to one another. The following dialogue between Minnie and Miss Leah exposes the contradictions inherent in the latter's remembrance of her past:

> MISS LEAH: Everybody knows them stories I got. Colored folks ain't been free long enough to have forgot what it's like to be a slave.
> MINNIE: But you didn't always talk about slavery. You talked about how blue the sky would be in the summertime and about how you and the children would sneak off from prayer meeting to play because you didn't want to work all week and pray all Sunday.
> MISS LEAH: And got beat for it just as regular as a clock.
> MINNIE: You used to tell me about how all your babies had such fat little legs, remember?
> MISS LEAH: And where are they now? All them babies. All them grandbabies? Gone! Every last one of 'em!
> MINNIE: But you loved them, Miss Leah. Who's going to know how much you loved them? (Cleage 39)

This exchange dramatizes the challenge of narrativizing traumatic memory both realistically and redemptively, but throughout the play Miss Leah capably meets the necessity of remembering past events selectively and interpreting them strategically. She tells her stories according to the demands of circumstance, consoling a wounded Minnie with memories of her own sexual objectification under slavery, redirecting a vengeful and impulsive Sophie with a story, and promising to regale her newborn granddaughter with the chronicles of "strong colored women makin' a way for little ol' you" (Cleage 86).

Despite Miss Leah's conflicted approach to her storytelling work, the narrative trajectory of *Flyin' West* remains basically linear and unambiguous. Paired with the aforementioned closing scene, in which Miss Leah welcomes her granddaughter and Sophie twirls in her yard "completely at peace" (Cleage 86), the enactment of the sisters' "ritual" helps establish the affective telos of Cleage's narrative (Cleage 44). In their call-and-response ritual the sisters grasp hands in a circle and communally memorialize their flight from Memphis and "declare [their] lives to be [their] own and no one else's" (Cleage 44). Like Miss Leah, they revisit the trauma of racialized violence by a process of narrativization, making the trauma submit to an aesthetic form in which they can manipulate it to productive ends. Coupled with Miss Leah's closing scene, the emotional force of this ritual, a communal act of solidarity and resistance, definitively privileges hope over despair for Cleage's women in their negotiation of traumatic memory.

At this point in a study of *Flyin' West*, Allan Feldman's work on the "technologies of memory" offers considerable insight regarding this play's critical reception (167). For Feldman, "technologies of memory" denote both the interpretative paradigms by which a culture narrativizes trauma in its midst and the power structures by which that culture enforces its favored metanarratives. His theoretical work informs Cleage's drama when he posits a "current cultural predilection for confessional trauma narratives" (Feldman 167), a generic form that "circulates and archives the experiences of terror and abuse as episodes scheduled for eventual overcoming through redemptive survival, recovery, and restorative justice" (Feldman 165)—and, most significantly for Cleage's readers, a generic form that *Flyin' West* is at least related to if not identical with. Feldman argues further that the confessional trauma narrative exhibits a "linearity [that] is meant to culminate in the cathartic 'break' with the past—establishing the pastness of prior violence, and managing and controlling the conditions and terms of its reentry into the present, usually through appropriate commemoration" (170). Indeed, the storytelling and ritual memorialization of history in *Flyin' West* serve to delineate such a "break" between past and present, oppression and freedom, and so imbues the future with promise. This narrative structure, more comic than tragic, distinguishes *Flyin' West* from the other two plays in Cleage's trilogy and may well account for its more favorable critical reception. This very optimism, though, which renders *Flyin' West* so agreeable to audiences, also presages the pessimism of Cleage's later plays.

Cleage predicates the safety of her women and the hope of Nicodemus—the grounds for this play's optimism—on an act of violence against Frank. Although Miss Leah talks Sophie out of the "messy business" of shooting Frank, the older woman does not balk at murder, opting to kill Frank more quietly by way of a poisoned apple pie (Cleage 78). The play frames this killing as the event that ushers Minnie's daughter into the Nicodemus community and ushers the white speculators out, hence a dawning era of prosperity and hope. This dynamic by which *Flyin' West* relates violence against and on behalf of black women adumbrates a trend that Feldman describes in his study of survival narratives—namely, the propensity to transform the survivor figure into a "rigidified subject position of the assaulted and aggrieved [that] can readily serve as the ontological ground for justifying and replicating renewed violence" (196). To fetishize the survivor of trauma makes it plausible "to legitimate new victims and new excuses for assault and harm—to commit violence 'in the name of'" (194). In *Flyin' West*, Sophie appropriates this formula when she says of Frank, "A colored man who will beat a colored woman doesn't deserve to live" (75).[2] Because the colored woman is Cleage's victim/survivor *par excellence*, an attack on her justifies, even requires, a reciprocal attack on the one who victimizes her. When Frank lies dead on the floor of the women's home, Cleage's stage directions dramatize Minnie's internal struggle to justify this "collective action" to which she consented:

> *She reaches out and touches him tentatively, realizing the enormity of what they have done. She draws back, but reaches out again, almost involuntarily, to touch Frank's arm, his hand, his shoulder. She moves through a complex set of emotions, ending with her knowledge of the monster Frank had become. Her face now shows resolve, and even her body seems to gain strength. She steels herself and reaches into Frank's pocket to withdraw the deed.* (Cleage 82–83)

Identifying Frank as a "monster" enables Minnie to justify his murder, and in the moral universe of *Flyin' West* her verdict legitimates this act of violence in defense of a victimized community. It appears quite simply as "what free people always have to do if they're going to stay free" (Cleage 76). This inscription of violence as a fundamental feature of the struggle for survival links *Flyin' West* to Cleage's later plays, which dramatize in narratives less readily redeemed the necessary recurrence of trauma in the lives of victims.

Blues for an Alabama Sky

Cleage structures *Blues for an Alabama Sky* in a manner that subtly announces this play's distinction from *Flyin' West*. Again, a geographical map lends this work its thematic shape, but where *Flyin' West* addresses the themes of violence and security in binary terms derived from the spatial opposition of South and West, with trauma located in a Southern past and freedom in a frontier present and future, *Blues* treats the same themes in terms of a three-tiered landscape that Cleage divides into Southern, Northern, and foreign spaces.[3] Set in Harlem in 1930, *Blues* reminds the reader of *Flyin' West* in its fixation on a geographical space "where Negroes could come together and really walk about" (Cleage 183), liberated from the indignities of a Jim Crow South. In 1930, though, "[t]he creative euphoria of the Harlem Renaissance has given way to the harsher realities of the Great Depression," and the once illustrious center of black culture struggles to sustain "a population whose most deadly disease is poverty" (Cleage 89). Harlem, therefore, does not correspond to *Flyin' West*'s Nicodemus as a domain where Cleage's characters are free. Rather, in *Blues*, the introduction of a third geographical space (Paris, France) defers the hope of black men and women's security to an imagined future in a foreign place. Since the play's action does not actually take the audience to Paris, the flight narrative that terminates in a free Nicodemus in *Flyin' West* never arrives at its destination in *Blues*. Hence, the later play charts a continuing, perhaps perpetual, flight from traumatic memory where the earlier play stages an ending to this movement.

In *Blues*, three refugees from the South reside at the center of the plot: Angel Allen and Guy Jacobs have fled to Harlem from a life of prostitution in Georgia, and Leland Cunningham has moved there to escape the memory of his deceased wife and their conjugal life in Alabama. *Blues* carefully sketches these characters' dreams of rebirth through flight but finally exposes the illusory quality of those dreams. Guy, a homosexual costume designer, stakes his dream of escaping Harlem on the graces of Parisian celebrity Josephine Baker by whom he hopes to be hired. Angel tolerates this fancy in her friend Guy, and if ever Josephine did send for him, Angel would certainly accompany him to Paris. Nevertheless, she repeatedly expresses frustration at Guy's fantasy, which she dubs the "myth of the magical Josephine" (Cleage 122); and when he cannot pay the rent for his apartment, where she is a squatter, Angel rails against his continuing hope of deliverance by the foreign celebrity: "Whatever presence you're feeling hasn't got anything to do with Josephine. We're not in Paris. We're in Harlem. We're not strolling the boulevard. We're about to be evicted!" (Cleage 167). Although Guy's dreams prove substantial when Josephine Baker does hire him and pays for his travel to Paris, Angel's skepticism about her friend's apparently outlandish hopes at least introduces a conceptual gap between dream and reality.

Angel's own hope rests on nothing more specific than a "chance to live free" (Cleage 175), but she imagines securing this privilege in relationship with a man, one who can write a "rent check that won't bounce" (Cleage 160). Positioned over against Guy and his alleged financial insolvency, Angel's suitor Leland Cunningham, a young widower from Alabama, in fact proves more susceptible than Guy to the perils of fantasy. He narrates his own story of meeting Angel this way:

> The night I found you, I went to bed early, like I always do, but I couldn't sleep. I was just laying there, wide awake. So I got up and went out for a walk. I was missing that Alabama sky where the stars are so thick it's bright as day. So, I looked up between the buildings and I thought I was dreaming. Didn't even look like Harlem. Stars everywhere, twinkling at me like a promise. And then I saw you. And that was all I saw. Just you. (Cleage 168)

Leland thus associates Angel with an idyllic past in Alabama and more specifically with his deceased wife Anna, whom Angel physically resembles. His story of first seeing Angel frames their ensuing relationship in a dreamlike, even make-believe, context. Angel, after all, cannot be a chaste reincarnation of Anna, and she finally loses patience with Leland's self-deception: "You want me to lie! That's all you ever wanted. Pretend I'm Anna. Pretend I love you. I'm through with it!" (Cleage 180). Thus, her hope of security with Leland founders on an inconsistency between reality and a "pretend" world of his fabrication. Guy's earlier warning that "[y]ou can't make it real just because you want it to be," a truism offered Angel in relation to an unlikely job opportunity, proves applicable with regard to Leland also and suggests that Angel's own fantasies about him contribute to their final disappointment as much as Leland's "dreaming" does (Cleage 118). Repeatedly wounded by the failure of her hopes, Angel apparently resigns herself to uninspired survival, declaring finally, "I'm tired of Negro dreams. All they ever do is break your heart" (Cleage 147).

By itself, this experience of disappointment does not distinguish the characters in *Blues* from Cleage's pioneers in *Flyin' West*; the negotiation of traumatic memory by the two casts does separate them, though, and outlines divergent thematic trajectories for the two plays. Where narrative and ritual render traumatic memory manageable and even useful in the earlier play, continual flight permits characters to defer psychological pain in *Blues*. In the later play, escape from pain constitutes an end in itself, so that the mere efficacy of one's avoidance strategy matters far more than its creativity or morality does. Accordingly, the opening scene in *Blues* introduces a utilitarian formula by which characters interact with traumatic memory throughout the play, as Angel enters the stage inebriated from a night on the town prompted by her lover's unexpected marriage to another woman. Though she initially claims to be "celebrating" the event (Cleage 94), she soon "*dissolves into helpless tears*" and confesses that her "heart is broken" (Cleage 94, 96). Angel's pursuit of oblivion in drunkenness represents one application of a formula to which she reverts in order to escape psychological pain. Any drug will suffice to "medicate" herself against psychological distress. When her friend Delia Patterson, a nurse advocating birth control in Harlem, begins to narrate the hardships of the poor women she works for, Angel's hungover response reinscribes her modus operandi concerning traumatic memory: "Please don't get her all worked up! I can't take the history of the downtrodden without some aspirin!" (Cleage 107). Hence, expedient forms of self-medication serve Angel in her determined and comprehensive evasion of traumatic memory.

The title of this play further informs the ethos that governs the characters' relationship to pain, for commentators on blues music often define the genre by its strategy of "laughing to keep from crying." In this pattern of blues music to divert pain by an appeal to humor, one finds the very structure framing this play's interaction with traumatic memory. Angel, a "former back-up singer at the Cotton Club," often sings blues songs, and when she dances with Delia during one of her impromptu performances, the women's friend Sam comments facetiously on Delia's family planning work, "I didn't realize your revolution left a space for dancing" (Cleage 112). Angel's response expresses the blues ethos pervading this play: "All revolutions leave a space for dancing. They just like to pretend they don't" (Cleage 112). The ostensible complementarity of dancing and social revolution suggests that struggle may not, of necessity, preclude happiness but that the two conditions, in all their varied forms, may sometimes coexist.

This position, a creative engagement of traumatic memory, finds its most vocal representative in Sam Thomas, the overworked obstetrician who instigates the above exchange with Delia and Angel. Known for his exuberant refrain—"Let the good times roll!"—Sam consistently works long shifts at Harlem Hospital, carouses late into the evening, and yawns irrepressibly during the day. To Delia's suggestion that he "should cut back on [his] nightlife," he replies, "That's the one thing I should not do," on the grounds that his nightlife "helps [him] remember that we're not just a bunch of premature labors and gunshot wounds" (Cleage 129). For Sam, "letting the good times roll" ostensibly discredits the conclusion he might otherwise draw from his work in Harlem Hospital that the district's residents amount to no more than walking traumas, to which "premature labors and gunshot wounds" metonymically refer. This defense against despair, though, betrays a logical instability. Before Sam initiates a romance with Delia, nightlife and hospital work constitute the two halves of his waking life, and he articulates the meaning of the former in terms of the latter. Nightlife, then, possesses no positive significance of its own that could be considered equal and opposite to the traumas Sam witnesses in the hospital; the meaning of the "good times" is essentially relative, derivative. The blues ethos that Sam embodies, an attempt to relate pain and elation in a binary alternating structure, elides the fact that in Cleage's Harlem the pain is primary and substantive; the elation of the nightlife is merely a negation. Hence, when Guy quips that "[e]verything is either-or," he seems to express the paradigm by which Cleage's play actually relates trauma and happiness; here, one invariably dominates the other.

In *Blues*, survival by self-medication and a self-deluding blues ethos cannot compare to the triumphant survival of Cleage's women in *Flyin' West*, a security won at the high price of violence against Frank. Accordingly, as the means of survival in *Blues* drain survival itself of its moral appeal, so the later play empties violence of any saving force it may have appeared to possess in *Flyin' West*. Once an effective resource for defending traumatized communities against further abuse, violence appears utterly destructive and futile in *Blues*. Rehearsing the black-on-black violence perpetrated by Frank in *Flyin' West*, black "hoodlums" in *Blues* "prove their manhood" by assaulting black homosexual men like Guy and literary star Bruce Nugent (Cleage 151). In *Blues*, though, such acts occur unpredictably on the plot's periphery, and on some level this diffuse quality of violence renders it more sinister than the violence so neatly contained (and eliminated) in Frank's character.

A violent act nearer the center of Cleage's plot, Angel's abortion of her baby by Leland, promises like Frank's murder to secure freedom from traumatic memory. Angel considers this abortion her "chance to live free" because it should enable her to leave Harlem for Paris with Guy, divested of "flesh and blood" reminders of her past (Cleage 175). Following the secret abortion, Leland references his own scarred history to account for problems in his relationship with Angel, but her blunt admission that she "got rid of" their baby and her response to his appeal for sympathy reveal a deep and general aversion to traumatic memory (Cleage 180):

> Listen to me, Alabama. This isn't about you and it isn't about all the dead mamas and all the dead babies and all the things that are supposed to move me. I'm not that kind of colored woman! I just don't want to think about all that anymore. I'm tired of it! I'm going away. From you. From Harlem. From all those crying colored ghosts who won't shut up and let me live my life! (Cleage 179–80)

Angel's fierce renunciation of Leland and her rejection of their baby provoke an equally violent response from Leland; his stunned anger drives him, in an ironic turnabout, to murder Sam, who performed the abortion despite his prediction that it would "kill" Leland (Cleage 175).

Thus, violence precipitates still more violence in *Blues*, and none of it effects freedom for anyone. Instead, Cleage's characters exhibit a tendency, widely acknowledged in trauma theory, for victims of trauma to revisit and recreate an original wounding. Allan Young describes this characteristic practice in *The Harmony of Illusions: Inventing Post-Traumatic Stress Disorder* (1995), where he notes that "victims of traumatic experiences may seek out circumstances that replicate their traumatogenic events" (25). Leland enacts this dynamic in that, having left Alabama after his wife's death, ostensibly for any change of setting, he pursues Angel precisely because, "You've got her eyes, her mouth, her smile" (Cleage 138). The same urge to return to the source of a past trauma impels Delia to "keep reading" the newspapers' coverage of Sam's murder case, a practice that appears to be "driving [her] crazy" (Cleage 182). Guy and Delia do leave for Paris, but Guy's pronouncement that all Harlemites are "[t]awdry and tainted and running for our natural lives" frames the transatlantic voyage, which was supposed to have been made with Angel, as a mere continuation of the desperate and probably perpetual flight begun when he and Angel first fled a life of prostitution in Georgia. Angel's repetitious movements spanning the arc of the play establish this rule of recurring trauma most definitively. Although her hope of freedom supplies the primary impetus behind the play's action, Angel does not escape to Paris where freedom supposedly resides. Rather, the last scene frames her life as a cycle of attempted flights and accompanying failures, as her final posture before an apartment window "is clearly reminiscent of the afternoon she first encountered Leland" (Cleage 185). The stage directions explaining that "[s]he has been faced with these same difficult decisions about how she will live many times" confirm that Angel has returned to a familiar position before this window, both spatially and psychologically, and the pattern of her life to date offers no hint of impending alteration. Instead of narrating progress from a traumatic past to a hopeful future, as *Flyin' West* does, *Blues* dramatizes an inertia that renders one's future tragically consistent with her traumatic past.

This cyclical narrative structure cannot satisfy audiences anticipating "redemptive survival, recovery, and restorative justice" (Feldman 165), the outcomes that Feldman finds most popular among witnesses to trauma and that a play like *Flyin' West* seems to afford. One should not infer, however, that Cleage's unwillingness in *Blues* to accommodate these critical expectations implies that she is unconcerned with audiences altogether. The play indicates quite the opposite by its emphasis on performance, a thematic concern introduced in the title that foregrounds blues music. At least three of Cleage's characters (Delia, Guy, and Angel) interact with clearly defined audiences, and these relationships make critical reception a central concern in the production. Delia's meeting with the deacons at Abyssinian Baptist Church, aimed at securing their support for a family planning clinic in Harlem, requires her to construct an appeal in language she would not ordinarily use. Practicing with Sam for this unfamiliar audience, she argues, "A woman shouldn't have to make a baby every time she makes love!" (Cleage 130). When Sam critiques this rhetorical approach, the stage directions indicate that "*She realizes he has been preparing her for the possibility of these hostile questions from the deacon board*," and Delia adapts her language accordingly:

> DELIA: No. I'm going to ask them for their help in building strong families with healthy mothers, happy children and loving fathers all over Harlem. Is that better?

> SAM: *(Smiling)*: Much better. That's the only approach they can buy. I don't think pleasure is the guiding principle at Abyssinian yet, despite the pastor's best efforts in that direction.[4] (Cleage 131)

These rhetorical adjustments prove effective in securing the deacons' support for the clinic, but they also alter the substance of Delia's appeal so that family replaces pleasure as the implicit good at its center.

Guy and Angel similarly find themselves catering to opinionated audiences. Guy resolves to "drive Josephine crazy" with costume sketches "until she sends for [him]" (Cleage 99), even though she has sent no response concerning his submissions in a year's time. Recently unemployed and waiting for Josephine's summons, he stoops to "measuring these chubby little chorus girls" at a costume shop named the Hole in the Wall, and his justification for assuming this demeaning post is telling: "The money was too good to turn it down. I sound like a whore, don't I?" (Cleage 117). Guy's language recalls his debased occupation in Georgia, and although his position at the Hole in the Wall represents a much shallower degradation, the structure of his relationship with Josephine Baker subjects him to a related form of indignity whereby her pleasure becomes his highest concern.

Angel experiences similar pressure to ingratiate herself with an audience. Out of work at a time when few singing jobs are available, she eagerly pursues the first audition offered her, but she suspects that her beloved blues will not earn the favor of Tony T., her prospective employer: "Those Italians don't care nothin' about no blues. They like hotsy-totsy girls, grinnin' and shakin' and singin' all at the same damn time" (Cleage 121). Angel decides to sing a blues song after all, but she compromises the musical form by performing it "real fast, almost double-time" in order to satisfy her listeners (Cleage 136). Her aesthetic decision finally makes no difference, though, for she discovers upon arriving at her audition that Tony T. has no interest in her vocal talents: "He wanted to keep a colored woman stashed up in Harlem so he could come by every now and then and rub her head for luck" (Cleage 147). Imagining this encounter to be her only opportunity to provide for herself financially, Angel responds warmly to his flirtatious advances, and while the play leaves the outcome of their suggestive banter uncertain, it effectively dramatizes the allure of audience approval even at the cost of aesthetic or personal integrity.

Despite the indeterminacy of Angel's charade with Tony T., her relationship to audiences elsewhere in the play functions as a model of Cleage's authorial posture in *Blues*. Angel finally repudiates those who would write their own scripts for her life. To Leland, who would make her a second Anna, she eventually responds, "You want me to lie! [. . .] Pretend I'm Anna. Pretend I love you. I'm through with it!" (Cleage 180). Even before throwing off this imposition, she rebuffs Guy on the opposite side for his judgment on Leland's sexual politics; to Guy's question, "Who gave [Leland] the right to vote on my love stories?" Angel replies, "Who gave you the right to vote on mine?" (Cleage 159). While *Blues* does not comfortably wear the "love story" appellation, Cleage's production resists assimilation to audiences' prefabricated trauma narratives as vigorously as Angel defies Leland's and Guy's scripts for her romances. This production departs from *Flyin' West* in its refusal to redeem the traumatic memories of its characters. No one in the play triumphs over the past or even incorporates it constructively into the present. If only at a symbolic level, though, Angel leaves behind a history of prostitution by withstanding the demands of her most intimate audiences and, in so doing, becomes a representative for the playwright of *Blues*, who does not demur at alienating audiences with representations of traumatic memory that remain immediate, messy, and unredeemed.

Bourbon at the Border

The third play examined in this chapter, *Bourbon at the Border*, announces its place in Cleage's trilogy by exhibiting a familiar correspondence between geography and consciousness, or form and content. Like *Blues for an Alabama Sky*, *Bourbon* manifests a three-tiered landscape oriented by the categories of Southern past, Northern present, and foreign future. The two primary characters, May and Charlie Thompson, have their physical residence in Detroit, Michigan, but their shared history from Mississippi's Freedom Summer of 1964 haunts both their lives. Twice during that summer, white police officers beat Charlie and, on one of these occasions, forced him to beat May himself and to watch them rape her afterward. Thirty-one years later, when the play is set, he struggles for his very sanity, having been hospitalized more than once after attempting to kill himself. Within sight of May and Charlie's apartment lies Canada, which exists in their imagination as a virgin territory conducive to new beginnings. Moreover, the "most striking feature" of the Thompsons' apartment, a view of the Ambassador Bridge connecting Detroit to Canada, represents a new element in Cleage's thematically weighted landscapes (Cleage 189). The image of this bridge, which at times "is almost a presence in the apartment" (Cleage 189), introduces a liminal space between the previously discrete locations associated with past, present, and future in *Flyin' West* and *Blues* and, more concretely, a structure facilitating movement between present and future. The word "border" in this play's title further accentuates the concept of liminality, and as early as the Playwright's Note introducing *Bourbon*, Cleage enlists the border as a trope to mediate between two paradigms for social protest, represented respectively by the Freedom Summer volunteers and LeRoi Jones's Clay from *Dutchman* (1964): Cleage posits, "Somewhere *in the space between* the nonviolent warriors and the powerless rage of the would-be poet, is the answer to the question W. E. B. Du Bois warned would shape the twentieth century: the question of the color line" (191, emphasis added). Thus, from the beginning the text sketches something of the structure from which its meditations on memory and trauma will take their shape.

As in *Blues*, traumatic memory in *Bourbon* cannot be relegated to the past or tidily compartmentalized in one's immediate consciousness. Rather, May and Charlie carry with them the trauma of physical and psychological abuses suffered during the 1964 summer campaign to register African American voters in Mississippi. After that summer, the harm that Charlie inflicts on himself and, eventually, on others suggests a sort of compulsion to resurrect and reenact a traumatic experience from the past, the same compulsion to which Leland and Angel succumb in *Blues*. Cathy Caruth calls this pathology the "endless *inherent necessity* of repetition" (63), likening it to a form of "possession" and a "taking over of the mind [. . .] by an event that it cannot control" (2, 58). Such a diagnosis aptly characterizes Charlie's experience, as he cannot forget the violence inflicted on him in Mississippi and will not deny its destructive reiteration in the present. Although May optimistically appraises Charlie's prospects for assimilation into ordinary society, commenting, "It's like one good thing brings another and another" (Cleage 256), her friend Rosa prophetically underscores the pathological pattern described above: "The opposite is true, too. Bad luck can multiply quicker than any winning streak I ever saw" (Cleage 257).

As in *Blues*, then, violence appears less like an instrument available for victims' conscious appropriation and more like a force originating in past trauma and thereafter exerting sway over the victim, both in the realm of the unconscious and the domain of the will. No more submissive to human calculation than a "winning streak," trauma replicates itself according to principles inaccessible to the conscious mind, and this apparent randomness renders the violence in *Bourbon* as menacing as that in *Blues*, where the havoc it wreaks is unexpected and disordered at the fringes of the plot. In *Bourbon*, a series of unsolved murders around downtown Detroit, in which each of the victims is white, provokes speculation among May and Charlie and their friends Rosa and Tyrone concerning the identity of the perpetrator and the motive attached to the crimes. The mystery surrounding these acts of violence appears to be "making folks nervous," prompting the white people Tyrone encounters to be "much friendlier than usual. Smiling and saying good morning like they wanted to make sure I didn't go off" (Cleage 240). Moreover, a tragic incident on a bridge in town, during which a minor automobile accident incites a man to beat the woman at fault so severely that she jumps off the bridge and drowns, heightens the sense of foreboding recently engendered by inexplicable violence across Detroit. Concerning the bridge incident, Rosa asks the obvious question: "Now how can somebody get that mad about a scratch on a damn car?" (Cleage 251). However, May's cryptic reply, "You know that wasn't about a car," discredits the myth of random violence and points to a rational, if deeply hidden, explanation for all such acts.

Allan Young's work offers some basis for locating the source of this violence in previous traumatic experiences: he claims that such experiences "are always charged with high emotion. Reactions to them—ranging from tears to acts of revenge—have the effect of discharging the attached affect" (36). Hence, trauma produces in its victim powerful emotions, which the victim, in turn, acts upon to "discharge" their intensity. One who witnesses this discharging may have no knowledge of the original trauma to which it is a response. May's assertion that the violence on the bridge "wasn't about a car" demonstrates her sensitivity to this contingency. Young, however, contends further that highly affective traumatic experiences often remain hidden from others or even from the victim. He calls traumatic memory "a kind of pathogenic secret," which the possessor wants not only to conceal from other people but also to forget or, at least, "to push [. . .] to the edges of awareness" (28). As Cleage's audience begins to suspect Charlie is responsible for the downtown murders, they find him practicing such methods of concealment in order to disarm traumatic memory, for he denies others access to his psychological history and hides the manner in which he reenacts the trauma of Freedom Summer—so effectively, in fact, that even a perceptive May suspects nothing.

Charlie's reserve concerning his traumatic past and its manifestations in the present must, nonetheless, be juxtaposed with his and May's sincere attempts to articulate their pain to one another. *Flyin' West* provides a model for the narrativization of traumatic memory, a model coinciding with some theories of therapy that posit storytelling as a constructive means of integrating traumatic episodes into a victim's broader life history and consciousness. After their experiences in Freedom Summer, May and Charlie aspire to narrativize their traumatic memories in this fashion. In 1995, thirty-one years after the events, May can tell Rosa their story coherently, but the audience does not know whether she has ever before accomplished this telling. More immediately after Freedom Summer, as May and Charlie labor to communicate with one another about what happened, Charlie manages to construct a story *about* their story, telling May that in their desperation he and she "were like desperadoes, drinking bourbon at the border and planning [their] getaways" (Cleage 263). In the final estimate, however, the couple meet with very little success in narrativizing their traumatic memories. They first try to communicate from a distance by telephone, but this arrangement proves fruitless: "Neither one of us knew what to say. He'd ask me how I was doing and I'd say better and then I'd ask him how he was doing and he'd lie and tell me he was okay. After that, we'd just sort of hold the phone until one of us started crying and then we'd hang up" (Cleage 263). Some time later, after May and Charlie's marriage, they still find it impossible to articulate their shared trauma:

> [W]e couldn't figure out a way to talk about what had happened to us in Mississippi and we couldn't find a way to talk around it. We just sort of hoped it would go away, but it didn't. It got bigger and scarier and bigger and scarier until Charlie couldn't touch me anymore without crying. (Cleage 264)

May's testimony about this communicative impasse accentuates the intransmissible and embodied character of the trauma that she and Charlie bear.

That *Bourbon* characterizes trauma in this way cannot be overlooked because it fundamentally distinguishes this play from *Flyin' West*, in which narrative contains and domesticates traumatic memory, and from much contemporary trauma theory. Amy Hungerford takes issue with Cathy Caruth's influential theory of trauma on precisely these matters of transmissibility and embodiment. She finds that Caruth's literary reading of trauma renders it all too symbolic and disembodied, and she contends, "By cutting experience free from the subject of experience [the actual trauma victim], Caruth allows trauma not only to be abstract in the extreme but also, by virtue of that abstraction, to be transmissible" (Hungerford 83). Likewise, in contemporary discourses on trauma, Allan Feldman detects a "general lack of specificity" in the "non-medical use of the term," a rhetorical looseness that makes trauma "both an object and a method of analysis," while tending to flatten and metaphorize all traumatic experience (184). Hence, such nonspecific and tropic language threatens to elide the trauma victim as it universalizes the trauma. *Bourbon* resists this effect not only by wrapping May and Charlie's traumatic memory in impenetrable silence so that it cannot be spoken, much less metaphorized, but also by inscribing trauma deep within these victims' bodies.

That Charlie "couldn't touch [May] anymore without crying" after Freedom Summer indicates what should be obvious—that the physical abuse May and Charlie endured not only wounded their minds but also marked their bodies indelibly, imprinting a memory of pain on their very skin. May recognizes that the embodiment of this trauma accounts for her family's distant regard when she returns from Mississippi: "They were afraid to even look at me. I was living proof of something so terrible nobody wanted to think about it, so they got mad at me instead" (Cleage 262). Significantly, the therapeutic response she craves from her father consists in embrace and physical protection: the way he could help was to "come and hold me" and to "promise that nobody was ever going to hurt me like that again" (Cleage 262). Charlie's body, too, announces its irrevocable difference after Freedom Summer. The police officers who assaulted him broke his leg in three places, and he walks with a "slight limp" thirty-one years later (Cleage 209). Neither can it be considered accidental that, for the past three decades at least, he revisits and repeats his traumatic memory by wounding his own body; as May explains to Rosa, "The only person he ever tries to hurt is himself" (Cleage 197). Such deep embodiment of trauma resists troping and the commodification that this literary usage can encourage.

Having affirmed the principle of intransmissibility, however, *Bourbon* dramatizes the metaphorical mapping of one traumatic experience onto another in Charlie's retelling of a trauma narrative culled from the history of North American slavery. In a contemplative moment at the end of the play, Charlie reminds May of the story of a shipload of African slaves who jumped overboard and drowned "because they believed their spirits would travel home to their ancestors as long as their heads were not separated from their bodies" (Cleage 266); he invokes the story in order to diagnose his own psychological condition. To make the narrative serve this purpose, however, Charlie must alter it slightly; he changes the phrase that expresses the slaves' doctrine, "as long as their heads were not separated from their bodies," to say in the following sentence, "As long as the head and the *heart* stayed together, they didn't give a damn about dying" (Cleage 266, emphasis added). The nearly imperceptible modification of the slaves' doctrine, which apparently concerns the specific problem of decapitation, enables Charlie to appropriate their history tropically, equating their experience to his own in which white police officers and misguided mental health practitioners "took my head and separated it from my heart, from my memories" (Cleage 267). *Bourbon* positions Charlie's sophisticated, albeit effortless, literary maneuver at the center of the mental processes that motivate his horrific repetitions of his Freedom Summer trauma.

Charlie confesses to May in this scene that he committed the three unsolved murders in downtown Detroit. His tropic appropriation of the slaves' trauma narrative represents far more than an act of literary violence, for it appears to catalyze—at the least, to rationalize—the process in which he "picked out three, just like those three in Mississippi picked us out, and [. . .] did what a man is supposed to do" (Cleage 268). The utter abandon afforded the slaves by their doctrine about the union of one's head and body ("they didn't give a damn about dying") inspires in Charlie a recklessness that renders murder comprehensible, even expedient. For him, restored sanity consists in the reunification of the head and the heart, or the memories. Charlie maintains that, in violently separating these constituents of identity, a racist society aims at "mak[ing] sure what you know doesn't fuck with you to the point where you might actually have to do something about it" (Cleage 267). When "what you know" is past traumatization, though, as it is for Charlie, "do[ing] something about it" threatens to entail violence. Cleage alludes to *Dutchman* at the opening of her text, but it is here at Charlie's confession where Clay's prescription for African Americans' mental health most forcefully resonates: "Crazy niggers turning their backs on sanity. When all it needs is that simple act. Murder. Just murder! Would make us all sane" (Jones 35).

LeRoi Jones's character Clay, of course, cannot be considered Charlie's lone ancestor. Cleage deliberately aligns her character with an African American past, a linkage first evoked when Charlie, promoting college students' participation in Freedom Summer, appeals to "the memory of our ancestors' bones" to motivate his audience (Cleage 201). Because a long history of violence against African Americans constitutes Charlie's cultural inheritance, the retrieval of his past ("my memories") portends violence at its reunion with his immediate consciousness ("my head"), for this confrontation involves individual and collective history. Indeed, Charlie's invocation of the slaves' story combines with his sense of historical accountability in driving him to murder: he apologizes to May not for killing three men but "For all those years I didn't kill anybody. I wasted thirty years. My father wasted seventy. My uncles made eighty and never killed a soul, so I owe, May" (Cleage 268). Charlie's murders, then, constitute an eruption of history into the present, an unexpected intrusion of black traumatic memory into the cultivated forgetfulness of collective white consciousness.

Returning, however, to the spatial-thematic landscape in *Bourbon*, the fate of the bridge symbol in the play problematizes the notion that Charlie's murder achieves the harmony of his head and heart or his present and past. The bridge symbolizes this hope of harmony and connectedness, as it spans liminal spaces and transcends borders, but the violent incident on one bridge in Detroit casts a shadow on this hope and figuratively renders the bridge impassable. If the bridge becomes a site of trauma, then, does the possibility of overcoming spatial, historical, physical, and mental division disappear from the play? *Bourbon* interacts with this question equivocally. One might note that the bridge on which the violent incident occurs is not the Ambassador Bridge seen from May and Charlie's window and connecting Detroit to Canada; it is the Belle Isle Bridge and may be considered less significant in the play's spatial-thematic landscape. Moreover, the stage directions frame the scene of Charlie's confession in terms that suggest an end to his internal division: "*Throughout this scene, there is about Charlie a strange and growing peace. He is not happy, but he is finally unafraid*" (Cleage 266). *Bourbon* does not utterly preclude a reading that makes Charlie's murders effective therapy for his traumatic memory, a harmonizing of his past and present, but Cleage diverts the audience from this interpretation by asserting in the Playwright's Note that the answer to the question of the color line must be found "in the space between the nonviolent warriors [of Freedom Summer] and the powerless rage of the would-be poet [*Dutchman*'s Clay]" (Cleage 191).

Moreover, *Bourbon* excludes the notion that Charlie's murders offer any hope for his (or May's) well-being in the future. In the closing scene, even as May rehearses for Charlie the familiar idyll of their imagined life in Canada, "*There is a sudden and very loud knocking on the door*" that is "*clearly the police*" (Cleage 270). Making no effort to escape, Charlie listens placidly as May describes the garden they intended to plant across the border, and the strange juxtaposition of her idealized narrative of Canada and the "*insistent*" knocking on the door dramatizes the couple's entrapment in a life rendered incoherent by traumatic experience. The once promising view of the Ambassador Bridge out their window now taunts May and Charlie, for the menacing police officers outside their door remind them of a painful past from which, in *Bourbon*, there can be no successful flight.

Such a grim outlook corresponds to Cleage's posture toward her audience in *Bourbon*, the most off-putting stance she assumes in the trilogy. Cleage courts an optimistic audience in *Flyin' West* before overtly confronting in *Blues* the perils of prostituting one's self for the critics. In *Bourbon*, however, the playwright presents her audience with an unprecedented challenge. Not only does the play deconstruct the belief that trauma may be faithfully narrativized and transmitted, but it also exposes the violence embedded in an audience's expectations for triumphalist representations of traumatic experience. Cleage levels this second critique in May's voice; having offered Rosa a history of her Freedom Summer, May identifies a gap between the truth of her experience and the heroic metanarrative that audiences anticipate from her: "There wasn't anybody to tell. Not just what happened. How it felt. People like to say how brave you are, but they don't want to hear about how scared you were. How you screamed so long you lost your voice and tried to close your mind so you could be someplace else, anyplace else, but there" (Cleage 264). May's desire to be "anyplace else" than in the throes of traumatic memory defies trendy constructions of survival as a rewarding destination in itself, and her commentary on the expectations frequently attached to survival stories recalls Feldman's "technologies of memory" (167), which require of such narratives "healing, trauma alleviation, justice, and collective catharsis" (170). Incapable of satisfying these generic requirements, May reverses the direction of expectation, demanding of her audience in Rosa, "Where were you when it was time to change the world, Rose? Where the fuck were you?" (Cleage 265). In this fierce challenge to her friend, May assumes the role of the critic, while her erstwhile audience undergoes interrogation. This swapping of roles, wherein the audience must account for its passivity, distinguishes Cleage's mature dramatic vision, a theory of the stage in which politically active playwrights like herself critique their audiences' performances in "chang[ing] the world."

Cleage's trilogy, then, charts a course through geographical spaces and historical eras to map the dynamics of traumatic memory, and it simultaneously traverses a critical landscape oriented around the spectacle of traumatic experience. As the playwright's perspective on her themes grows increasingly drear, suggesting the futility—if not the impossibility—of flight from traumatic memory, Cleage's authorial stance becomes increasingly aloof as she confronts the violence implicit in any staging of traumatic experience. Audiences may well prefer the sanguine tone of *Flyin' West* to the oppressive atmosphere of *Blues* and *Bourbon*, but the latter two plays construct a necessary critique of traumatic witnessing. The disappearance of strong frontier women, sisterly rituals, and homemade apple pies "to die for" renders trauma far less accessible and domesticable in the plays that follow *Flyin' West*. Such distinctions between the first play and the second two cannot entirely disrupt the trilogy's continuity, though, for Cleage's three plays about trauma and the spaces it occupies collectively comprise not a flight from but "a sinking down into the past, into the interiority of memory" (duBois 105)—in this case, an African American collective memory scarred by violence in every historical period. This historical continuity explains why her African American characters in disparate settings are all flyin' "anyplace else" (Cleage 264), but Cleage denies her audiences the same option of disengagement, demanding instead that they renounce critical detachment and permit her characters' traumas to interpellate them in some corresponding, "flesh and blood" struggle for freedom (Cleage 175).

Notes

1. In the Gospel of John, a Pharisee named Nicodemus discusses with Jesus the nature of salvation, and Jesus teaches him that "unless one is born again he cannot see the kingdom of God" (John 3:3). This concept of spiritual rebirth resonates in the name of the all-black Kansas town where Cleage's women intend to establish their independence from racial oppression.
2. In *Saints, Sinners, Saviors: Strong Black Women in African American Literature*, Trudier Harris identifies the same either-or dynamic in *Flyin' West* and in representations of "strong black women" generally, arguing that "in order for [such female characters] to be strong, black men must be absent, expendable, or diminished" (150).
3. Although London represents a third geographical space in *Flyin' West*, the play constructs this city as a negation. It claims only tangential significance in the trajectory of the plot and, thus, constitutes a no-place, a utopia in the sense that it possesses no reality for any of the protagonists except Minnie.
4. Guy's suggestion that Reverend Powell at Abyssinian Baptist Church "ought to quit preaching and go on into full-time show business" indicates that the preacher, too, operates in a tension between his congregation's expectations for spiritual nourishment on the one hand and sheer entertainment on the other (Cleage 107).

Works Cited

Carroll, Rebecca. *I Know What the Red Clay Looks Like: The Voice and Vision of Black Women Writers.* New York: Carol Southern, 1994.

Caruth, Cathy. *Unclaimed Experience: Trauma, Narrative, and History*. Baltimore, MD: Johns Hopkins University Press. 1996.

Cleage, Pearl. *Flyin' West and Other Plays*. New York: Theatre Communications Group, 1999.

duBois, Page. *Torture and Truth: The New Ancient World*. New York: Routledge, 1991.

Feldman, Allan. "Memory Theaters, Virtual Witnessing, and the Trauma-Aesthetic." *Biography* 27 (2004): 163–202.

Harris, Trudier. *Saints, Sinners, Saviors: Strong Black Women in African American Literature*. New York: Palgrave, 2001.

Hungerford, Amy. "Memorizing Memory." *Yale Journal of Criticism* 14 (2001): 67–92.

Jones, LeRoi. *Dutchman and the Slave: Two Plays by LeRoi Jones*. New York: Morrow, 1964.

Young, Allan. *The Harmony of Illusions: Inventing Post-Traumatic Stress Disorder*. Princeton, NJ: Princeton University Press, 1995.

7

"A World Made in My Image"

Romare Bearden's Collagist Technique in August Wilson's *Joe Turner's Come and Gone*

JOHN M. HANNAH

In his forward to Myron Schwartzman's *Romare Bearden: His Life & Art* (1990), August Wilson recounts two seminal moments in his artistic development. First, his discovery of the blues provided an aesthetic model that allowed him to represent the black experience in a way that elevated as well as celebrated its many nuances and contradictions (8). Second, through his encounter with Romare Bearden's art, Wilson found inspiration that enabled him to translate the blues aesthetic within a narrative form that captured the essence of African American culture and its traditions. In Bearden's work, Wilson writes:

> I saw . . . black life presented on its own terms, on a grand and epic scale, with all its richness and fullness, in a language that was vibrant and which, made attendant to everyday life, ennobled it, affirmed its value, and exalted its presence. (8)

Paying homage to the artist whose six decades of paintings and art scholarship shaped if not defined the study of African American art in the twentieth century, Wilson names Bearden as his artistic role-model, stating that he sought to fashion his plays as the dramatic equivalents of the collagist's works (9).

If Bearden's collagist form and artistic practice hold such an important position in Wilson's estimation, then how does the playwright manifest this influence in his own work? Although critics have discussed Wilson's direct observations concerning Bearden's influence, none have particularly addressed the ways that

Wilson applies Bearden's aesthetic approach and artistic practices within the context of a specific play. For example, in "Romare Bearden, August Wilson, and the Traditions of African Performance," Joan Fishman addresses the ways Bearden and Wilson reference a common set of communal rituals and images to represent the black American experience within the practice and invocation of African performativity (137–45). Although she observes that "[n]ot unlike Bearden, Wilson builds his plays from small pieces, in a collagist style," Fishman focuses instead on the ways each enacts "the creation of traditional performance" (137).[1] Joan Herrington, in "The Four 'B's': August Wilson's Inspiration," discusses the images that Wilson draws from Bearden's paintings (22–25). Mark Rocha, in "August Wilson and the Four B's: Influences," argues that Bearden "serves Wilson as a kind of father-figure . . . [and] a personification of the ideal for a black artist," briefly listing specific elements that Wilson borrows from Bearden's works (10–12). In "Finding One's Song: *Joe Turner's Come and Gone*," Sandra Shannon notes in passing that "*Joe Turner* also owes a structural debt to the collage, for it reflects the seemingly incoherent patchwork that is Bearden's hallmark" (125), but to suggest that either Bearden's or Wilson's works are even "seemingly incoherent" ignores the important interplay of tensions that exist between the part and the whole as well as the larger unity that simultaneously emerges from out of that fragmentation.

In fact, through this collagist tension—the continuous and simultaneous interplay between fragmentation and unity—Bearden and Wilson contextualize and represent the African American experience. By replicating and therefore revising the processes of fragmentation arising out of successive forced migrations and ever-changing forms of institutionalization, both articulate the possibilities for unity and balance through a hybrid African American identity, a complex confluence of African retentions and Western appropriations. Indeed, as other critics have observed, Wilson's and Bearden's works do intersect on two distinct levels. First, each engages the folk forms, themes, and imagery of a larger African American artistic tradition, drawing extensively from the oral tradition, the black vernacular, and the blues. Second, Wilson draws extensively from, or riffs, Bearden's art as an intertext, invoking specific Bearden works in his plays. More importantly, however, Wilson embraces and puts to use specific elements of Bearden's aesthetic, his artistic sensibility, and his formal craft as a playwright. In *Joe Turner's Come and Gone* (1988),[2] one particular example, Wilson constructs the play as a collage, invoking the collagist tensions to reveal the forces of fragmentation created out of white hegemony as well as the possibility for recovery and self-assertion located within the community. Through the interaction between the individual and the community, the part and the whole, furthermore, Wilson suggests the possibility for a prevailing hybrid African American identity as represented in the figure of Herald Loomis.

To address Bearden's specific use of collage and the ways it influences and informs Wilson's plays, a brief overview of the theory and technique of collage will position its development within the Western art tradition. In "Collage in the Twentieth Century: An Overview," Katherine Hoffman defines collage "as a quintessential twentieth-century art form with multiple layers and signposts pointing to a variety of forms and realities, and to the possibility or suggestion of countless new realities" (1).[3] As a process, collage first serves as a "breaking away from an established [representational] order" by bringing to bear the processes of "chaos—disintegration, fragmentation, [and] dislocation"—in contesting and questioning the nature of "time, space, and reality" (1) within any cultural representation. The very act of de(con)struction, however, allows "for the transformation of one reality into another" (7) as the collagist negotiates alternative perspectives and identities through the reordering of these cultural fragments. This complex interplay between the forces of chaos and fragmentation and those of order and recovery, the collagist tension itself, resists essentialism in the way that it both disrupts and renegotiates authorized or privileged representational forms.

The mixing of different forms, genres, and media, therefore, creates a distinct ontological tension within collage as the relationship between the individual and society, the part and the whole, the old and the new, and the past and the present becomes indeterminate, subject to negotiation, context, and perspective. Donald Kuspit describes this tension as being the complex interplay between the objective and the subjective in that the artist must first begin with the objective, the assumed or accepted cultural forms and assumptions, in order to resist and move beyond them to negotiate the subjective as an act of becoming (47–48). Accordingly, "collage demonstrates rebellion against determining beliefs in the very act of articulating them through the choice of fragments" (48). As a representational form, therefore, collage is also "double-voiced" (xxiii) as detailed in Henry Louis Gates Jr.'s *The Signifying Monkey* (1989) in that it "speaks" to and interacts with multiple voices, artistic forms, and traditions, simultaneously reifying and revising them.

Thus an artistic practice that simultaneously resists and yet enables cultural representation, collage particularly empowers the African American artist—one who engages in cultural representation across any number of forms and mediums—to claim, recover, and renegotiate a sense of self and community from within a self-authorizing, oppressive, white cultural hegemony. Through the collagist act, Colin Rowe and Fred Koetter suggest that the artist may negotiate the restrictions of binary essentialism in that "[s]ocieties and persons [are able to] assemble themselves according to their own interpretations of absolute reference and traditional value; and up to a point, collage accommodates both hybrid display and the requirements of self-determination" (144–45). Within the collagist tension, the African American artist challenges and disrupts an assumed, unified Western subject by dismantling and deconstructing traditional and privileged representations of cultural identity. By revising Western forms, therefore, the black artist may negotiate both identity and historical perspective. The processes of regeneration and recovery inherent to collage thereby allow the African American artist to contest and renegotiate the fragmentation arising out of the Western hegemonic processes manifested in the slave trade and slavery and reinscribed through forced migration, systematic institutionalization, and economic marginalization.

Within the African American literary tradition, W.E.B. Du Bois most clearly defines the fragmentation that shapes the African American experience as "double-consciousness" (11), casting the struggle within terms suggestive of the collagist tension. In his oft-cited passage from *The Souls of Black Folk*, Du Bois observes that "this American world . . . yields [the Negro] no true self-consciousness. . . . [Thus] [o]ne ever feels his two-ness,—an American, a Negro; two souls, two thoughts, two unreconciled strivings; two warring ideals in one dark body, whose dogged strength alone keeps it from being torn asunder" (10–11). Contextualizing the African American experience within the strictures of white hegemonic essentialism, Du Bois observes further:

> The history of the American Negro is the history of this strife,—this longing to attain self-conscious manhood, to merge his double self into a better and truer self. In this merging he wishes neither of the older selves to be lost. He would not Africanize America, for America has too much to teach the world and Africa. He would not bleach his Negro soul in a flood of white Americanism, for he knows that Negro blood has a message for the world. He simply wishes to make it possible for a man to be both a Negro and an American. (11)

The question then implied within Du Bois' writing is how might the black artist represent the black experience within the tyranny of the copula, the privilege assumed within Western essentialism to name, and thereby authorize, what "is" and "is not."[4]

Both Bearden and Wilson respond to this tension within their art, representing the particularities of the African American experience to resist the fragmenting forces in American society. In describing his artistic purpose, Bearden contextualizes his art in terms of American racial negotiation:

> [I work] out of a response and need to redefine the image of man in the terms of the Negro experience I know best. I felt that the Negro was becoming too much of an abstraction rather than the reality that art can give a subject. . . . What I've attempted to do is establish a world through art in which the validity of my Negro experience could live and make its own logic. (Patton 6)

Similarly, Wilson's desire to represent the "nobility [inherent] to the lives of blacks in America" (Moyers 63) arises out of the struggle against the residual forces of slavery in contemporary American society. Praising "the resiliency of their spirit" (64), Wilson, in restating Du Bois, points out the particularity of black experience: "We are Americans. But first of all, we are Africans. . . . We have different philosophical ideas, different ways of responding to the world, different ideas and attitudes, different values, different ideas about style and linguistics, different aesthetics" (68–69). In negotiating this difference, therefore, both artists contend with the cultural tensions arising out of the African American experience.

In doing so, Bearden defines the artist's role in representing experience: "The thing is that the artist confronts chaos. The whole thing of art is, how do you organize chaos?" (Schwartzman 197).[5] For Bearden, this chaos manifests itself in the fragments that enter into his art, the tensions created out of the African American experience, the ideals of an America ever in a state of becoming, Africa and its art and ideas, and the Western intellectual and artistic traditions. To organize this chaos, Bearden revises, juxtaposes, and fuses these fragments—the objects of the African American experience—as a hybrid manifestation emerging out of the collagist form, negotiating a sense of unity and perspective—an African American subject—from the synthesis of these disparate, often antagonistic fragments of experience. In doing so, Bearden draws from the found objects gleaned from the disparate physical, spiritual, and intellectual elements that intersect his life—the African American folk tradition, his personal past, African and Western art, a collective American past. Suggesting the tenuous nature of any artistic enterprise, Bearden's collage reflects the tensions of the black experience in America as an act of becoming, the simultaneous movement between the part and the whole, chaos and order, and fragmentation and unity.

Within his writings, Bearden establishes a hybrid aesthetic perspective useful for exploring both Wilson's drama in particular and the artistic representation of the African American experience in general. In *The Painter's Mind* (1969), for example, Bearden defines the basic terms of his aesthetic approach suggesting that the artist must seek "a rationale of order" to establish a "vision of the world" (7–9) from within the chaos of competing perspectives, interests, and experiences.[6] The manipulation of "structure and space" (20–21) then allows the artist to create or reorder human experience within the "totality, or total unity of a work of art" (17). Although he invokes the Aristotelian notion of unity, Bearden revises this foundation of Western privilege—the authority to define that which is complete, valid, and acceptable—expanding the possibilities for representing experience outside of authorized hegemonic narratives.[7] The collagist generates a world of his or her choosing "in which all the parts are related," and in being complete, one "that must be considered on its own terms" (18).

Negotiating the collagist tension, Bearden produces his art as a hybrid form that mediates and balances the forces inherent to Western binary essentialism. In prefacing his discussion of structure and space, Bearden asserts that art speaks to and comes out of other art, an idea that he borrows from André Malraux (*Painter's* 12), suggesting that art is in conversation with other works and forms, an intertexuality that arises out of repetition, riffing, and redefining.[8] Expanding upon this idea in "Rectangular Structure in My Montage Paintings," Bearden notes "that modern painting progresses through cumulative destructions and new beginnings" (12), indicating the negotiation of chaos and order that takes place in borrowing and revising elements from other works of art. In defining "structure," Bearden considers "four great structural elements," repetition, tempering of volumes, tension, and overlapping of planes (*Painter's* 43–44). In doing so, he does not so much as assert a prescriptive formulation for physical arrangement as much as emphasize the negotiation of balance, unity, and equilibrium within an artwork. Relating the complex relationship between the tensions emerging out of "opposition" and "equilibrium" (44), he emphasizes the artist's role in bringing order to the elements—the fragments, found objects, and appropriations—that enter an artwork.

Contextualizing artistic "space" as a reflection of the human "desire for relationship and order" (*Painter's* 97), Bearden contends that the artist shapes and negotiates space through "movement and countermovement" (95), another restatement of the collagist tension. Whereas structure involves the elements brought into a work, the negotiation of space involves the ordering of those elements into some larger whole. Writing that "order is space and space is order" (99), Bearden establishes an ontological foundation for representing experience as a function of perspective and context. Through this negotiation, Bearden indicates, "[I am able] to paint the life of my people as I know it . . . to reveal through pictorial complexities the richness of a life I know" ("Rectangular" 18). In depicting the African American experience, therefore, Bearden invokes but revises the master's discourse within the Western artistic tradition to assert and open up the possibilities for self-representation.

Although using a structuralist and essentialist vocabulary, Bearden invokes a poststructural and postmodern sensibility. While asserting that the artist may represent "a truth" (*Painter's* 21), Bearden describes truth relative to context and perspective, suggesting the possibilities for negotiating alternative realities—alternative subjectivities—within a work of art. Although he assigns agency and authority to the artist through the choice of subject and form, Bearden also recognizes the Derridean notion of the text, or artwork, as an encountered object, stating explicitly that "whatever the image, the only visual reality present is the structure" (20), thus art is an "illusion" created within the presence of a text or work.[9] Suggesting that art is polysemous "with its multiplicity of images," he writes, "Not all who look see the same thing . . . [but] each according to his temperament, his imagination, and his spiritual needs" (20). In accounting for subjectivity, agency, and textuality, therefore, Bearden suggests that a work of art enables and mediates social negotiation by bringing together the artist's created world with the agency of a viewer or reader, creating a shared experience from out of that interaction. Within the negotiation of difference emerges a shared experience, one that includes the percipient, the reader or viewer, as participant and sharer.

With influences ranging from George Grosz, Diego Rivera, Grant Wood, and the Dutch masters to Chinese classical painters, African design, and the African American folk tradition ("Rectangular" 11–15), Bearden's artistic development reflects the complexities of the African American experience as well as the hybridity of his collage. In her introduction to the catalog for the Bearden exhibit *Narrations* (2002), Sharon Patton relates the varying elements that shape his paintings, "African art . . . provides a spiritual impetus for modern artists as it did for their European counterparts, [Bearden] claimed. He adapted African art as a formal element and African-American folk culture . . . as subject matter and aesthetic, combining these with the techniques of abstract modernism in his works" (7).

Wilson likewise demonstrates a collagist disposition in the way that he approaches his plays. When asked whether he considered *Fences*, his most economically successful and recognized endeavor, to be his "signature play," Wilson emphatically stated no: "My signature play would be *Joe Turner's Come and Gone*. Most of the ideas of the other plays are contained in that one play. . . . *Fences* is the only one that's not an ensemble play" (Shannon and Williams 194). In contrast to *Fences*, a play developed around Troy Maxson, a single character, Wilson's ensembles reflect the workings of community as the drama's themes develop out of the complex interplay of multiple characters. As parts of a larger whole, therefore, the characters' actions and experiences echo the dramatic rhythms emerging out of the repetition, juxtaposition, and opposition that move the play forward.

Furthermore, when discussing how he writes his plays, Wilson illustrates the way that he negotiates the collagist tensions in bringing together the fragments of experience, from both his own life and those of the African American collective, into a larger, meaningful whole:

> You're either wrestling with the devil or Jacob's angel, the whole purpose being that when you walk through that landscape you arrive at something larger than you had when you started. And this larger something should be illuminating and as close to the truth as you can understand. (Powers 10)

Invoking the African American folk tradition, a world in which the devil and God both regularly interact with humans and through which the tensions and conflicts represented within the pairing come under constant negotiation, Wilson invokes the processes of collage as he addresses the tension between chaos and order and the way the experiences of life, the fragments, come together to form some larger meaningful whole. In referring to the idea of truth, Wilson echoes Bearden's allusion to a truth that emerges out of an individual's experience and perspective. In fact, describing how he created *Joe Turner* in the same interview, Wilson essentially paraphrases Bearden's notion of the unified artistic vision as well as his delineation of the four elements of structure in *The Painter's Mind*: "I knew I wanted to create . . . a whole other world. It's a blending together, an overlap" (10).

Like Bearden, Wilson claims numerous influences—African, European, and American—revising Du Bois's notion of "double-consciousness" to suggest hybridity of identity and artistic form. Of course, in the "four B's—Bearden, Baraka, Borges, and the Blues"—Wilson asserts what Mark Rocha calls the playwright's "theory of African American literature" (4). In *The Ground on Which I Stand* (2001), a speech presented to the Theater Communications Group Conference in 1996, Wilson specifically speaks to the hybridity of his work. Noting his Western dramatic ancestors, Wilson lists the pantheon of canonical dramatists: "Euripides, Aeschylus, . . . Sophocles, . . . Shakespeare, . . . Shaw, Ibsen, . . . Chekov, . . . O'Neill, . . . Miller, . . . [and] Williams" (11). In naming his African American sources, however, Wilson first names his models of self-assertion and resistance—"my grandfather,. . . . Nat Turner, . . . Denmark Vesey, . . . Martin Delaney, Marcus Garvey, and the Honorable Elijah Muhammed" (11). Later in the speech he positions himself within literary black nationalism as represented by "Ron Milner; Ed Bullins; Philip Hayes Dean; Richard Wesley; Lonne Elder, III; Sonia Sanchez; Barbara Ann Teer; and Amiri Baraka," his self-described African American literary ancestors (20). For both Wilson and Bearden, the naming of influences becomes an act of self-definition, a kind of collagist negotiation in itself.

As does Bearden, Wilson also uses his art to negotiate order and balance within the chaos of human experience. Observing the differences between African and Western epistemologies and ontologies, Wilson suggests that the African worldview privileges the collective and the communal as opposed to the primacy of the individual: "Western culture sees man as being *apart from* the world, and African culture just sees man as *a part* of the world" (emphasis in text, Sheppard 106). Wilson takes this point further, "Whites see man against a world that needs to be subdued. Africans see man as a part of the world, as a natural part of their environment" (Savran 34).[10] Addressing the tensions of Western binary essentialism, both Bearden and Wilson invoke an African ontology, one that positions the part within the whole and the individual within the community as a movement toward balance. As a result, Wilson invokes Bearden's application of collage—negotiating the sources and processes of fragmentation that operate simultaneously with those of order and recovery—as a reflection of the distinct African sensibility that informs the black experience in America.

Addressing this negotiation of the collagist tension in her analysis of *Joe Turner*, Sandra Richards argues that Wilson revises the tyranny of the copula in that "[t]he binary of either/or is replaced by the principle of both/and" (101), implying that the negotiation of self is ongoing within a complex interaction of forces positioned as polarities of Western binary essentialism. Taking this idea further in his analysis of *Joe Turner*, Kim Pereira invokes the collagist tension as a function of the Yoruban cosmology, asserting that Wilson invokes the complex relationship existing between the "complimentary" gods Eshu, "associated with disorderliness and confusion," and Ifa, "whose function is to promote orderliness in the world," a reflection of the tensions within and between the individual and society (65). Explaining this further, Pereira writes, "Each of them alone would present a one-dimensional world of either order or chaos. Together they furnish the complexities of life and living that derive from daily renegotiations of the very oppositions represented by them" (65).[11] Within Pereira's description, both Bearden and Wilson demonstrate a distinct African sensibility in the way each negotiates the simultaneous tensions inherent to order and chaos, unity and fragmentation, and balance and imbalance in the context of Western binary essentialism.

In creating their art, Bearden and Wilson demonstrate a shared historical sensibility in representing the varied fullness of the African American experience. Both assert a persevering black identity within the fragmentation arising out of white hegemony by challenging Western discourse to recover and renegotiate a past marked by slavery, forced migration, and institutionalization. Wilson sums up the centrality of history to the African American experience, asserting that "[i]dentity means understanding your political . . . as well as your social history" (Grant 178). Perhaps echoing Ralph Ellison's pronouncement in *Invisible Man* that "the end is in the beginning and lies far ahead" (6), Wilson observes, "[I]f we're going to be pointed toward a future, we must know our past" (Savran 27). Observing this anachronistic quality in Bearden's work, art historian Mary Campbell defines his art in terms of "its reliance on memory and history, its storytelling narrative technique, [and] a nostalgic attempt to recreate the Black American past" (10), a reflection of Bearden's "fierce assertion of his own cultural identity and history" (11). "What makes Bearden's art particularly difficult to grasp," Campbell observes, "is that even as [it] points to the future, it also wholeheartedly embraces the past" (11). Thus in the way that his collage moves toward identity, unity, and self—an art that resists rather than replicates the forces of fragmentation—Bearden's paintings reflect the quality that marks African American artistic production in distinction to other late twentieth-century works. In fact, when most artists were breaking away from the past in the early 1970s, Bearden began developing his art around themes concerning the early decades of the last century, the 20s and 30s. Wilson, in creating a play to represent each decade of the last century, similarly follows Bearden's model.

As part of this recovery, Bearden and Wilson invoke the African American folk tradition and its accompanying rituals as a means to sustain a black community resisting the processes of fragmentation in American society. In *From My People: 400 Years of African American Folklore* (2002), Daryl Dance contends that for African Americans, folklore is a kind of living history that represents the shared experiences of being black in America and counters hegemonic distortions and erasures that would deny such a history exists (xxxiv–xxxvii). In *Going to the Territory* (1986), Ellison describes Bearden as capturing the essence of a black "humanity that has struggled to survive the decimating and fragmentizing effects of American social processes" (234–35). In what could easily be a reference to Wilson's plays, Ellison elaborates upon Bearden's evocation of African American folk forms that include his visualization of the blues "including the familiar trains . . . and the conjure women . . . who evoke the abiding mystery of the enigmatic women who people the blues" (235). Most important, Ellison suggests, "are renderings of those rituals of rebirth and dying, of baptism and sorcery which give ceremonial continuity to the Negro American community" (235).

In entering this tradition, moreover, Bearden and Wilson also invoke the processes and forces that gave rise to it, similarly exposing a shared American history that includes the theft, institutionalization, and exploitation of the black body, the rise of the urban and industrial, and the fragmentation and dislocation of forced migration brought about by the terrorism of lynch mob, the imposition of Jim Crow, and the exploitation of cheap labor. Through the artistic act, however, Bearden and Wilson invoke and reinscribe the human strength and fortitude that gave rise to and continues to sustain the folk tradition, using the transformative and creative powers of collage to negotiate unity and wholeness within these processes of fragmentation. As Joan Fishman observes, Bearden's and Wilson's particular use of the African American oral tradition—the storyteller, the preacher, music, and the "repeated rituals of everyday life"—bring together the secular and the sacred in their works within a hybrid of African, Western, and American practices and thought (139–42). In bringing these elements together in their art, each is able to bridge the past and the present, invoking a shared, cotemporaneous community sustained by its own logic, practice, symbology, and vernacular.

The most important form of the folk tradition that informs Bearden's and Wilson's artistic practice, however, is the blues, a foundational source that reflects the same structural and ontological tensions as collage. In his famous pronouncement from *Shadow and Act* (1964), Ellison defines the blues as "an impulse to keep the painful details and episodes of a brutal experience alive in one's aching consciousness . . . to transcend it, not by consolation of philosophy but by squeezing from it a near-tragic, near-comic lyricism. As a form, the blues is an autobiographical chronicle of personal catastrophe expressed lyrically" (78–79). In the way it allows for a hybrid negotiation of the tension existing between the tragic and the comic, the blues enables its performer to resist the Western binary essentialism upon which white authority and privilege exists.[12] In *Stomping the Blues* (1976), Albert Murray takes a slightly different approach from Ellison, observing that despite "its preoccupation with the most disturbing aspects of life," the blues has "the express purpose to make people feel good" as well as "to generate a disposition that is both elegantly playful and heroic in its nonchalance" (45). By confronting the processes of loss and fragmentation represented in the blues, the blues player takes control of those forces and thereby revises and repositions them. As Daryl Dance observes, "The blues enables transcendence. One old bluesman is quoted as saying, 'the blues regenerates a man'" (72).

Within their respective forms, both Bearden and Wilson draw heavily upon the unifying and regenerative power of the blues. In "The Visual Equivalent of the Blues," Albert Murray particularly notes that Bearden's "aesthetic statement had been conditioned by the blues idiom in general and jazz musicianship in particular" (18).[13] During the 1950s, in fact, Bearden co-authored several popular jazz-influenced songs (Schwartzman 173–75). With the blues informing his "compositional approach to collage," Bearden frequently populates his works with blues imagery and jazz performers (Campbell 15).[14] Ultimately, Murray elaborates upon his friend's blues sensibilities most clearly:

> And of what *is* A Bearden emblematic if not the fundamental rituals of the blues idiom and the way it conditions one to survive? . . . And what more graceful, more stylishly heroic method of survival can there be than by expressing flexibility through elegant improvisation? . . . [Bearden's representation] works on the beholder not only as a work of art but as something deeper: a totemistic device and talisman for keeping the blues at bay. (Murray's capitalization, "Visual" 28)

In his essay on Bearden, Wilson similarly describes the blues as the artistic tradition that informs his plays ("Foreword" 8). Calling it "the book of black people," Wilson suggests that "the blues is the African American's cultural response to the world. . . . I've found that whatever you want to know about the black experience in America is contained in the blues" (Livingston 58).

In bringing together their varying influences—the African, Western, and African American—Bearden and Wilson share a similar artistic practice and compositional sensibility reflected in the collagist's negotiation of the part and the whole. Positioning the blues within the context of Western art, Bearden draws upon the form's mimetic qualities through the use of repetition, improvisation, and variation. Albert Murray relates Bearden's description of his creative process:

> You have to begin somewhere, . . . so you put something down. Then you put something else with it, and then you see how that works, and maybe you try something else and so on, and the picture grows in that way. One thing leads to another, and you take the options as they come, or as you are able to perceive them as you proceed. . . . Once

> you get going . . . all sorts of things begin to open up. Sometimes something just falls into place, like piano keys that every now and then just seem to be right where your fingers happen to come down. ("Visual" 18–19)

Working in a similar fashion, Wilson gathers the materials for his play from the objects and fragments that he finds in the world around him. In doing so, he relates how he begins with a single image or idea—"it can be a line of blues lyric, a painting, an image" (Livingston 54)—upon which he expands and builds his plays.

In bringing order to the fragments manifested in their respective artworks, Bearden and Wilson similarly identify themselves as participants in dialogue with the represented characters and figures.[15] Bearden, for example, describes how his collages develop and emerge into a completed whole, referring to the figures that enter his art as guests invited to a party: "If you work in an art, it wants to help you, but you must follow where it leads. . . . I now don't 'do' a collage in the sense of rational, predetermined composition. I just invite some of the people I knew to come into the room and give it an ambiance" (Schwartzman 187). Similarly, Wilson relates how the interaction with his characters is a kind of conversation where his characters come and go as if in a room, "I trust the characters. . . . I just write down what I hear that the characters say. I have a premise; everything they say is true. . . . The more they talk, the more I learn about the characters" (Shannon, "Wilson Explains" 224). In doing so, each positions and thus represents himself within his art, drawing upon personal experience as kind of found object. In representing the black experience, Wilson asserts, "What you confront is part of yourself, your willingness to deal with the small imperial truths you have accumulated over your life" (Powers 10).

With the showing of his "Projections" in 1964, Bearden makes his first major statement as a collagist (Schwartzman 209–12), demonstrating to full effect many of the numerous tensions negotiated in his art—chaos and order, fragmentation and unity, movement and countermovement, and part and whole. In contending with the tensions inherent to Du Bois's double-consciousness, Bearden represents the breadth of African American experience, marking its origins in slavery and the agrarian South as well as documenting the Great Migration and the movement North to the urban centers of Pittsburgh and Harlem. Within these works, he portrays the images that support his artistic vision: baptism and the rituals of black life, blues players, guitars, trains, "conjur" women, animal familiars, spirits, and urban street-scenes ("Rectangular" 15–17).[16]

With each of the "Projections" a hybrid in terms of form and construction, Bearden sought "maximum multiplicity" (15), the artist's term for multiple, competing layers of form, media, and ultimately voice. Producing first a series of eight-by-ten-inch collages that he named "montage paintings," works constructed out of photo fragments, found objects, and painted images, Bearden then created black and white photostat enlargements of the smaller paintings. By adding another layering of form and media, Bearden at once invokes the collagist tension in that he adds additional elements, additional fragments, as he simultaneously unifies those elements by photographing and then enlarging the works (14–15). In describing this process, Bearden explains how he actually expands meaning when an element "is taken out of its original context and is fractured and integrated into a different space and form configuration" (17). By integrating the fragment into another work, Bearden then expands the meaning of the fragment while "extending the larger rhythms of the painting" (17). In her analysis of the Projections, art historian Lee Stephens Glazer illustrates and explains how Bearden appropriates and revises specific artworks from several European masters to represent the African American experience. Citing Houston Baker's *Modernism and the Harlem Renaissance* (1987), Glazer suggests that Bearden's demonstrated "deformation of mastery," manifested by Bearden's appropriation and revision of historical artworks, enables him to achieve his "mastery of form" in representing the black experience. Within the resulting hybridity, therefore, Bearden's "borrowings and revisions subvert hegemonic claims to formal values, even as they pay homage to the art-historical past" (419).

Embracing this same practice, Wilson draws directly from Bearden's works, fragmenting, riffing upon, and reshaping specific elements within his own contexts. In the case of *Joe Turner*, Wilson explains in very specific detail how he draws upon Bearden's *Mill Hand's Lunch Bucket* (1978), incorporating these features as types of found objects:

> It was a boarding house painting, and in the center . . . was this man sitting in this chair with his coat and hat on, in this posture of abject defeat, and there is a man reaching for his lunch bucket. There is a child . . . [and] a woman standing with a purse as if she is about to go shopping. . . . [A]nd I said, "Everyone is going to leave . . . And what he needs most is human contact." And then I began to wonder who he was and why he was sitting there like that. . . . He became Herald Loomis. (Sheppard 111–12)

In using *Mill Hand's Lunch Bucket*, Wilson replicates Bearden's process of fragmentation and composition by first breaking the work into usable elements in order to revise it, forging a new order and unity within a representation that both speaks to and differs from the original.

Addressing the ways he revises Bearden's original context, Wilson invokes and then positions the blues as another kind of found object in *Joe Turner*, incorporating it as a means to contest and resist the forces of fragmentation impacting his protagonist Harold Loomis:

> I was listening to . . . *W.C. Handy Sings and Plays His Immortal Hits*, and one . . . was a song called "Joe Turner." "They tell me Joe Turner's come and gone, got my man and

> gone, and with forty links of chain, got my man and gone." And so I said, "Oh, I see, this is what happened to this character." And then ultimately I changed the name of the play from *Mill Hand's Lunch Bucket* to *Joe Turner*. . . . (Sheppard 112)

In doing so, Wilson revises and repositions Bearden's collage, Handy's blues, and the elements of the Judeo-Christian tradition demonstrating the processes of fragmentation imposing upon the black experience while representing the possibilities for recovery. Importantly, he also evokes the tension existing between the secular and the sacred, what Albert Murray suggests is the tension between the blues form's "Saturday Night Function" as defined by the "blue devils" and its "Sunday Morning Service" that reflect the "Holy Ghost" (*Stomping* 23), further suggesting a hybridity that mediates elements of binary essentialism.

Beyond their shared artistic sensibilities and interests, however, Wilson draws more from Bearden than just inspiration. According to Sandra Shannon, "*Joe Turner* presents a kaleidoscopic view of black men and women who are themselves so culturally disoriented that only fragments of their characters are revealed. Thus, the play is a patchwork of episodes in the lives of post-Reconstruction blacks as they attempt to start new lives or, as Wilson puts it, 'find their song, in a strange northern territory'" ("Finding One's Song" 120). Whereas Shannon's description generalizes the play's structure, Wilson, more appropriately, creates the play as a collage where the characters' fragmented lives come together to reveal a larger whole from across the patterns of repetition played out within the canvas of the Holly boardinghouse. The play thereby invokes the collagist tensions as the characters individually and collectively attempt to negotiate the powers of fragmentation at play in their lives in seeking a sense of balance and wholeness.

In drawing Bearden's works as inspiration and intertext in *Joe Turner*, Wilson shows himself to be a collagist on a number of different levels. First, the playwright positions and brings together the fragmented lives within the confines of the Pittsburgh boardinghouse, itself becoming a collagist canvas as a site that simultaneously mirrors the processes of dislocation and recovery, an image borrowed from Bearden's life and art.[17] Next, through the indeterminacy and transience implied by the boardinghouse, Wilson merges the past, present, and future in the way that the unreconciled impact of slavery shapes the characters' lives, a tension made manifest with each reading or performance of the play. Through his negotiation of the collagist tensions that underlie the play—the force that seeks to balance the disparate, often antagonistic fragments of experience against the desire for and movement toward recovery and wholeness—Wilson fuses the African with the American. Evoking the conjurer, the blues figure, the Juba, the notion of conversion as reflected in blood sacrifice and baptism, and the ghosts of the dead both known and unknown, moreover, he demonstrates the hybridity that naturally emerges from intersection of the African and the Western manifested in these continuing presences.

Through the play's setting, Wilson establishes the ontological tension resulting from the constant, complex interplay between the forces of chaos and fragmentation and those of order and renewal, the very same tension inherent to Bearden's collages. In evoking "Pittsburg, 1911," Wilson writes:

> The sun falls out of heaven like a stone. The fires of the steel mill rage with a combined sense of industry and progress. Barges loaded with coal and iron ore trudge up the river to the mill towns that dot the Monongahela and return with fresh, hard, gleaming steel. The city flexes its muscles. Men throw countless bridges across the rivers, lay roads and carve tunnels through the hills sprouting with houses. (*Joe Turner* n. pag.)

Suggesting a movement toward chaos, Wilson's sun, the supposedly fixed center of the universe, stands apart from the heavens, fragmented and dislodged as a stone from the earth. The coal and ore, literally stones wrenched from the soil, extend Wilson's sun metaphor as being fragments removed from their natural setting. Fed to the "fires of the steel mill," the coal and ore become offerings to "industry and progress," the twin gods of American materialism, undergoing even further fragmentation into their elemental components. Among the raw materials required for this effort is labor, a need that similarly rends men and women from their homes, dislocating and drawing them in their hope for social and economic gain.

Like the sun, the coal, and the iron ore, therefore, "the sons and daughters of newly freed African slaves" also stand fragmented, "[i]solated, cut off from memory, having forgotten the names of the gods" ("The Play"). By identifying the African, Wilson chronicles a contentious history shaped by the diasporic forces that continue to impact the black experience in America, one that begins with individuals stolen from their various homelands and cultures under the auspices of Western hegemony to support white economic gain. Describing the Great Migration as the next major shift, the exodus "[f]rom the deep and the near South," Wilson represents another layer of black fragmentation created out of the political betrayal that brings an end to Reconstruction in order to maintain a Republican White House in the aftermath of the contested 1876 elections.[18] Having established this tension and demonstrating its impact upon the play's characters, Wilson indicates they are "[f]oreigners in a strange land" created from "a long line of separation and dispersement," reflecting the diasporic processes, "which informs their sensibilities and marks their conduct" ("The Play").[19]

With these processes of fragmentation, however, Wilson also posits the processes of order and recovery, the complimentary forces that together make up the collagist tension, an element that organizes and moves the play to the conclusion. Through his allusion to Exodus, Wilson first invokes an important element of the

African American folk tradition in the story of Moses, who leads the Israelites out of slavery from Egypt, a metaphor of resistance in both the spirituals and the black preacher tradition that speaks to the possibilities of finding the promised land in the present. In undergoing an exodus, African Americans are in a state of becoming, freed from slavery but not free from its influences, fragmented but recognizing the possibilities for unity. Appropriating and revising the Judeo-Christian story, he establishes an important affirming intertextuality with a Western tradition that would otherwise deny the possibilities for individual and collective recovery in its ability to authorize what "is" and "is not."

As another metaphor of this process, the steel mills first rage and devour in order to create, transforming the coal and ore into steel. The steel in turn becomes the bridges that span the rivers and impose human order upon the natural world, another transformation and tension manifested within the play. Thus "dazed and stunned" from the processes of fragmentation, Wilson's characters "search for ways to reconnect, to reassemble" a sense of self and community ("The Play"). Returning to the metaphor of fire, Wilson suggests that the "fiery blasts of the coke furnace" not only break elements down, but they provide his characters with "a way of bludgeoning and shaping the malleable parts of themselves into a new identity" ("The Play"). To support the act of self-creation, something that must take place within the individual, the characters also bring the elements that will enable their survival, a "heart kicking in their chest with a song worth singing" as well as their "Bibles and guitars" ("The Play"). With their faith and folk expression, therefore, Wilson suggests they may reorder and recover their lives even as the processes of fragmentation impose upon them.

At the play's beginning, Wilson's characters stand fragmented in search of someone or something that might offer some larger, meaningful whole, seeking to find a sense of self or completion in a world thrown out of balance by either the incursions and intrusions of white oppression or its manifestations within the black community. In relating the part to the whole, Wilson connects the tensions experienced by each individual character as a repetition of the collective experience shared with the others in the Holly boardinghouse, representing in turn the black experience in American society upon which it both rests and proves itself resistant. Each character, therefore, stands as a representation, a repetition or retelling, of the process by which Herald Loomis becomes aware of a self fragmented by slavery and its aftermath. As the embodiment of black fragmentation, therefore, Loomis emerges from his seven-year imprisonment at the hands of Joe Turner robbed of his song, stripped of his faith, and lost without a sense of self, family, or community. Wilson represents Loomis as a man fragmented by the same collagist tensions that operate within the play. Being "in search for a world that speaks to something about himself," he has no balance and thus "is unable to harmonize the forces that swirl around him" (14). Similar to the way that Bearden defines the artist's role in his collagist aesthetic, Loomis "seeks to recreate the world into one that contains his image" (14).

If Loomis stands at the play's center as an embodiment of the African American experience, then Joe Turner represents the ubiquitous white oppression that underlies the processes of fragmentation and separation, serving as a metaphor of slavery itself.[20] Through the historical figure of Joe Turner, a man Loomis never directly observes during his seven-year de facto enslavement and who never physically appears in the play, Wilson invokes and collapses the white hegemonic forces that stymie each of the play's characters into a single representative figure. In fact, because Loomis has internalized white hegemony, Joe Turner need not appear directly. The white oppressor's presence is almost visceral when Bynum confronts Loomis as being "one of Joe Turner's niggers" to which Loomis responds, "How you see that? I got a mark on me? Joe Turner done marked me to where you can see it?" (71). Though he is a constant threat and tension, Turner exists beneath the surface and at the boundaries of the play. Wilson manifests white oppression in the same manner through which Ellison suggests Bearden's art "reveal[s] the unseen through the seen" (*Going* 237). Thus positioned beneath the play's surface as is the white canvas or wood sheeting that supports a collage, Joe Turner is both an absence and a presence.

In applying the collagist technique, moreover, Wilson reinscribes this tension of the unseen Joe Turner by piecing together the individual actions of the play's white characters as they interact with, impose upon, or impact the residents of the Holly boardinghouse. Loomis, for example, the man most clearly connected to and defined by Joe Turner states, "I ain't never seen Joe Turner. Seen him to where I could touch him" (73). Instead, it is Joe Turner's "whole mess of men" (72), the guards and subalterns, who establish and enforce white hegemonic authority. Even before his imprisonment, Loomis is trapped in peonage, working as a sharecropper for Henry Thompson, a man who evicts Martha, after her husband gets sent to the work-farm (72). For Jeremy, it is "Mr. Piney's boys" who arrest him after his payday to take his money (13) as well as the "[w]hite fellow" who forces the black workers to "give him fifty cents to keep hold their jobs" (64). In seeking his dream of economic independence, Seth Holly must scrape and plead with the white keepers of business—Mr. Johnson and Sam Green—as he seeks capital to set up a pot-making business (3). In preventing Seth from starting his own business, the white businessmen insure that he must continue working for Mr. Olowski, the white boss who places Seth on the nightshift (4). Each incursion is, therefore, a reification of white oppression, a repetition of what Bearden would suggest is a basic rhythm manifested throughout the play.

Identifying with the white oppressor adds another tension and fragmentation that impact interactions within the black community. Although oppressed, Seth has also internalized aspects of the oppressor, causing him to judge negatively and antagonize others who come through his boardinghouse, an irony given that he makes his living off of their business. Suggesting his own self-loathing in being black, Seth views those migrating northward with disdain, being perhaps only one generation removed from the South and poverty himself. First, he denies the folk practices and beliefs represented by Bynum, the conjurer, as being "that mumbo jumbo nonsense" (1). Defensive about his relationship to slavery and the South, he lists the differences that separate him from the "niggers coming up here with that old backward country style of living" (5): "I ain't never picked no cotton. I was born up here in the North. My daddy was a freedman. I ain't never even seen no cotton!" (70). Although he knows how the police profile and prey upon black men, Seth harangues and blames his boarder Jeremy for falling victim to white oppression (13). In essence, he judges the young man negatively for being black and suffering its consequences in a white society, suggesting his own self-loathing. First, the boardinghouse owner wants to succeed in accordance with white economic standards. After describing his business aspirations, he states, "I can't get nowhere working for Mr. Olowski and selling Selig five or six pots on the side" (3). In nearly every aspect of identification, Seth negates and denies his black identity. Wilson reasserts this tension in the way that Bynum, a man who has found a sense of balance in being African and American, greets Seth and his wife every morning. Saying "[m]orning, Seth. Morning, Sister Bertha" (4, 34, 59), Bynum suggests that unlike Bertha, who as a sister is a family member or a fellow-practitioner of a shared faith, Seth is not. In not being a brother, he is therefore an outsider.

In creating Seth Holly, Wilson also reflects Bearden's collagist practices by incorporating a number of experiences from his own life as found objects within the play. One particularly striking source is "Mr. B," Wilson's tenth-grade history teacher who the playwright relates "was one of those black teachers who did not like black people" (Livingston 43).[21] Like Seth Holly, the ambitious Mr. B held three jobs in his attempt to realize the American dream "to make it . . . [and] be somebody" (45). All of these jobs, however, similar to Seth's nightshift job with Mr. Olowski, are dead-ends. Describing his own entrance into Pittsburgh's "Connelly Trade School," an institution that gave blacks the skills needed for low-paying, manual labor jobs, Wilson tells that because the "auto mechanics . . . class was filled up, . . . [t]hey put me in sheet metal . . . making tin cups" (43), the same skill practiced by Seth.

The most direct representative of white oppression in the play, however, is Rutherford Selig. Though seemingly sympathetic with the blacks to whom he sells his wares and provides his services, he proves himself to be another enforcer of white hegemony. Although Selig, as with his grandfather the slave-trader and his father the slave-catcher, does not set the terms of white hegemony, he is complicit as one in a long line of "[b]ringers and finders" (41). A representation of the very worst of the inhumanity imposed upon African Americans—the processes of the slave trade and the enforcement of the Runaway Slave Act—Selig characterizes the work of his father and grandfather in the same way that one might relate the mundane routine of a day at the office (41). Calling himself a "People Finder" (15), Selig is merely one of a long line of black exploiters, a man who, as Bertha suggests, gives someone a ride and then charges a dollar to tell where he has dropped the individual (42).

In creating the character of Selig, moreover, Wilson appears to bring another experience from his personal past as a found object by drawing upon his experiences with a white businessman named "Herb Glickman" who first went door-to-door selling to the blacks on credit and then would come around monthly for the regular payments (Livingston 47–48).[22] Suggesting his own ambivalence, Wilson praises and problematizes Glickman and other white businessmen as being simultaneously sympathetic and oppressive, representing this same arrangement in the relationship existing between Selig and the blacks in the boardinghouse. Suggesting that the white incursion is fragmenting in terms of what these businessmen took out of the community (48), Wilson, within the same response, relates how they also supported the community:

> Herb . . . wasn't a bad guy. . . . He would buy the merchandise for $39 and sell it to you for $49, because he was willin' to take the risk . . . [and] come every week and get $2 until you finished payin' him. So he earned every dime of that extra that he charged. And had it not been for him, there was a whole lot of blacks who wouldn'ta had nothin'. (Livingston's punctuation, 48)

Whereas the white businessmen provide needed goods, they do so under circumstances that exploit a black community left with no other outlets for fair, competitive service.

Even Rutherford Selig's name is a kind of found object within which Wilson invokes historical elements of white oppression.[23] In drawing the character's first name, Wilson suggests Rutherford B. Hayes, who being in nearly a dead-heat with his Democratic opponent Samuel Tilden wins reelection as Republican president after agreeing to end Reconstruction, to withdraw federal troops from the South, and to place a southerner in his cabinet, an act of betrayal that signals the beginning of Jim Crow.[24] In the character's last name, Wilson suggests William N. Selig, 1864–1946, a pioneer of the motion picture industry, who in the early 1890s, "formed a minstrel troupe, 'Selig and Johnson's Colored Minstrels,' a company of twelve who traveled the state by horse-drawn wagon" (Slide 27). Of note, Selig hired comedian and entertainer Bert Williams around 1893, who during his employment met George Parker, the man who would become his vaudeville partner (Smith

9–13). Though not widely remembered today, his Selig Polyscope Company was one of the first great movie studios responsible for many landmark events in early cinema; Selig frequently collaborated with W. D. Griffith, whose *Birth of a Nation* incited white racist activism nationwide (Slide 26–30).[25] Rutherford Selig's name resonates with the white political forces that maintain white hegemony as well as the forces of popular culture that reinscribe black stereotypes.

In situating the figure of Joe Turner as the representation of the forces of fragmentation and chaos, Wilson positions his character Bynum Walker as a representation of the forces of order and balance. Interpreting *Joe Turner* within the Yoruban cosmology, Kim Pereira examines the relationship between chaos and order, arguing that Loomis is a manifestation of Eshu, the representation of chaos and disorder in the text (66). While Loomis stands fragmented and imbalanced, he exists that way only as a result of Joe Turner, Wilson's manifestation of the ubiquitous white oppression that underlies the African American experience. In asserting the forces of recovery and renewal, however, Pereira rightly argues that Bynum represents the figure of Ifa, the agent of order who helps mediate between humans and the gods (65–66). In seeking to restore order and balance between the individual and the world, a function that parallels the relationship between the part and the whole in collage, Bynum both represents and is a link to a severed and forgotten African heritage, offering an outlet for self-creation and self-determination outside of imposing circles of white power.

Functioning as a helping guide who enables Loomis's movement toward recovery and order, Bynum's agency brings and "binds [people] together" (10) as a kind of collagist in the way he helps others find a sense of unity and wholeness. Bynum acts, therefore, as a counterbalance to the fragmenting diasporic forces in the play, choosing his binding song to help the "people walking away and leaving one another" (10). "That's why they call me Bynum," the conjurer asserts; "Just like glue I sticks people together" (10). As the glue that binds the lives of those in the play together, that binds the African with the American, and similarly binds the fragments within the larger whole of the collage, Bynum represents the opportunity for recovery of the natural balance lost to the forces of "industry and progress" ("The Play"), the processes of white hegemony that recast the black body as object and resource through enslavement, peonage, and institutionalization.

As a conjurer, Bynum helps those in need to recover and negotiate a sense of wholeness within the confines of the natural world, a reflection of the collagist's artistry. In highlighting the need to find a mutually sustaining relationship between the individual and the community, one of balance and unity, Wilson invokes an African worldview and sensibility in distinction to the Western focus on the individual. In doing so, Bynum reifies the negotiations inherent to the collagist tension. Whereas he states that he can upset the natural order with his "roots," the results will make for greater individual fragmentation (22). As a conjurer, therefore, Bynum must guide those he helps within the natural order. In telling how he helps those who seek his services, Bynum fashions himself as a collagist, stating, "Depend on how all the circumstances of the thing come together. How all the pieces fit" (21). As the central example within the play, both Bynum and Loomis seek to complete a shared vision that neither can reconcile individually. Early in the play Bynum relates his vision wherein coming to an ocean, he sees "something I ain't got words to tell you" (10). Later, Loomis states, "You don't know what I done seen. Herald Loomis done seen some things he ain't got words to tell you," collapsing in a trance-like state (52–53). Separately, neither man can give words to his vision, each complements and completes the other's story. Only when Loomis and Bynum combine their fragmented stories, merging them into a single narrative through call and response can they fully articulate the vision of the bones, those lost during the Middle Passage, that rise up out of the ocean and become flesh (52–56). This recovery of the past represented by the merging of Loomis's and Bynum's visions begins the final movement toward which each finds affirmation and finally realizes a sense of self.

The process by which Bynum recovers his own "powerful song" (21), moreover, serves as the model through which Loomis recovers his own sense of balance and self, a repetition echoed throughout the play. In doing so, Bynum relates his first encounter with the "shiny man," whose blood ritual and baptism foreshadows and parallels that which Loomis ultimately reenacts (9). In referring to the shiny man as "John" (8), Bynum tells how the man "had this light coming out of him," something that makes Bynum "cover up [his] eyes to keep from being blinded" (9). In doing so, Wilson invokes several important biblical intertexts that demonstrate the possibilities for transformation, suggesting the bestowal of some holy purpose.[26] Most importantly, Bynum identifies his shiny man as John the Baptist, "the One Who Goes Before and Shows the Way" (10), also invoking the story of Christ, an important element that speaks to Loomis's regeneration and transfiguration in the wake of his own blood sacrifice.[27] In that Bynum's story brings together the African and the Judeo-Christian, Wilson suggests a hybrid construction that allows for a negotiation of the tensions of double-consciousness.

Wilson's shiny man also suggests the folk hero Shine from the African American toast tradition, making it a kind of found object taken from the black oral tradition. As a figure recovered and transformed from the grotesque white stereotype, Shine's strength, mother wit, and self-sufficiency enable him to swim to shore after the sinking of the Titanic as the characters representing white hegemony drown, showing themselves weak and needy.[28] Like the bones emerging from the water and becoming flesh in Loomis's and Bynum's shared vision, so too does Shine emerge from the ocean recovered and unscathed. In fact, the figure of Shine appears throughout the writings of a number of Black Arts Movement–related figures with whom Wilson would have been familiar.[29] Stating that Shine is "part of the private mythology of Black America," Larry Neal asserts, "Shine is US" ("Shine Swam On" 7). In his poem "Shine Touched by Death's Whisper," another possible source for Wilson's shiny man and the vision of the bones, Neal not only invokes the toast, but he represents many of the same elements that resonate throughout Loomis's and Bynum's vision in *Joe Turner*. Particularly, Neal addresses the troubled African American past revitalized in the present by a visitation of ancestral spirits that warn of the need to recover and maintain the strength and power represented within the heritage shaped by the black experience in America (176). Relating the importance of song in reviving the past, Neal also addresses his reader as a singer who might recover and thereby access the transformative, sustaining magic invoked within these ancestral voices (176), an idea echoed in *Joe Turner* in terms of the individual's song that becomes a manifestation of self-assertion and identity.

Through the shiny man, Bynum gains an awareness of the possibilities for self-creation and affirmation that position him to determine "the Secret of Life" (8–9). Relating the central element of the vision, Bynum describes encountering his father:

> I looked over and seen my daddy standing there. He was the same size he always was, except for his hands and his mouth. He had a great big old mouth that look like it took up his whole face and his hands were as big as hams. Look like they was too big to carry around. . . . Said he had been thinking about me and it grieved him to see me in the world carrying other people's songs and not having one of my own. Told me he was gonna show me how to find my song. (9–10)

Through the vision, Wilson illustrates the importance of the past and its relationship to the present by positioning Bynum generationally. Bynum, therefore, returns to and recovers his ancestral past through his encounter with his father in his vision, a link that connects him to the African American collective past and the larger history of the African diaspora represented in the bones rising up from the ocean. Only by recovering and contextualizing this past can Bynum and Loomis each recover his song.

On another level, Bynum's vision also illustrates how Wilson draws upon Bearden's art directly within the visions and dreams shared by members of the community. Wilson, who like Bearden spent much of his childhood and youth in Pittsburgh, clearly addresses the artist's influence on his drama in terms of the painter's particular works that inspired and made their way into his drama ("Foreword" 9). In addition to the boardinghouse setting that he borrows from *Mill Hand's Lunch Bucket*, Wilson also draws the names of Seth and Bertha Holly from Bearden's *Mr. Seth and Miss Bertha* (1978); he also invokes and signifies upon

Bearden's *The Piano Lesson* (1984) in his own play of the same name (9).

One particular stylistic element that Wilson borrows here is Bearden's emphasis on and exaggeration of the head and hands that result from the artist's collagist technique. The enlarged hands suggest their power and ability to construct and create; the heads, created out of a mixture of African masks, suggest the fractures and fragments that make up the African American experience.[30]

Through song, Wilson not only bridges the present with the past, but he demonstrates how one might find strength in the past to console in the present and to guide in the future. As the play's title suggests, the blues in general and the title song in particular serve as a metaphor of selfhood, representative of the individual's ability to sustain and heal the self in contesting the forces of fragmentation and chaos.[31] By identifying the source of the blues within Joe Turner, the representation of an imposing white hegemony, Wilson renegotiates and thus repositions these forces of fragmentation and chaos within the collagist tension by invoking the healing powers of the blues. In fact, the tension of the blues echoes those of collage, the simultaneous interplay of fragmentation and healing, being "both a wail and a whelp of joy" ("The Play"). In relating how he regains his song, furthermore, Bynum's description suggests the construction of a collage: "I looked long back in memory and gathered up pieces and snatches of things to make that song. I was making it up out of myself"(71). This "powerful song" (21) then is the source of his strength—the source that reasserts his existence and ensures his survival—coming from inside the individual. Only by recovering the past and connection to the community can Loomis and Bynum each find what they had been looking for individually, becoming transformed and made whole in the process. Wilson asserts, therefore, that in recovering the past, one can understand the ways it enters into the present and shapes the future, a process reflected in the way the playwright conflates the history of slavery with its implications in a timeless present created out of the play's performance.

In the end, Herald Loomis, as his name suggests as a kind of collagist construction in itself, becomes a bearer of light and truth as he regains his song and recovers a self stolen by the processes of white hegemony. Through Bynum's help, therefore, Loomis may bleed for, baptize, and cleanse himself, a repetition and reenactment of Bynum's vision in the blood ritual at the play's end as well as a revising of Christ's sacrifice (92–93). In doing so, Loomis frees himself, escaping both the tyranny of Joe Turner and the shackles of Christianity as he conflates Turner and Christ as manifestations of the forces of chaos and fragmentation.[32] Only then can the conjure-man exclaim, "Herald Loomis, you shining! You shining like new money!" (94). If the Bible connects three shining men—Moses, Elijah, and Christ—in relationship to the movement toward redemption, Wilson appropriates these elements and revises them to demonstrate the relationship between his three shiny men—the man in Bynum's vision, Bynum, and Loomis—who likewise become transfigured, recovering a sense of wholeness and balance in transcending the fragmenting forces of white hegemony.[33]

Ultimately, Wilson reinscribes the patterns of repetition that guide the play's characters, suggesting the collagist process by which the parts reflect and come together to represent a greater whole. As Molly Cunningham points out in Act Two, "Most folks be what they daddy is" (61), suggesting the return and repetition of generational forces and circumstances. Selig, with a long line of exploiters who profit from the black body in his family tree, also takes advantage of precarious economic circumstances within the black community. In the future, the people of Selig's ilk will be pawnbrokers, absentee landlords, credit givers, and bail bondsmen. Bynum, whose father also was a conjurer, has passed some of himself, his power, and his authority, onto Loomis, a man who stands ready to confront the world. Zonia and Reuben may reinscribe the separation and searching lived out by Loomis and Martha (78–84), a repetition implied when Reuben states, "When I get grown, I come looking for you" (84). Although Loomis and Mattie Campbell appear poised on the verge of forming what Bynum suggests is "a whole world there" (45), Jeremy and Molly remain unfixed and unfocused, joining together out of restless self-interest and physical desire. Stating that "[h]is ambition is to 'trace the odyssey of the black male in American society'" (Livingston 39), Wilson extends the play's movement and rhythms, binding the past, present, and future, by suggesting that the relationship shared between Bynum and Loomis will likely play itself out in Jeremy. A young man "[a]bout twenty-five . . . [with] the world in his hand," Wilson specifically writes that Jeremy's "spirit has yet to be molded into song" (12). As with the lack of resolution and open-endedness inherent to collage, so ends the play with Jeremy positioned to experience his own trials and tribulations as he finds his song.

Within each of their respective forms, Bearden and Wilson prove themselves to be conjurers, story-tellers, bluesmen, preachers, and tricksters—the same figures that appear prominently in their respective works—as each represents the African American experience by drawing upon its many creative possibilities and outlets. In the ways that Bearden's plastic art makes use of the African American oral tradition and its musical forms, the blues, jazz, the spirituals, so too does Wilson's drama make use of formal elements from Bearden's art, each mirroring the flexibility, spontaneity, and interplay of the larger African American artistic traditions and its many manifestations. Certainly, each achieves the quality for which, as Bearden asserts, every great artist should strive, "a simplicity that often makes us wonder at the very majesty of something that should appear commonplace" (*Painter's* 218). Having captured the pulse, vernacular, and sensibilities of the black experience, painter and the playwright have each created an art that attests to the strength, creativity, and perseverance that informs the individual who, paraphrasing W.E.B Du Bois, must negotiate the tensions of being African and American. In doing so, each creates a form that both represents and transcends its many influences and traditions.

Ultimately, the exploration of Bearden's aesthetic and artistic practice opens up new possibilities for considering the larger notion of an African American artistic tradition. Addressing the complexities inherent to the black experience in America, Bearden and his art asserts both a framework and demonstrates the possibilities for negotiating a sense of self and community across multiple, simultaneous levels of contestation that include race, class, gender, sexuality, and nationality. Yet as cultural critic Homi Bhabha asserts, the negotiation of identity is both hybrid and "performative" in that it is neither fixed nor essential; a continuous process, identity and its representation must necessarily reside as "neither One nor the Other but something else besides, in-between" (313). Drawing upon and speaking to its many influences Western, African, and American, Bearden's art revises and therefore resists the imposition of hegemonic binary essentialism. Whereas the trajectory of Western art marks the movement from nineteenth-century essentialism to twentieth-century postmodernism fragmentation, Bearden's art seeks balance in negotiating the tensions constantly in play between fragmentation and unity, chaos and order, imbalance and balance, presence and absence, part and whole, subject and object, African and American, and black and white.

The fact that two important African American writers with very different social, artistic, and political sensibilities—Ralph Ellison and August Wilson—claim Bearden as sharing a common aesthetic purpose and artistic practice alone suggests the need for an extended consideration of the artist's work and methodology. Ellison, whose episodic, hybrid *Invisible Man* clearly fits within the collagist framework, asserts that Bearden achieves the universal in the way he evokes the black experience within his technical mastery of Western forms. Relating the way that Bearden's art brings together defining elements of the African American experience, Ellison observes:

> Through his creative assemblage he makes complex comments upon history, upon society, and upon the nature of art. Indeed, his Harlem becomes a place inhabited by people who have in fact been *resurrected*, re-created by art, a place . . . where the sacred and profane, reality and dream are ambiguously mingled. (Ellison's italics, *Going* 235)

Wilson, however, the self-proclaimed black nationalist, sees Bearden evoking an authentic African American identity that represents its fullness and diversity. Upon seeing the painter's work for the first time, Wilson recalls finding "a world made in my image" ("Foreword" 9).

Beyond Ellison and Wilson, two representative examples particularly suggest the relevance of Bearden's aesthetic and artistic practice as an analytical framework worthy of further consideration. First, Frederick Douglass's *Narrative of the Life of Frederick Douglass, an American Slave, Written by Himself* (1845), arguably the most important of the slave narratives, functions as a hybrid form of self-representation that speaks to and resists Western racist essentialism. Drawing upon and revising aspects of the captivity and the conversion narrative forms, the jeremiad, the abolitionist tract, the picaresque novel, and Benjamin Franklin's autobiography, Douglass's narrative clearly reflects the social and artistic negotiation theorized by Bearden and demonstrated in his collage as the former slave inverts the moral and philosophical arguments asserted by pro-slavery apologists.[34] One particular incident that demonstrates the collagist tension involves the fight with Edward Covey, the "'nigger-breaker'" (42) upon which Douglass makes his famous pronouncement: "You have seen how a man was made a slave; you shall see how a slave was made a man" (47). Marking a shift in Douglass's sense of self, the portion of the narrative leading up to the pronouncement documents the processes of fragmentation imposed by an American slave society that defeats the individual and denies his or her basic humanity, conditions that include physical and psychological abuse, rape, inadequate food and rest, and the breaking apart of families. The portion of the narrative after the pronouncement, however, documents Douglass's physical journey northward to freedom and signals his psychological movement toward self-assertion and control.

A second example, Toni Morrison's *Beloved* (1987) reflects Bearden's framework in the way the novel invokes the imposing, fragmenting forces of slavery that continue to shape and impose upon the present. Demonstrating the characters' inability to articulate the brutality and inhumanity of their lives under slavery, the desire to name and thereby somehow move beyond the past, Morrison establishes a basic rhythm in the negotiation of chaos and order that organizes and resonates throughout the novel. In attempting to assert an aspect of order over the chaos that dominates an individual's experience, each character subsequently suffers some further, more imposing injustice or setback. Sethe's escape from slavery combined with the miracle of the celebration feast gives way to communal anger and jealously, a manifestation of internalized defeat created out of white oppression (135–38). Unable to reconcile Baby Suggs's apparent bounty within the loss and suffering experienced by each individual, the black community allows schoolteacher to intervene without prior warning, somehow equalizing the shared sorrow. Sethe's assembly and disassembly of her wedding dress from the scraps and articles around Mrs. Garner's kitchen (59) suggests both the practice of collage as well as the constant negotiation of fragmentation and unity in the way the woman assembles these disparate found objects to revise the dehumanizing imposition of slavery. Echoing this fragmentation as a manifestation of the collagist tension across the novel as a whole, Morrison describes Beloved, a representation of slavery, as being "[d]isremembered and unaccounted for" because "[r]emembering seemed unwise" (274), lost in a story too painful "to pass on" (275). Whereas the characters within the novel cannot contend with the brutality of slavery, the reader may in part recover and account for the "Sixty Million and more" represented by Beloved within a relationship mediated through the novel, one in which Morrison turns the text back on itself and passes the story on to the reader.

Ultimately, Bearden's art demonstrates the possibilities for negotiating and thereby asserting the terms and conditions for representing the African American experience. As Ellison suggests, Bearden is able to transcend culture, form, and temporality in the way he demonstrates "the irrepressible thrust of a people to endure and keep its intimate sense of its own identity" (*Going* 237). "For the artist [to do so]," the painter argues, "the world has to be remade in his/her own terms" to capture the "larger truth" of experience asserted within in a work of art (Rowell 446). Rather than essentializing and thereby narrowing the black experience, Bearden's aesthetic and artistic practice points to its many complexities and possibilities. Providing both a call and a response, Bearden invites negotiation and interaction as the hybridity of his art, the relationship between the part and the whole, positions individual experience as both constructing and reflecting the communal.

Notes

1. Fishman argues that Bearden and Wilson share "a similar method of creation . . . [in that] [a]s a community or its key members prepare a performance, bits and pieces of their life and culture, such as a recurring event, a traditional costume, a familiar song, are brought together to create a whole" (137).
2. Through to the end of this chapter, I will refer to the play as *Joe Turner*.
3. Hoffman credits Pablo Picasso and Georges Braque as being the first to use collage "as a fine art form" (6); art historians consider Picasso's *Still-Life with Chair Caning* (1912) to be the "first Cubist collage" (5).
4. In *The Rule of Metaphor* (1977), Paul Ricoeur argues that metaphor is a distinctly social construction from which Western privilege and authority has evolved. In doing so, he addresses how the Western tradition has brought the philosophical and the metaphysical together through the use of metaphor. According to Ricoeur, "the 'place' of metaphor . . . is . . . the copula of the verb *to be*. The metaphorical 'is' at once signifies both 'is not' and 'is like'" (6 italics in text). The essentialist foundation upon which Western philosophical discourse resides, therefore, is within the ability to authorize what "is" and "is not."
5. Ralph Ellison, Bearden's longtime friend, also defines the artist's role in addressing chaos. In *Shadow and Act*, he describes the human need to rise "up out of the chaos of the universe" from which the artist may represent "the triumph of the human spirit over chaos" (20). In *Going to the Territory*, he cites the specific role of art: "We cannot live . . . in the contempla-

tion of chaos, but neither can we live without an awareness of chaos, and the means through which we assert our humanity most significantly against it, is great art" (246).

6. Bearden co-wrote the book with friend and fellow artist Carl Holty to address the question, "How is a painting put together?" (7).
7. In *The Poetics*, Aristotle reinscribes Western authority through his assertion of binary essentialism in distinguishing between the tragic and the comic (223–43).
8. In *Shadow and Act*, Ellison relates how Langston Hughes loaned him two of Malraux's books shortly after he arrived in Harlem. Throughout his essays, Ellison describes the French intellectual "as a literary 'ancestor'" (162).
9. Bearden explicitly states, "The desire to consider art as dealing only with art cannot exclude the artist or all the things that affect him" (*Painter's* 14).
10. Wilson reiterates this position in a 1990 interview with Vera Sheppard, "August Wilson: An Interview" (106).
11. Pereira notes, "These two traditions that operate simultaneously within the African cosmology are to be found at the heart of many cultures—Apollo and Dionysius in ancient Greece, Vishnu and Siva in Hindu Mythology, Yin and Yang in Chinese philosophy" (65).
12. In *The Poetics*, Aristotle establishes a binary relationship between tragedy and comedy. Tragedy, the privileged form, "represent[s] noble actions . . . and noble personages" whereas comedy represents "the actions of the ignoble" (227). As "an imitation of men worse than the average," comedy reflects "the Ridiculous," which according to Aristotle, "is a species of the Ugly" (229).
13. Murray wrote the essay specifically for the retrospective exhibition *ROMARE BEARDEN: 1970–1980* which took place in the Mint Museum in Charlotte, North Carolina, from October 1980 to January 1981.
14. In one interview, Bearden describes his compositional practice within the music vernacular: "Let's say, this is a full note, this maybe a quarter note, faster, and another quart note, so this would be: da dee di da, you see. And already you're starting a melody. . . . But this is what I mean: that these are repetitions developed into rhythm. The melody is in the spacing that I did . . . this is the way I do it." (Rowell 445).
15. Fishman makes a similar observation suggesting that "both . . . are guided by the characters who appear in their paintings and play" (138).
16. In his writing, Bearden used "conjur" rather than "conjure." Many of his Projections appear in Schwartzman (210–15) and Bearden's "Rectangular Structure in My Montage Paintings."
17. Schwartzman reports that in 1920, Bearden lived with his maternal grandmother who ran a boardinghouse in Pittsburgh (44).
18. Du Bois details the post-bellum political forces, particularly "the revolution of 1876," that significantly shaped the black experience in America (12–13).
19. In Genesis 2:22, Moses, in recounting his days in Egypt, states, "I have been a stranger in a strange land."
20. Wilson describes Loomis's seven-year enslavement with Joe Turner as "represent[ing] the four hundred years of slavery" (Powers 9).
21. "Mr. B" is an important figure in Wilson's lore as being the teacher who accuses him of plagiarizing a research paper on Napoleon. After receiving a failing grade on the paper, Wilson

quit high school (Livingston 43–45).

22. In *Fences* (1986), Wilson references "Mr. Glickman" as being the man who sells furniture to Troy Maxson on credit (20).
23. James Keller, in "The Shaman's Apprentice: Ecstasy and Economy in Wilson's *Joe Turner*," points out that "Selig . . . in German, means 'blessed' or 'ecstatic,'" arguing that Wilson uses the term ironically to describe a man who seems to worship capitalism (472–73).
24. See note 18.
25. Although addressing only Ellison's *Invisible Man* (1952) in interviews, Wilson would have also been familiar with Ellison's *Shadow and Act*, which addresses the "Hayes-Tilden deal of 1876," and Griffith's *The Birth of a Nation* as representative of the film industry as being complicit in "the dehumanization of the Negro" (275–77).
26. Exodus 34:29–35 tells the story of Moses who, aglow from being in God's presence, must veil his face to speak with the Israelites. Matthew 17:1–6, Mark 9:2–8, Luke 9:28–36 describe how Christ assumes God's brightness at the transfiguration, an event that coincides with the appearance of Moses and Elijah.
27. Isaiah 40:3–5 and Malachi 3:1 and 4:5–6 prophesize the one who will precede the coming of the savior. Matthew 11:13–14, Luke 3:3–6 and 7:24–27, and John 1:23 mark its fulfillment in the New Testament.
28. See Bruce Jackson's *Get Your Ass in the Water and Swim Like Me* (35–38).
29. H. Rap Brown, in *DIE NIGGER DIE!* (1969), asserts that the most practical and important part of his education came in learning such toasts as "Shine and the Titanic, Signifying Monkey, . . . and Piss-Pot-Peet" (30). In "Dark Prophecy: I Sing of Shine," Etheridge Knight recasts the toast in his own poetic form (49).
30. In addition to Bynum's vision, Reuben similarly describes his vision of Miss Mabel, Seth's dead mother, as she admonishes him to release his friend Eugene's pigeons: "[She wore a] white dress. Ain't even had no shoes or nothing. Just had on that white dress and them big hands . . . and that cane she hit me with" (79). In developing Reuben's vision, Wilson incorporates Bearden's remembrance of a friend Eugene who died and left his doves to the artist (Schwartzman 52–56) as a found object in the play.
31. As Trudier Harris suggests, "Joe Turner" may be the earliest blues song (59); if so, then Wilson fashioned Loomis to be the essential blues figure.
32. In "The Necessary Binding: Prison Experiences in Three August Wilson Plays," Trudier Harris argues that Loomis transcends and moves beyond both Joe Turner and Christianity and therefore can define himself (136–37).
33. See note 25.
34. Henry Louis Gates Jr.'s "Binary Oppositions in Chapter One of *Narrative of the Life of Frederick Douglass an American Slave Written by Himself*" considers the origins and importance of the slave narrative, arguing that Douglass destabilizes the binary essentialism manifested in the institution of slavery and its practices (80–97). William Andrews's *To Tell a Free Story: The First Century of Afro-American Autobiography, 1760–1865* (1986) describes the influences of the slave narrative in general (7–22) and Douglass's influences in particular (123–38).

Works Cited

Andrews, William L. *To Tell a Free Story: The First Century of Afro-American Autobiography, 1760–1865*. Urbana: University of Illinois Press, 1986.

Aristotle. *The Rhetoric and the Poetics of Aristotle*. Trans. W. Rhys Roberts and Ingram Bywater. New York: Modern Library, 1984.

Bearden, Romare. "Rectangular Structure in My Montage Paintings." *Leonardo* 2.1 (1969): 11–19. April 19, 2006 <http://www.jstor.org/search>.

Bearden, Romare and Carl Holty. *The Painter's Mind: A Study of the Relations of Structure and Space in Painting*. 1969. New York: Garland, 1981.

Bhabha, Homi K. *The Location of Culture*. London: Routledge Classics, 1994.

Brown, H. Rap. *DIE NIGGER DIE!*. New York: Dial, 1969.

Campbell, Mary Schmidt. "History and the Art of Romare Bearden." *Memory and Metaphor: The Art of Romare Bearden 1940–1987*. New York: Oxford University Press, 1991. 7–17.

Dance, Daryl Cumber, ed. *From My People: 400 Years of African American Folklore*. New York: Norton, 2002.

Douglass, Frederick. *Narrative of the Life of Frederick Douglass, an American Slave, Written by Himself.* 1845. Ed. William L. Andrews and William S. McFeely. New York: Norton, 1997.

Du Bois, W.E.B. *The Souls of Black Folk*. 1903. Ed. Henry Louis Gates Jr. and Terri Hume Oliver. New York: Norton, 1999.

Ellison, Ralph. *Invisible Man*. 1952. New York: Vintage, 1995.

———. *Shadow and Act*. 1964. New York: Vintage, 1972.

———. *Going to the Territory*. 1986. New York: Vintage, 1995.

Fishman, Joan. "Romare Bearden, August Wilson, and the Traditions of African Performance." *May All Your Fences Have Gates: Essays on the Drama of August Wilson*. Ed. Alan Nadel. Iowa City: University of Iowa Press, 1994. 133–49.

Gates, Henry Louis, Jr. "Binary Oppositions in Chapter One of *Narrative of the Life of Frederick Douglass an American Slave Written by Himself*." *Figures in Black: Words, Signs, and the "Racial" Self.* New York: Oxford University Press, 1987. 80–97.

———. *The Signifying Monkey: A Theory of African-American Literary Criticism*. New York: Oxford University Press, 1988.

Glazer, Lee Stephens. "Signifying Identity: Art and Race in Romare Bearden's Projections." *The Art Bulletin* 76 (1994): 411–26. March 9, 2006 <http://www.jstor.org/search>.

Grant, Nathan L. "Men, Women, and Culture: A Conversation with August Wilson." 1993. *Conversations with August Wilson*. Ed. Jackson R. Bryer and Mary C. Hartig. Jackson: University Press of Mississippi, 2006. 172–87.

Harris, Trudier. "August Wilson's Folk Traditions." *August Wilson: A Casebook*. Ed. Marilyn Elkins. New York: Garland, 2000. 49–65.

Harris-Lopez, Trudier. "The Necessary Binding: Prison Experiences in Three August Wilson Plays." *South of Tradition: Essays on African American Literature*. Athens: University of Georgia Press, 2002. 121–39.

Herrington, Joan. "The Four 'B's': August Wilson's Inspiration." *"I Ain't Sorry for Nothin' I Done"*: August Wilson's Process of Playwriting. New York: Limelight Editions, 1998. 20–40.

Hoffman, Katherine. "Collage in the Twentieth Century: An Overview." *Collage: Critical Views*. Ann Arbor: University of Michigan, 1989. 1–37.

Jackson, Bruce. *Get Your Ass in the Water and Swim Like Me: African American Narrative Poetry from Oral Tradition*. 1974. New York: Routledge, 2004.

Keller, James R. "The Shaman's Apprentice: Ecstasy and Economy in Wilson's *Joe Turner*." *African American Review* 35 (2001): 471–79. May 20, 2006 <http://www.jstor.org/search>.

Knight, Etheridge. "Dark Prophecy: I Sing of Shine." *The Essential Etheridge Knight*. 1986. Pittsburgh, PA: University of Pittsburgh Press, 1994. 49.

Kuspit, Donald B. "Collage: The Organizing Principle of Art in the Age of the Relativity of Art." *Collage: Critical Views*. Ann Arbor: University of Michigan, 1989. 39–57.

Livingston, Dinah. "Cool August: Mr. Wilson's Red-Hot Blues." *Conversations with August Wilson*. Ed. Jackson R. Bryer and Mary C. Hartig. Jackson: University Press of Mississippi, 2006. 38–60.

Morrison, Toni. Beloved. 1987. New York: Plume, 1988.

Moyers, Bill. "August Wilson: Playwright." *Conversations with August Wilson*. Ed. Jackson R. Bryer and Mary C. Hartig. Jackson: University Press of Mississippi, 2006. 61–80.

Murray, Albert. *Stomping the Blues*. 1976. New York: Da Capo Press, 2000.

———. "The Visual Equivalent of the Blues." *Romare Bearden: 1970–1980*. Charlotte, NC: Mint Museum, 1980. 17–28.

Neal, Larry. "And Shine Swam On." *Visions of a Liberated Future: Black Arts Movement Writings*. Ed. Michael Schwartz. New York: Thunder's Mouth Press, 1989. 7–23.

———. "Shine Touched by Death's Whisper." *Visions of a Liberated Future: Black Arts Movement Writings*. Ed. Michael Schwartz. New York: Thunder's Mouth Press, 1989. 176.

Patton, Sharon F. "Romare Bearden: Narrations." *Romare Bearden: Narrations*. Purchase, NY: Studley Press, 2002. 4–16.

Pereira, Kim. *August Wilson and the African-American Odyssey*. Urbana: University of Illinois Press, 1995.

Powers, Kim. "An Interview with August Wilson." *Conversations with August Wilson*. Ed. Jackson R. Bryer and Mary C. Hartig. Jackson: University Press of Mississippi, 2006. 3–11.

Ricoeur, Paul. *The Rule of Metaphor: The Creation of Meaning in Language*. 1977. Trans. Robert Czerny. London: Routledge Classics, 2003.

Richards, Sandra L. "Yoruba Gods on the American Stage: August Wilson's *Joe Turner's Come and Gone*." *Research in African Literatures* 30.4 (1999): 92–105. April 19, 2006. <http://muse.jhu.edu>.

Rocha, Mark W. "August Wilson and the Four B's: Influences." *August Wilson: A Casebook*. Ed. Marilyn Elkins. New York: Garland, 2000. 3–16.

Rowe, Colin, and Fred Koetter. *Collage City*. Cambridge, MA: MIT Press, 1978.

Rowell, Charles H. "'Inscription at the City of Brass': An Interview with Romare Bearden." *Callaloo* 36 (1988): 428–46. April 19, 2006 <http://www.jstor.org/search>.

Savran, David. "August Wilson." *Conversations with August Wilson*. Ed. Jackson R. Bryer and Mary C. Hartig. Jackson: University Press of Mississippi, 2006. 19–37.

Schwartzman, Myron. *Romare Bearden: His Life & Art*. New York: Abrams, 1990.

Shannon, Sandra G. "August Wilson Explains His Dramatic Vision: An Interview." *The Dramatic*

Vision of August Wilson. Washington DC.: Howard University Press, 1995. 201–47.

———. "Finding One's Song: *Joe Turner's Come and Gone*." *The Dramatic Vision of August Wilson*. Washington DC: Howard University Press, 1995. 119–42.

Shannon, Sandra G. and Dana A. Williams. "A Conversation with August Wilson." *August Wilson and Black Aesthetics*. Ed. Dana A. Williams and Sandra G. Shannon. New York: Palgrave Macmillan, 2004. 187–95.

Sheppard, Vera. "August Wilson: An Interview." *Conversations with August Wilson*. Ed. Jackson R. Bryer and Mary C. Hartig. Jackson: University Press of Mississippi, 2006. 101–17.

Slide, Anthony. *Early American Cinema*. Rev. ed. Metuchen, NJ: Scarecrow Press, 1994.

Smith, Eric Ledell. *Bert Williams: A Biography of the Pioneer Black Comedian*. Jefferson, NC: McFarland, 1992.

Wilson, August. *Fences*. New York: Samuel French, 1986.

———. *Joe Turner's Come and Gone*. New York: Plume, 1988.

———. "Foreword." Myron Schwartzman's *Romare Bearden: His Life & Art*. New York: Abrams, 1990. 8–9.

———. *The Ground on Which I Stand*. New York: Theatre Communications Group, 2001.

8

Signifying *Raisin*

Hansberry's *A Raisin in the Sun* and Wilson's *Fences*

JOHN M. HANNAH

With the death of August Wilson in October 2005, America lost its great dramatist of the African American experience, whose work chronicles and illuminates the defining social issues that continue to impose upon our individual and collective consciences. In the course of his productive career, Wilson's unrivaled success garnered him every important American dramatic award. Similar to Wilson, Lorraine Hansberry, the first African American playwright to achieve critical and popular success, also suffered an early death, succumbing to cancer in 1965 after having broken several barriers with *A Raisin in the Sun* (1959). Whereas Hansberry created the first successful African American drama performed on Broadway, Wilson created the most successful non-musical drama on Broadway in *Fences* (1986), both plays being huge financial successes with long production runs.[1] Additionally, both plays—each described as being "universal"—are traditionally constructed family dramas bounded by social realism, qualities that have moved critics to compare the two plays to Arthur Miller's *Death of a Salesman* (1949).[2] Coming out of a larger African American dramatic tradition, furthermore, the two plays address the social, political, historical, and economic tensions of being African and American as they incorporate black folk practices and elements of the black oral tradition.

Despite these similarities, critical analysis connecting the two playwrights involves little more than passing mention that Lloyd Richards, whose June 2006 death ended a career that included such accomplishments as being dean of Yale

School of Drama from 1979 to 1991 and Artistic Director of the National Playwrights Conference at the Eugene O'Neill Theater from 1968 to 1999, directed Hansberry's *Raisin* and several Wilson plays. Although Wilson commonly refers to his main influences as the "four 'B's'"—the blues, Romare Bearden, Amiri Baraka, and Jorge Luis Borges (Herrington 39–40)—he offers little on the significance of Hansberry as source of inspiration and provides no comment to suggest that *Raisin* was a model for any of his plays.[3] Not mentioning Hansberry at all in his now famous 1996 speech to the Theatre Communications Group National Conference,[4] Wilson's most direct reference appears in a 1987 interview with Dinah Livingston; in generalizing about the African American dramatic tradition, he states, "I certainly couldn't have written my plays without Lorraine Hansberry, and Ed Bullins, and Ron Milner, and Amiri Baraka, and all of those playwrights who have preceded me. Because they did their work, that enables me to do mine" (55). When comparing *Raisin* and *Fences*, however, the reader discovers that the two plays share more than just the commonalities that would result from a shared literary tradition. In fact, a close reading demonstrates that Wilson's *Fences* speaks to and signifies upon Hansberry's *Raisin* directly in the ways that it engages, responds to, and revises several specific structural and thematic elements of the earlier play from a masculinist perspective.

Although Wilson addresses *Fences* as being different from his other plays, he provides no insight into the playwrights or plays who might have influenced his play. In several interviews, he asserts that *Fences* is the odd play out of his self-described cycle of ten plays that represents a decade of the African American experience across the twentieth century (Lyons 208; Pettengill 167; Rosen 201; Shannon and Williams 194; Watlington 88). When asked whether he considered *Fences*, his most economically successful play that earned him the most awards, his "signature play," Wilson emphatically states "No." "My signature play would be *Joe Turner's Come and Gone*. Most of the ideas of the other plays are contained in that one play. . . . *Fences* is the only one that's not an ensemble play" (Shannon and Williams 194). By Wilson's account, he set out to write a more traditional play with a strong central character in response to reviews that questioned these elements in *Ma Rainey's Black Bottom* (1985) (Pettengill 167; Watlington 88): "After telling people that I knew how to write that kind of play, I asked myself, Do I really know how to write that kind of play? So I wrote *Fences* in answer to the challenge that I'd given myself" (Watlington 88).

Despite Wilson's relative silence, several relationships connect him with Hansberry and *Raisin*. When he began writing *Fences* in 1982, Wilson had already been working with Lloyd Richards at the Eugene O'Neill Playwrights Conference on *Ma Rainey*, a play that Richards chose for production at the Yale Repertory Theatre (Herrington 63). Relating the impact of Richards's fatherly relationship (Shannon, *Dramatic* 216–17; Watlington 87), Wilson observes, "Lloyd has been important not only as director of the plays, but important to my whole career, and important to my understanding of theatre. I have learned a lot about theatre over the past six years in working with him" (Sheppard 114). If Wilson began writing *Fences* "on the bus heading home from the [O'Neill] Conference" as Joan Herrington asserts in *I Ain't Sorry for Nothin' I Done: August Wilson's Process of Playwriting* (1998), then he would have most likely consulted Richards concerning ways to approach writing a more conventional play. Given that Richards had directed the most successful African American drama produced on Broadway, a very traditional, conventionally constructed play in the tradition of American domestic drama, he would have logically pointed Wilson to *Raisin* as a model.

In another connection, Amiri Baraka, one of Wilson's four self-described influences, positions Hansberry as an important, influential antecedent to his "Revolutionary Theatre" in writings from the 1980s.[5] As a founder of the Black Arts Movement, the cultural wing of the Black Power Movement,[6] Baraka joined with other intellectuals to devise appropriate and relevant critical standards that supported black artistic production, formulating the framework for the Black Aesthetic.[7] In "A Critical Reevaluation: *A Raisin in the Sun*'s Enduring Passion," an essay that marks the play's continuing importance on its twenty-fifth anniversary, Baraka praises Hansberry on the way her play "reflects more accurately the real lives of the black U.S. majority than any work that every received commercial exposure before it, and few if any since" (9). Describing *Raisin* as a classic, Baraka suggests that it represents the "class and ideological struggles" of its time and "still remains overwhelmingly popular and evocative of black and white reality" (19). Comparing *Raisin*'s seemingly "'conservative' . . . form and content" with that of James Baldwin's *Blues for Mr. Charlie* (1964) and his own *Dutchman* (1964), Baraka contends that Hansberry provides "the accurate telling and stunning vision of the real struggle" of race in America (19). If, as Wilson states in *The Ground on Which I Stand*, Baraka is representative of the "warriors on the cultural battlefield [of the 1960s] that affirmed their self-worth. . . . [and] found themselves sufficient and secure in their art and their instructions" (20), then Hansberry too fits that lineage. Even before Baraka, other Black Aesthetic proponents embraced Hansberry. Playwright Loften Mitchell, whose essay "I Work Here to Please You" appears in the important Black Arts Movement anthology *The Black Aesthetic* (1971), praises *Raisin* as being "honest, moving, human drama" and asserts that Hansberry "well deserved the acclaim accorded her" (301).[8] With Baraka's own production of "Revolutionary Theatre" being more experimental and less traditional, Wilson would have to go further back in the African American drama tradition to find a suitable antecedent; Hansberry's *Raisin*, by Baraka's account, is that antecedent.

In addition to coming out of shared African American dramatic and literary traditions, a close comparative reading of *Fences* and *Raisin* suggests that Wilson engages Hansberry directly on a number of different levels within his play. Highlighting the playwright's remarkable productivity with *Fences* on the verge of its 1987 Broadway opening, Samuel Freedman, a *New York Times* columnist, makes a passing comparison between Wilson and Hansberry: "In Wilson's plays, the black middleclass exists only as an object of contempt; if he had written '*A Raisin in the Sun*,' the Younger family would not have moved to the suburbs, it would have joined either the Blackstone Rangers street gang or the Nation of Islam" (49). Misreading both playwrights, Freedman first fails to recognize Hansberry's remarkable ability to identify the social tensions and complexities that would define the 1960s, missing the double-voiced militancy of *Raisin* in the way that it resonates differently for white and black audiences.[9] More importantly, Freedman does not recognize the ways that *Fences* speaks to and signifies upon Hansberry's work as Wilson incorporates and revises elements from the earlier play, particularly reinscribing Big Walter, the deceased Younger patriarch, in his own Troy Maxson.

Following Hansberry's lead, Wilson also sets his play in the urban North at the same historical moment as *Raisin*, just on the precipice of the great social change and upheaval of 1960s that will reshape American race relations. Set in 1957, moreover, *Fences* begins the same year that Hansberry completed *Raisin* (Kappel 163); ending in 1965, *Fences* concludes in the same year that Hansberry dies. While these details may be coincidental, Wilson nonetheless invokes *Raisin*'s historical context directly and bounds his play in accordance with Hansberry's career as a playwright. Although both plays invoke the migration narrative by tracing the black exodus out of the agrarian South to the urban North, an element that places them within the larger African American historical and literary traditions, Wilson echoes elements specific to *Raisin*. In doing so, Hansberry and Wilson invoke W.E.B. Du Bois's question of being black and American, exploring the presence of an imposing, unresolved past and the unfulfilled promises of American democracy.[10] Particularly, the idea of home ownership serves as a metaphor of the American dream in both plays, a sign of success, security, and stability. Early in *Raisin*, Mama Lena first voices her desire to buy a house in a discussion with her daughter-in-law, Ruth: "Been thinking that we maybe could meet the notes on a little old two-story somewhere, with a yard where Travis could play in the summertime. . . ." (44). In the opening of *Fences*, Wilson similarly describes the Maxson house as being "an ancient two-story brick house. . . . [with] a small dirt yard" (7). The cost of each house, moreover, comes down to the worth of the black body, a central conflict in both plays.

As traditionally constructed domestic dramas, the most obvious connection linking *Raisin* and *Fences*, both plays trace the struggles and conflicts within an African American family as its members confront the social and generational change that brings each to the brink of collapse. Addressing the full spectrum of familial interactions, both plays explore the relationships between parent and child, husband and wife, siblings, and male and female across multiple generations. In *Raisin*, Hansberry clearly asserts a dominating female presence in that one or more of the three female characters—the Younger family matriarch Mama Lena, her daughter-in-law Ruth, or her daughter Beneatha—are on the stage at all times. Set within the home, a traditionally female space and Mama Lena's center of authority, the first speaking character is Ruth and the last is the dominating Lena. In addressing the dynamics of these relationships in *Fences*, Wilson mirrors but inverts Hansberry's formulation by shifting the familial authority to Troy, the Maxson family patriarch, thereby generating a distinct masculine presence that recontextualizes the family conflict. Setting the play outside the immediate boundary of the home in the adjacent yard, a distinctly masculine space dominated by Troy, Wilson revises Hansberry, creating a distinct male presence and dominance in the play with five major male roles and only one adult female. Thus in *Fences*, one or more of the male characters, mostly Troy as the play's dominating figure, appear on stage at all times.

Among the many structural parallels that connect the two plays, Wilson draws his characters in a manner that closely reflects and overlaps those in *Raisin*, reflecting many of the same family dynamics and conflicts as Hansberry. In particular, Troy Maxson reflects Big Walter, as family patriarch, and Mama Lena, as the play's dominant figure. Similarly, Hansberry's Lena and Wilson's Rose find themselves as the heads of their respective families after their husbands die, each becoming the keeper of her late husband's legacy. In the way that Hansberry's Walter Lee, the play's only major adult male character, is constantly at odds with at least one of the female characters, arguing with, needling, or seeking something from each as he struggles to assert himself in the overcrowded apartment, Rose Maxson, the only adult female character in *Fences*, finds herself constantly interceding between her husband and the other male characters. With Walter Lee being in his mid-thirties and Lyons being thirty-four, the two characters also correspond in the way that each becomes more like his father as life progresses. Both characters similarly attempt to escape the pressures of work and home by retreating to a local bar, each seeking comfort and expression in music. The relationship and marital struggles that take place on stage between Hansberry's Walter Lee and Ruth resonate, moreover, in the off-stage struggles to which Wilson alludes between Lyons and Bonnie. In that Cory is approximately the same age and at the same juncture in life as Hansberry's Beneatha, each similarly seeks independence and identity, hoping to take advantage of opportunities not afforded their parents, particularly college. Finally, the children—*Raisin*'s Travis and *Fences*'s Raynell—figure importantly in representing an undetermined future that will emerge as the past and its lingering forces of oppression bear upon the conflicts of the present.

Wilson also speaks to *Raisin* in the ways that *Fences* renegotiates the physical space within and beyond the immediate stage setting to shape and define the larger conflicts driving the family toward collapse. With the entirety of *Raisin* taking place within a crowded, roach-infested apartment in which tenants share a common bathroom, Hansberry creates a space bounded and defined by the sites of oppression, frustration, and denial. Although the audience does not see the workplace where the adults go to be domestics and chauffeurs, the neighborhood where kids chase rats with sticks, and the bars where people go to escape their lives, it does see the claustrophobic, poorly lit apartment where the conflicts converge upon and shape familial relations.[11] In *Fences*, Wilson similarly contextualizes the play's stage setting within the boundaries of conflict that physically and metaphorically surround and bear down upon the Maxsons—Troy's workplace defined by the monotony and physicality of emptying trashcans, the ever-present threat of prison as a form of white institutionalization, the baseball field as a site of white oppression and denial, and the bar where Troy meets and becomes involved with Alberta. Although the apartment in *Raisin* and the yard in *Fences* should be a site of freedom and self-authority for each play's respective family, each place becomes another site of enclosure and incarceration.

By including three generations of African Americans, Wilson further parallels Hansberry, shaping the play's dramatic conflict within the inter-generational tensions created out of a long-standing history of racial conflict imposed by a white oppressor and internalized by the black oppressed. In both plays, the senior generation—Mama Lena and Big Walter in *Raisin* and Troy Maxson and his friend Jim Bono in *Fences*—participates in the Great Migration to escape peonage, Jim Crow, and the South's racist terrorism in the hope of securing a better life in the North. This older generation, however, does not fully appreciate the changes it helped bring about in having reshaped American society and the attitudes and expectations of its own children. In confronting the present in accordance with the experiences that defined it, the senior generation, in turn, generates another source of familial tension. Having benefited from the social and economic improvements brought about by the older generation, the middle generation, represented by Walter Lee, Ruth, and Beneatha in *Raisin* and Lyons and Cory in *Fences*, will then be the first to have its members live their entire lives in the North as well as the one that will help usher in the Civil Rights and the Black Power Movements. The youngest generation—Travis and his unborn sibling in *Raisin* and Raynell in *Fences*, will in turn be the first to negotiate a post–Civil Rights Movement America where the forms of oppression and the rules for survival will change, becoming more complex and ambiguous.

After benefiting from the social and economic improvements brought about by the previous generation's trials and sacrifices, each successive generation develops greater individual expectations and higher aspirations for its participation in society. In *Raisin*, Lena pointedly articulates the circumstances that shaped her generation's worldview as well as the different perspective held by her children:

> Once upon a time freedom used to be life—now it's money. . . . In my time we was worried about not being lynched and getting to the North if we could and how to stay alive and still have a pinch of dignity too. . . . Now here come you and Beneatha—talking 'bout things we ain't never even thought about hardly. . . . You ain't satisfied or proud of nothing we done. I mean that you had a home; that we kept you out of trouble till you was grown; that you don't have to ride to work on the back of nobody's streetcar—You my children—but how different we done become. (74)

Although the social change may seem small, Lena illustrates the impact of the Great Migration as she articulates her children's shifting expectations, suggesting a process of change predicated on the advances and gains of each African American generation from slavery through the present.

In *Fences*, Troy similarly remains fixed within the boundaries of oppression that shaped his early manhood. Upon arriving in Pittsburgh, Troy discovers that he cannot access the same jobs and wages as white laborers, a reality that turns him to crime as he attempts to support his family. Sent to prison for his crime—institutionalization being a self-fulfilling prophecy that reinscribes hegemonic stereotypes concerning the black male—Troy learns and excels at the game of baseball, but despite his talent, he cannot play in the segregated major leagues. Although escaping the peonage of sharecropping and thereby opening different opportunities for his children, Troy can only envision his son in terms of the forces that shaped his own life. Despite Rose and Bono reminding Troy that those circumstances have changed (14–15, 41), he cannot see how Cory will benefit from attending college on a football scholarship. In what becomes his final pronouncement, Troy states, "He ought to go and get recruited in how to fix cars or some thing where he can make a living" (14). In joining the Marines, one of the young man's few viable options, Cory also enters a form of hegemonic institutionalization, a parallel of Troy's prison experience, with his father being complicit in the process.

This generational conflict factors significantly as both plays address the question that Langston Hughes posits in "Harlem," "What happens to a dream deferred?" (Hansberry, *Raisin* 3). Following Hansberry's lead, Wilson critiques the American dream and the supporting economic practices that commodify the black body, a precedent set during the slave trade, and impose black peonage that guarantees the cyclic recurrence of poverty in the North and South. In *Raisin*, each of the Youngers places his or her individual dream—a business for Walter Lee, a college education for Beneatha, and home ownership for Mama Lena and Ruth—in terms of the dollar value placed on Big Walter's life who, despite his long years of work, could not impact or advance his family economically without the insurance payment. Commenting upon this reality, Asagai, the Nigerian college student, states, "Then isn't there something wrong in a house—in a world—where all dreams, good or bad, must depend on the death of a man?" (135). Even then, after making a thirty-five-hundred-dollar down payment on a house, the play's central metaphor of the American dream, Mama Lena can only afford a house in all-white Clybourne Park because economic and social practices allow a white-controlled real estate market to limit the areas where blacks may buy and then restrict access to homes in black residential areas through price gouging (92–93). Illustrating the ways that cyclic black poverty creates a peonage as insidious as tenant farming in the South, Hansberry demonstrates how even when Big Walter was alive, four of the five Younger adults worked unskilled jobs to provide for the six people living in the small apartment (44, 71–73, 129).

In *Fences*, Wilson clearly speaks to Hansberry's evocation of these social and economic tensions, recontextualizing and revising several elements that directly parallel *Raisin*. Troy too must not only defer his dream of playing professional baseball, a process that becomes even more embittering given his chronological proximity to the breaking of baseball's color barrier, but he directly impacts and frustrates the dreams of his family. Placing three-thousand dollars down on his house (31), nearly the same amount as Mama Lena, Troy likewise can do so only after the commodification and exploitation of the black body, drawing upon his brother Gabriel's compensation for war wounds. Whereas Mama Lena legitimately deserves the insurance payment from Big Walter's death, Wilson revises the element by positioning Troy as a possible exploiter of the exploited. In what has become part of the Maxson family lore, Troy states, "Man go over there and fight the war . . . messin around with them Japs, get half his head blown off . . . and they give him a lousy three thousand dollars. And I had to swoop down on that. . . . That's the only way I got a roof over my head . . . cause of that metal plate" (31). In doing so, he not only demonstrates the internalization of American racism, but he expresses his own sense of guilt in feeling complicit with the hegemonic forces that placed a dollar value on his brother's well-being. Similar to the Youngers, the Maxsons achieve home ownership—a defining element of the American dream—not through the hard work and aspirations of the individual, the essence of the dream itself, but rather through the physical exchange of the black body.

Wilson also follows Hansberry's representation of a controlling white hegemony that imposes a de facto segregation that limits all interaction between blacks and whites to some economic exchange benefiting white interests. In *Raisin*, four of the five adults living in the Younger household before Big Walter's death must work as servants—domestics and chauffeurs—in white homes, their only interaction with white America. Despite their efforts, they are only able to rent one very small apartment without its own bathroom and to provide minimally for the family's other material needs. The only instance when a white individual enters into the black neighborhood occurs when a representative of these controlling hegemonic forces wants to take something it values. Specifically, Karl Lindner comes to the Younger household seeking to keep the family from moving into the all-white Clybourne Park by offering monetary incentives to maintain the prevailing segregation.

Fences reinscribes Hansberry's formulation of black exploitation, expanding it to include the recruitment of black athletes, another commodification of the black body. First, Wilson introduces a work arrangement where Troy, his friend Bono, and his son Cory perform low-paying, unskilled jobs outside the black community. Next, he describes the elements of white hegemony that enter into black neighborhoods to take what little money might be available, contributing to the cyclic recurrence of poverty. Introducing Mr. Glickman, a white door-to-door salesman who sells furniture to blacks on time installments and profits by offering credit when furniture stores will not (19–20), Wilson indicates how economic forces add another layer of cost and inconvenience to inhibit black participation. Next, Wilson demonstrates how the police and the courts, as Troy Maxson indicates, regularly arrest individuals out on the street, reasserting hegemonic control by extracting fines from those who can afford them and jailing those who cannot (57, 62). *Fences* also questions the commodification of the black athlete where, in providing opportunities to attend college and transcend economic barriers, the recruitment process reflects the same historical elements that bartered for slaves on the auction block. As with *Raisin*, Wilson illustrates how white-controlled economic forces shape racial interaction, maintain segregation, and reimpose the cycle of generational poverty.

As in *Raisin*, *Fences* features an imposing, overbearing figure within the senior generation who sets the terms and conditions of intergenerational familial relations, adding to the larger conflict within the play. Called "a tyrant" by her daughter,[12] Mama Lena is "a strong woman" who runs the house with an iron fist, regulating her children's lives and challenging her daughter-in-law's child-rearing abilities (52). Asserting her familial authority, she states her position clearly: "There are some ideas we ain't going to have in this house. Not long as I am at the head of this family" (51). When unable to get what she considers an appropriate response from her cajoling, she invokes her dead husband's authority. That failing, Lena physically bullies her children. When Beneatha espouses secular humanism, Mama Lena "*slaps her powerfully across the face*," stating, "Now—you say after me, in my mother's house there is still God" (Hansberry's italics 51). Later, she similarly begins beating Walter Lee after discovering he has lost the majority of his father's insurance benefit payment (129). Even at the play's end, Walter Lee "comes into his manhood" only after his mother shames him into confronting Karl Lindner in front of Travis, his son (147–51).

In keeping with his masculine revision, Wilson revises Hansberry's matriarch and magnifies her antagonism and aggressiveness in his character Troy Maxson, the dominating figure in *Fences*. Following the same approach as *Raisin*'s Lena, Troy also cajoles and bullies his family, resorting to physical force when he fails to get what he considers an appropriate response. When Lyons, Troy's oldest son from a failed first marriage, seeks either to borrow money from or return it to his father, Wilson's protagonist initiates what has become a family shaming ritual, cajoling the son to force a confrontation. When Troy tells Rose that his girlfriend is pregnant, he grabs his wife forcefully and threatens her when she challenges his selfishness (68). Unlike Lena, however, Wilson's protagonist does not actually strike one of his children during the play. Though nearly coming to blows twice with his son Cory, Troy exercises great physical restraint as the young man attempts to assert himself when confronted with his father's aggressiveness (68–69, 82–83). As with Lena, Troy expects his family to follow his authority without question, being the force with whom his family must reckon.

In developing the conflict between Troy and his son Cory, Wilson closely follows Hansberry's formulation of the tension that arises between Lena and her son Walter Lee; in asserting familial authority so forcefully, the older generation becomes another impediment that in effect reinscribes white oppression. In *Raisin*'s first act, before Walter Lee attempts to discuss with his mother his plans for opening a liquor store, he first asks his wife Ruth to talk to Lena about his plan (32–35) as he clearly understands the household power relationships. When Ruth briefly speaks to her mother-in-law, Mama Lena has already decided that she will not support the plan (41–42). Even though she recognizes the poverty that envelops her family, she cannot envision a different existence, having internalized the limitations imposed and enforced by white oppression, immediately replying, "We ain't no business people, Ruth. We just plain working folks" (42). Later, in response to Walter Lee's attempt to explain his plan, Lena flatly dismisses him in the manner of one addressing a child, stating, "I don't aim to have to speak that again" (71). After his mother puts the down payment on the house and seeks his affirmation, Walter Lee responds, "You the head of this family. You run our lives like you want to. . . . So what you need for me to say it was all right for? . . . So you butchered up a dream of mine—you—who always talking 'bout your children's dreams" (94–95). Although Walter Lee's plan for entering business is problematic, his desire to break the cycle of poverty through a means that his parents could not have realistically considered demonstrates this generational conflict.

In *Fences*, Wilson reinscribes this same tension in terms of Cory's desire to play college football, closely paralleling *Raisin*. Early in the first act, Rose too attempts to intercede for her son who, like Hansberry's Walter Lee in his dealings with his mother, is not able to discuss the issue directly with his father. Later, Cory indicates that he, as Walter Lee does with Ruth, asks his mother to speak on his behalf (32). Although asserting that racism will not allow Cory to play or benefit from football (14, 37), Troy himself, acting in a manner similar to Mama Lena, becomes the agent of the white oppression that he fears, having internalized the forces that denied his own aspirations in playing baseball. The exchange between father and son then closely follows that between mother and son in *Raisin*. When Cory tries to talk with his father about the football scholarship, Troy, who has already made up his mind to prevent his son from taking advantage of this opportunity, dismisses his son: "I don't care what nobody else say. I'm the boss . . . you understand? I'm the boss around here. I do the saying what counts" (38). After his father tells his coach that he can no longer play football, Cory echoes Walter Lee's emotional outburst of frustration, stating, "Why you wanna do that to me? That was the one chance I had" (55).

Signifying upon Hansberry's Lena, Wilson reinscribes her sense of self-sacrifice and responsibility in his own Troy Maxson who similarly uses it as a means to bully and impose his will upon his family. Throughout *Raisin*, Mama Lena contextualizes her and Big Walter's life in terms of their two children often to gain their compliance or acquiescence in some issue. Even when giving Walter Lee the remaining insurance benefit and telling him to take charge of the family, she has already made the down-payment on a house in the all-white Clybourne Park. Without consulting anyone else, therefore, she commits the family to an endeavor that will require everyone's economic participation and may expose them to white violence, stating, "What you ain't never understood is that I ain't got nothing, don't own nothing, ain't never really wanted nothing that wasn't for you" (106). In *Fences*, Troy similarly wields his commitment and responsibility as a means to intimidate and antagonize his family while justifying his own problematic behavior. When Cory seeks his father's support and acceptance, Troy can respond only by threatening and belittling the young man:

> Like you? I go out of here every morning . . . bust my butt . . . putting up with them crackers every day. . . . It's my job. It's my responsibility! . . . A man got to take care of his family. You live in my house . . . sleep you behind on my bedclothes . . . fill you belly up with my food . . . cause you my son. You my flesh and blood. . . . Cause it's my duty to take care of you. I owe a responsibility to you! (39–40)

After Troy tells his wife that his girlfriend is pregnant, Rose challenges his selfishness. Grabbing her forcefully, he responds, "You say I take and don't give. . . . I done give you everything I got" (68). As with Hansberry's Lena, Troy justifies his aggressiveness and his selfish actions in terms of his own sense of sacrifice.

Reasserting Hansberry's representation of the African American family, Wilson similarly challenges the hegemonic master discourse that maintains that the black family is dysfunctional as a result of an absent, and therefore irresponsible, black male.[13] In *Raisin*, Hansberry represents the poor, inner-city black family as a functioning unit consisting of a father, a mother, and their children, extended only as a result of the poverty imposed by an oppression that allows only menial, low-paying work and overpriced, poorly maintained housing. Contesting the stereotype of the absent black father, two generations of Younger men stand by their families. Big Walter's absence, moreover, comes as a result of an early death brought on by oppression's erosive processes in his attempts to provide for his family. In *Fences*, Wilson similarly portrays two generations of Maxson men who, despite their many failings, uphold their responsibilities toward their families. In recentering patriarchal authority within a masculine space, Wilson asserts that Troy's defining presence, as problematic as it may be, demonstrates commitment and responsibility to his family, a revision of white stereotypes concerning the black male (Savran 30–31). Whereas Troy's and his father's failings reflect the oppression and imposed limitations that shape their characters, each acts upon an instinct to support his family, seeking to teach and correct his children. The human failings of Troy and his father become manifest, however, as each bullies and demeans his family in the process. Wilson takes his revision even further and reverses the image of the long-suffering, self-sacrificing black mother in that Troy's sharecropper father remains with his family after his mother flees the older Maxson's "evilness" (50).

In developing Troy Maxson, Wilson particularly appears to draw from and expand upon Hansberry's description of Big Walter. Although Lena demonstrates that she is revising her late husband's memories, forgiving and letting go any troublesome aspects to emphasize instead his positive qualities in supporting his family and confronting the manifestations of oppression, she provides Ruth with a brief insight into the complexities of his character:

> God knows there was plenty wrong with Walter Younger—hard-headed, mean, kind of wild with women—plenty wrong with him. But he sure loved his children. Always wanted them have something—be something. . . . Yes, a fine man—just couldn't never catch up with his dreams, that's all. (45–46)

In that Troy Maxson fits each of these descriptions, even in the concern for his children though manifested in often questionable and problematic ways, Wilson creates a protagonist that clearly parallels Big Walter. Suggesting a common disposition and physicality between the two men, Walter Lee's statement that his father "almost beat a man to death" (147) parallels Troy's recollections of killing a man during a failed robbery attempt intended to provide for his family (53). Participants in the Great Migration, furthermore, Big Walter and Troy leave the agrarian South with the hope of finding greater opportunity and escaping Jim Crow. Upon arriving in the North, each similarly finds himself trapped within the ubiquitous American racism that prevents the two men from achieving their respective dreams. In that Big Walter's death precedes the beginning of *Raisin* and *Fences* culminates with the death of Troy Maxson, Wilson in effect revises Hansberry's play to retell the story from the patriarch's perspective, providing a kind of prequel that might reflect the circumstances and conflicts that lead up to Big Walter's death given the similarities between the two characters.

Big Walter and Troy also fit within the man of words tradition, a key similarity, in their observed or demonstrated verbal skills that reflect the African American oral tradition.[14] Although the audience may access Big Walter only through the filter of his wife, Hansberry suggests that in being denied other outlets to direct his creativity and interests, the Younger patriarch possessed certain verbal skills. In several instances, Lena quotes her husband directly, citing his views on restrictions and oppressions imposed on blacks in America. Relating his views on the opportunities afforded blacks to achieve their dreams, for example, Lena comments on her husband's ability to use words, stating, "He could talk like that, don't you know" (45–46). Although Big Walter's interrogation and critique of American oppression comes filtered through his wife, his addressing the issues of equality, justice, and fairness places him squarely in the African American preacher or orator tradition.[15] Lena's assertion that he was wild with the women might also suggest that Big Walter used his powers to articulate and persuade in several different contexts.

In *Fences*, Wilson's Troy Maxson repeatedly demonstrates his verbal dexterity directly as he uses his skills to define and shape the world around him. Repeatedly called a "liar" by his wife and his friend Bono, a term applied to able storytellers,[16] Troy uses his stories to humor, negotiate, instruct, and sometimes threaten those around him. Whereas *Raisin*'s Lena acknowledges Big Walter's verbal skills and hints at his infidelity, Troy demonstrates his complexity—his nobility and his fallibility—as a man of words. At work, he turns the codified language of white authority, the words and processes proscribed by the union and the sanitation department, back on itself to negotiate social change, ending the practice that denies blacks the opportunity to drive the garbage trucks (8–9, 42–46). At Taylors', the bar where he meets Alberta, Troy beats out the other men in competition for her attentions (10–11). In recounting his experiences with his share-cropper father, a man he calls "the devil himself" (51), Troy also constructs the family lore of male generational conflict that plays itself out in each of the male Maxsons (50–52). As a reflection of the storytelling and preacher traditions, Troy's description of his battle with death takes on epic and biblical proportions (16–18, 72–73). At the play's ending, Rose, like *Raisin*'s Lena, takes up her late husband's words for herself; similarly, Troy's children take up their late father's words in terms of his particular folk expressions as well as the song about Blue, the dog, handed-down from Troy's father.

Even to the extent of his early death at age sixty, Troy is approximately the same age as Big Walter given Lena's age at the beginning of *Raisin*. Alluding to the impact of oppression on Big Walter, Mama Lena states that her late husband "was fighting his own war with this here world" (45), a conflict echoed in Troy Maxson's self-described struggle with "Death," the personification of white oppression manifested in terms of his frustrations and disappointments concerning baseball, his father, prison, and his brother. Whereas Hansberry's Lena can only report on her husband's struggles, Wilson's revision of *Raisin* allows for a deliberate first-person description of the process from his patriarch's perspective. Telling how he wrestles with Death "for three days and three nights" when sick with pneumonia (17), Troy's struggle takes on biblical proportions as he invokes the story of Jonah in the belly of the whale as well as Christ's time in the grave.[17] In his story, Death notably wears "a white robe with a hood on it" (17), evoking the central symbol of white racism within the image of the Ku Klux Klan and its related violence and terrorism. Thus, in attempting to stave off the racist antagonism and conflict that surround him, Troy finally builds his fence to protect himself and his family from its intrusion.

Responding to Hansberry's representation of African American opportunities in relation to the American work ethic, individual ability, and identity, Wilson directly invokes elements of *Raisin* in Troy's efforts to become a garbage truck driver and Cory's job at the supermarket, jobs specifically referenced in the earlier play. In *Raisin*, Hansberry deconstructs the myth surrounding the American work ethic—a prerequisite for achieving the American dream—in which hard work, a willingness to learn, and perseverance will allow an individual to rise within a chosen field. While demonstrating all of these qualities, Walter Lee, as his father before him, cannot move beyond societal proscriptions that only allow blacks access to low-paying, menial jobs. Thus suggesting how his chauffer job offers no possibility for advancement, personal satisfaction, or positive identity, a job that does not even enable him to provide for his family, Walter Lee tells his mother, "I open and close car doors all day long. I drive a man around in his limousine and I say, 'Yes, sir; no, sir; very good, sir; shall I take the Drive, sir?' Mama, that ain't no kind of job . . . that ain't nothing at all" (73). Later, Mama Lena echoes her husband's assessment of the jobs available to African Americans, an assertion of his legacy, seeing into her own as well as her son's condition:

> My husband always said being any kind of a servant wasn't a fit thing for a man to have to be. He always said a man's hands was made to make things, or to turn the earth with—not to drive nobody's car for 'em—or—(*She looks at her own hands*) carry they slop jars. (Hansberry's italics 103)

In that all of the Youngers work as domestics, jobs that reflect the same kind of servitude first installed during slavery, *Raisin* indicates how little has changed by the 1950s in terms of black opportunity.

In *Fences*, Wilson riffs upon Hansberry's critique of a post–World War Two America that failed to extend the same opportunities for economic advancement to blacks, drawing specific elements from *Raisin*. First, Troy's assertion that his son Cory should "learn how to fix cars or build houses," getting a trade that allows him to use his hands doing something "[b]esides hauling people's garbage" (37) directly paraphrases Big Walter's philosophy concerning what makes for fitting work. Whereas Walter Lee's growing frustration and lack of fulfillment in being a chauffer pushes him to despair, Wilson signifies upon *Raisin* in the way Troy aspires to become a driver after laboring eighteen years as a garbage man, a menial, back-breaking job that at its best parallels the physicality of picking cotton. In that Troy struggles to break a color barrier that allows only whites to drive the trucks and blacks to empty the cans, Wilson makes Walter Lee's job seem almost luxurious in comparison to one that destroys Troy's body and spirit. In another instance, Wilson invokes Hansberry's Travis, who plays one parent against another in seeking to earn money for school by helping people with their bags at the local supermarket (29–31). In *Fences*, Cory similarly works a part-time job at the A&P to help with school costs. Reflecting the family dynamics in *Raisin*, Cory asks his mother to intercede on his behalf with his father, so he can cut back on his after-school job to play football, a move that sparks the conflict that forces him to leave home.

Wilson also draws upon Hansberry's representation of the erosive processes of oppression that reduce and destroy the individual. Indicating these very forces in *Raisin*, Lena describes their impact on her late husband, a man muted and silenced by these forces, over time:

> I seen him . . . night after night . . . come in . . . and look at that rug . . . and then look at me . . . the red showing in his eyes . . . the veins moving in his head . . . I seen him grow thin and old before he was forty . . . working and working and working like somebody's old horse . . . killing himself. (129)

In *Fences*, Wilson gives voice to the family patriarch in a passage that echoes Lena's reading of Big Walter's body. Contextualizing his life in terms of the tedious, unfulfilling repetitive work that shapes his existence, Troy states:

> I come in here every Friday. I carry a sack of potatoes and a bucket of lard. You all line up at the door with your hands out. I give you the lint from my pockets. I give you my sweat and my blood. I ain't got no tears. I done spent them. . . . I get up Monday morning . . . find my lunch on the table. I go out. Make my way. Find my strength to carry me through to the next Friday. . . . That's all I got to give. I can't give nothing else. (41)

Given the many parallels between Big Walter and Troy, the reader may reasonably consider *Fences* as representing the conditions and circumstances in which *Raisin* begins.

With home becoming a site of contention for Walter Lee, Wilson invokes *Raisin* in the way that the domestic space serves as another site of dispute and tension that imposes upon Troy. In both plays, the men attempt to escape their failure to find decent, rewarding work and the tensions subsequently generated at home by seeking release in bars, a shared space outside of each of the play's staged context. The bar, therefore, becomes a space where men seek to escape the pressures of home and work as well as one that potentially puts home and work in jeopardy. When Mama Lena warns Walter Lee that "[i]t's dangerous . . . [w]hen a man goes outside his home to look for peace," particularly "in some other house," she may speak from experience given her statement concerning Big Walter's problem with women (73). Noting her husband's increasing reliance on drink as a means to escape (72), Ruth identifies that Walter Lee is moving down the same path as his father when she observes that he is changing, and she no longer can provide him comfort and solace at home (42). Whereas Hansberry suggests another kind of generational repetition between Big Walter and Walter Lee in terms of the processes that seem to drive them from their home, Wilson revises *Raisin* in the way Troy's frustrations and desires play out in his relationship with Alberta. After confessing his relationship to his wife, Troy states, "She gives me a different idea . . . a different understanding about myself. I can step out of this house and get away from the pressures and problems . . . be a different man. . . . I can just be a part of myself that I ain't never been" (66). Speaking to the routine of his life, Troy states, "I done locked myself into a pattern trying to take care of you all that I forgot about myself" (66); in response, Rose echoes Mama Lena, stating, "You should have stayed in my bed, Troy. . . . You should have held me tight. You should have grabbed me and held on" (67). Instead of offering relief and escape, the home becomes another site of conflict for Troy, one from which he selfishly seeks escape.

Following Hansberry's lead, Wilson, in addition to marking the changes that distinguish the generations, represents the erosive processes of oppression that repeat generationally. Invoking the same physical mannerisms that described her husband's movement to an early death, Lena suggests that her son is following a similar pathway, telling him, "You get all nervous acting and kind of wild in the eyes" (72). Suggesting that his own fate is converging with his father's, Walter Lee asserts, "Sometimes it's like I can see the future stretched out in front of me—just plain as day. . . . Hanging over there at the edge of my days. Just waiting for me—a big, looming blank space—full of *nothing*. Just waiting for *me*" (Hansberry's italics 73). Frustrated and unfulfilled at work and home, he confronts the prospect of a life defined by menial labor and endless domestic conflict as he and his wife repeat the cycle of poverty and oppression that trapped his parents and drove his defeated father to an early death. By extension, Ruth, his wife, similarly confronts her own fate as she finds herself pregnant with their second child, realizing the emotional, physical, and economic burden she will have to bear. Given that her second child and Travis will share the same age difference as Walter Lee and Beneatha, Ruth finds herself slowly becoming Mama Lena. Only Beneatha seems to have the immediate opportunity to break the cycle of poverty as she works to complete college and enter a profession. Whether Travis, as representative of the next generation, will break this cycle remains open to question.

In a passage that echoes Hansberry's Walter Lee, Wilson's Troy Maxson similarly recognizes and articulates the stifling conditions imposed by oppression that slowly wear down his spirit: "It's not easy for me to admit that I been standing in the same place for eighteen years" (67). Although Troy repeatedly describes his own father's apparent meanness and disregard, a conflict that he cannot resolve, his actions demonstrate that he too has become his own father in the way he bullies and manipulates his family. At the play's end, Cory also attempts to come to terms with his father, becoming, as his mother asserts, "Troy Maxson all over again" (89), a statement that echoes Mama Lena's description of Big Walter's influence on Walter Lee, "That's where Brother gets all these notions, I reckon" (45). In a similar vein, Lyons and Cory become like their father as each finds himself institutionalized. Whereas Lyons goes to jail for writing bad checks and loses Bonnie, Cory wrestles with his father's presence. As with *Raisin*'s Travis, only Raynell appears poised to transcend the limitations that define her father and her brothers.

In the way that Troy allows insight into Big Walter, *Raisin's* Lena Younger similarly parallels Wilson's Rose Maxson as each becomes the head of her family following the death of her husband. Throughout *Raisin*, Lena attempts to keep her family together, contending with the changes that take place in the wake of Big Walter's death. As the keeper of her husband's memory, furthermore, she begins to position his legacy within the Younger family lore, only briefly mentioning Big Walter's flaws as she repeatedly cites his wisdom to help assert her authority and guide the family. Establishing this same pattern in *Fences*, Wilson positions Rose to contend with her own mixed emotions as she confronts Troy's death within the context of her anger and sense of betrayal. Indicating her role as head of the family, for example, Rose acknowledges Troy's strengths and demonstrates that she has let go of some of her anger when she describes how she will raise Raynell, "I'm gonna do her just like your daddy did you . . . I'm gonna give her the best of what's in me" (91). Although she does not resort to physical violence, she quickly asserts her authority when Cory states that he will not attend his father's funeral, telling him, "I ain't going to listen to that kind of talk this morning. . . . Just take [your anger] and set it over there on the shelf and forget about it" (89). Echoing a line from *Raisin,* moreover, Wilson suggests that Rose has reconciled some of her ambivalence toward her late husband in a manner similar to Hansberry's Mama Lena as she tells Cory, "Your daddy wanted you to be everything he wasn't . . . and at the same time he tried to make you into everything he was. I don't know if he was right or wrong . . . but I do know he meant to do more good than he meant to do harm" (90).[18]

In another parallel, both plays address the legacy of a family patriarch who even in death remains a force that weighs heavily upon and continues to shape the family in the present. In *Raisin*, the death of Big Walter becomes the very catalyst that brings the family to the brink of collapse in terms of familial change and the issues concerning the use of the insurance benefit that it brings about. While signaling that another generation has failed to fulfill its aspirations, a repetition that directly connects the Youngers to the forces of oppression and racism initiated during slavery, Big Walter's death also provides an opportunity for his family in terms of the insurance policy payment, an opportunity that the patriarch could never provide during his life. Invoking many ambiguous, contradictory responses, the family must contend with such competing emotions as bereavement, hope, bitterness, desire, anger, despair, and optimism. When speaking with Ruth about Walter Lee's aspirations to succeed, Mama Lena quotes her husband, "Seem like God didn't see fit to give the black man nothing but dreams—but He did give us children to make them dreams seem worth while" (45–46). These words prove to be prophetic, resonating as a presence within the repetition of oppression and betrayal manifested by Walter Lee's inability to achieve his dream after Willy Harris steals the money intended to open the liquor store.

Whereas Hansberry's Big Walter becomes an absent presence whose death sets the conditions for the family crisis, the physical presence of Wilson's Troy Maxson drives the family to collapse with his death setting the conditions to bring the family back together. Extending the impact of generational influence established in *Raisin*, Wilson adds another layer of patriarchal and generational influence in the way that Troy Maxson's antagonistic relationship with his family becomes a repetition of his own relationship with his sharecropper father. In what could easily represent Troy's relationship with his father, Cory states, "Papa was like a shadow that followed you everywhere" (89), indicating the presence his late father continues to exert. In the same way that Troy confronts his father's legacy, one that is simultaneously troublesome and affirming, so too must his family confront Troy. Although his often selfish and questionable behavior brings his family to the point of collapse, more importantly Troy's legacy—manifested in the song about Blue the dog received first from Troy's father and then handed down to his children (43–44, 91–92)—not only bonds his three children with one another but with the two previous generations of Maxson men as well. As with *Raisin*'s Lena, Rose too begins to shape her late husband's legacy, emphasizing his strengths in her attempt to make his memory relevant to the living. In both plays, therefore, the dead patriarch becomes an object of memory—serving as example and warning—shaped by those who must move on and reconcile this change.

Echoing *Raisin*'s representation of the processes of social change, Wilson likewise addresses the impact and negotiation of racial barriers from the perspective of the working class. Rather than focusing on a sensational act of racial violence, a very real threat that exists at the play's boundaries in first the South from which the senior generation of Youngers escapes and then the white neighborhood into which the family will move, Hansberry interrogates American racism and the oppression it manifests from the perspective of a black working class denied access to the opportunities of the post–World War Two era. In *Raisin*, change occurs, not in the context of the grand social movements led by the young that would define the 1960s and 1970s, but through the actions of one family that pressures a resistant hegemonic order to apply and enforce its rules and processes fairly. With Mama Lena putting the money down on a house in an all-white neighborhood, Hansberry actually positions the senior generation as the instigator of change. Whereas Walter Lee and Beneatha might represent the different perspectives for black uplift that Booker T. Washington and W.E.B. Du Bois represent respectively, the son's focus on materialism and status and the daughter's interest in cultural identity and awareness do not directly attend to the most pressing needs of the black working class. Instead, Lena's more immediate act of self-assertion in seeking safe, adequate housing sets the processes of change in motion.

By invoking Jackie Robinson's dramatic entry into segregated baseball in 1947, a sensational action that did impact racial negotiation in America, Wilson speaks to and revises Hansberry's representation of social change, indicating the slow pace of change as well as the depth of oppression. In that his protagonist at one point had the talent and the desire to support his unrealized dream of playing in the major leagues, Wilson illustrates the fundamental shortfalls of the American democratic ideal and the notion of rugged individualism which, according to the myth of the American dream, suggests that the best qualified will rise to the top of a chosen endeavor. Even though *Fences* begins ten years after the desegregation of baseball, Troy Maxson must still confront the city sanitation department's whites-only hiring practice that prevents blacks from being garbage-truck drivers. Wilson thereby illustrates how little in society has actually changed, marking the layers of insidious and imposing oppression that continue to confront the black working class. Only after filing a union complaint questioning the practice of hiring whites-only as drivers (8–9) does Troy ultimately move the sanitation department to change the job description. As in *Raisin*, therefore, one individual's act of self-assertion brings change to the hegemonic forces that bear down upon him. Whereas Troy dies embittered in not having the opportunity to play professional baseball, he opens up opportunities for other blacks, being, so to speak, the Jackie Robinson of the Pittsburgh sanitation department. Although change occurs in both plays, Wilson, like Hansberry, demonstrates this change coming in the efforts of the play's senior generation, highlighting the struggles as well as the heroic nobility of the black working class.

Although a minor detail, the issue of licenses as a hegemonic manifestation that excludes and controls enters prominently in both plays. In *Raisin*, Hansberry represents the possible corruption and nepotism guiding the state liquor licensing process as a metaphor of a prevailing hegemony that uses its many levels of governance and bureaucracy to inscribe white authority. The audience never knows whether the liquor licensing process requires bribery, but regardless of the actual circumstances, Willy Harris, as a kind of trickster, clearly plays upon Walter Lee's internalized expectations of having to confront a corrupt hegemonic authority. Willy Harris may con Walter Lee and Bobo by convincing them of the need to bribe the licensing authorities, but in reality they succumb to yet another manifestation of oppression. In *Fences*, Wilson also invokes the license as a representative layer of hegemonic control, signifying upon Hansberry in the way that his protagonist Troy who, as a trickster rather than victim, subverts white authority. Even though he secures a driving position after successfully filing a union complaint (45–46), Troy, an illiterate who does not possess a driver's license, never clearly obtains the necessary authorization that would allow him to operate a garbage truck. Troy not only uses one kind of hegemonic force to battle another in the way his union complaint challenges the practices of the sanitation department, but he rises above the layers of bureaucratic hegemony that defeat Walter Lee.

Wilson also appears to borrow from and speak to *Raisin* in the way he addresses the implications of poverty and incorporates domestic ritual. Both plays early on address the complexities arising from the lack of a private household bathroom, a circumstance that indicates poverty and substandard housing. *Raisin*'s opening scene presents the difficulties of negotiating a single shared bathroom among the two families who reside on the same floor, a defining daily ritual in the Younger household (25–35). Wilson similarly references this issue in *Fences* when Troy's friend Bono relates the burdens of not even having access to indoor plumbing:

> Me and Lucille was staying down there on Logan Street. Had two rooms with the outhouse in the back. I ain't mind the outhouse none. But when that goddamn wind blow through there in the winter . . . that's what I'm talking about! To this day I wonder why in the hell I ever stayed down there for six long years. But see, I didn't know I could do no better. I thought only white folks had inside toilets and things. (13)

Wilson likewise echoes Hansberry in the way ritual of household cleaning appears prominently in both plays. In *Raisin*, the Saturday morning cleaning is a family ritual with each person given particular responsibilities (54–60). In *Fences*, Wilson expands the Saturday morning ritual to include the building of the fence that eventually encloses the Maxson yard, setting the majority of the family's confrontations within this context. Not only does Troy's infidelity coincide with his failure to uphold this weekly ritual, but his conflicts with his son Cory take place during the time allotted for this ritual. Likewise, Troy tells his wife about his relationship with Alberta and her pregnancy on Saturday morning. An untimely pregnancy, furthermore, is also a source of conflict in both plays. In *Raisin*, Ruth's announcement coincides with and adds to the family tensions (57–60, 70–75). In *Fences*, Troy's announcement that Alberta will have his child and his bringing home of the baby further isolate him from his family and friends (63, 72–75).

As a final structural parallel, each play appears to reach a resolution concerning the family's immediate conflict, but in doing so positions its families to contend with even larger social issues. After being on the brink of total collapse, the Youngers unite physically on the stage and spiritually in purpose at the play's end, surviving the immediate crises created out of Big Walter's death and the circumstances surrounding the life insurance benefit. Whereas some critics have suggested that *Raisin* ends tidily with the Youngers moving upward as a representation of universal middle-class sensibilities,[19] in actuality the family confronts an uncertain future that will in all likelihood include hostile encounters with the "Chicago peckerwoods" described by Mrs. Johnson, the accommodationist busy-body who lives next door and seems to delight in her predictions concerning the Younger's fate (101–2). In a letter to the *New York Times* included in *To Be Young, Gifted and Black: Lorraine Hansberry in Her Own Words* (1969), Hansberry describes from her own experience what happens when black families move into white neighborhoods. Even though her "father and the NAACP 'won' a Supreme Court decision" that challenged racist practices that prevented blacks from buying homes in white neighborhoods, Hansberry observes:

> That fight also required that our family occupy the disputed property in a hellishly hostile "white neighbourhood" in which, literally, howling mobs surrounded our house. One of their missiles almost took the life of the then eight-year-old signer of this letter. My memories of this "correct" way of fighting white supremacy in America include being spat at, cursed and pummeled in the daily trek to and from school. And I also remember my desperate and courageous mother, patrolling our house all night with a loaded German luger, doggedly guarding her four children. (20–21)

Thus having transgressed the North's de facto segregation, the Youngers, as Hansberry suggests, must now confront the physical realities of white racism, an open-ended, uncertain endeavor at best.

Echoing Hansberry's staging, Wilson also concludes *Fences* with the Maxson family physically reuniting in the final scene, an action that seems to counterbalance Troy's often divisive presence. As in *Raisin*, *Fences* provides a sort of immediate familial resolution as each of the Maxsons begins sifting through very particularized, often ambivalent perspectives to reconcile Troy's death. In that his protagonist's death occurs in 1965, Wilson also marks the larger social changes taking place in America as the Civil Rights Movement begins giving way to black militancy and the Black Power Movement in a year that brought the murder of Malcolm X and escalation of the American presence in Viet Nam. For the Maxons, the play ends with each of the characters—except for Raynell—institutionalized. Having just turned fifty, Rose resigns herself to living through the church and raising Raynell. The three Maxson men find themselves within hegemonic institutions expressly noted for controlling the black male. As a marine, Cory will likely participate in Viet Nam making him complicit with American hegemony and positioning himself to suffer death or wounding, a repetition of his Uncle Gabriel, or some other long-term effect such as posttraumatic stress syndrome or drug and alcohol abuse. Following the same path as his father, Lyons is in the workhouse, a form of incarceration, for writing bad checks. Addled by wounds received during World War Two and committed to a state hospital, Gabriel is essentially in prison, having no legal recourse or limits set for his incarceration. Thus contained, each of the Maxsons must deal with the fences that set one off from another.

With Wilson being so outspoken on his work throughout his lifetime, reviewers and critics have largely focused on the playwright's self-described influences, the "four B's," rather than comparing his works with those of other playwrights in the American or African America dramatic traditions. Although Wilson never directly claims Hansberry as a source or influence, *Fences* and *Raisin* share too many commonalities to ignore, even when considering that both come out of shared literary and artistic traditions. In fact, throughout his published interviews, Wilson very guardedly acknowledges many specific influences outside those previously mentioned. Of course when questioned about the ways that *Fences* speaks to and signifies upon Miller's *Death of a Salesman*, a play that he clearly invokes,[20] Wilson responds, "I am not familiar with *Death of a Salesman*. . . . I very purposefully didn't read [it]" (Savran 23). As with Ralph Ellison and *Invisible Man* (1952), Wilson engages more sources than he acknowledges.

Although Hansberry is a seminal figure in African American drama, a rather modest amount of scholarship has emerged in addressing her larger influence on the tradition. As Amiri Baraka observes:

> The truth is that Hansberry's dramatic skills have yet to be properly appreciated—and not just by those guardians of the status quo who pass themselves off as dramatic critics. For Black theater artists and would-be theorists especially, this is ironic because the play is probably the most widely appreciated—particularly by African Americans—black drama that we have. (10)

In fact, a comparative close reading of other plays within the African American dramatic tradition that follow *Raisin* similarly reflects the same kinds of connections, suggesting that Hansberry has had a larger and more pronounced influence on the black playwrights in terms of structure, characterization, thematic development, and dramatic movement.

Adrienne Kennedy's *Funnyhouse of a Negro: A Play in One Act* (1969), as one example, revises Hansberry's family drama by internalizing the polyvocal sources of family conflict into a single character, complicating and extending the contradictions of double-consciousness. In what could be a retelling of Beneatha's attempts to define herself—she specifically tells Asagai, "I am looking for my identity" (62)—Kennedy's "Negro Sarah" negotiates multiple identities and voices as the young woman attempts to balance a conflicted self that is black, educated, American, and African. Many of the elements from *Raisin* similarly make their way into *Funnyhouse*. Beneatha's pan-Africanism demonstrates itself in Kennedy's invocation of Patrice Lumumba. Her rejection of Mama Lena's faith similarly enters the play through the interactions with an internalized figure of white Jesus. Kennedy's negotiation of double-consciousness reflects Beneatha's two love interests, the assimilationist George Murchison and the African Asagai. The Negro Sarah also tells of getting married and going to Africa (7–8), something that Beneatha specifically considers. Kennedy's recurrent image of hair that falls out of her characters' heads is another connection, reflecting Beneatha's decision to cut off what Asagai calls her "mutilated hair" (61). Kennedy's later cycle, *The Alexander Plays* (1992), similarly explores these same themes from the perspective of a young black college woman who eventually marries and travels to Africa.

Alice Childress's *Wedding Band: A Love/Hate Story in Black and White* (1973) also is a female-dominated family drama set within a distinctly female space. Taking on the issue of miscegenation and interracial relations, Childress revises *Raisin* by invoking the same family relationship to include a matriarch, her son, and her daughter but in making them white puts the mother at odds with her son's black mistress. Having been with Herman for ten years (51), nearly the same amount of time that Walter Lee and Ruth are married (34), Julia parallels Ruth as the de facto daughter-in-law and must confront her lover's mother, a white matriarch who, as Mama Lena, bullies her family through threats and intimidation. In the same way that Lena receives Big Walter's insurance payment, so too does Herman's mother receive control of the family savings after her husband's death (48). Similar to Walter Lee seeking money from his mother to start a business, so too does Herman borrow money from his mother to open a bakery (48). At the play's end, echoing the way that Walter Lee "come(s) into his manhood" (151), so too does Herman take responsibility for his relationship with Julia, something confirmed when she quotes the speech from John C. Calhoun, "men are not born—men are made" (61).

Ntozake Shange's *for colored girls who have considered suicide/ when the rainbow is enuf* (1976), like *Raisin*, is a family drama that considers the situation of black women across multiple generations. Shange explores the full spectrum of familial relationships, addressing not only the men and children who populate women's lives but also the important relationships between women in confronting social circumstances. In doing so, the play could in certain ways be a retelling of the circumstances of Mama Lena in her relationship with Big Walter, Ruth in her relationship with Walter Lee, or Beneatha in her relationship with either George Murchison or Joseph Asagai. Addressing the abuses of "bein betrayed by men who know us" (19), Shange could extend or detail the circumstances experienced by any of three women in the play, particularly Lena's vague assertion of her late husband's meanness and wildness. Paralleling to an extreme Ruth's concern that she cannot provide her husband with what he needs, Shange's "lady in red" confronts the physical abuse of "beau willie," a man eroded by white oppression and institutionalization who also is looking for something no woman can provide (55–60). While taking Walter Lee's drinking to another level, beau willie becomes a metaphor of the abuse and oppression that black women potentially face at the hands of black men. The black woman's consideration of selfhood and self-assertion also resonates throughout the play. Whereas Lena and Ruth are in many respects defined by their relationships with men, Beneatha clearly seeks to explore, assert, and define herself in her own terms, a desire echoed by each of Shange's characters.

George C. Wolfe's *The Colored Museum* (1985) directly parodies *Raisin* in the scene entitled, "The Last Mama-on-the-Couch Play." His treatment of the play most clearly acknowledges *Raisin* as a definitive African American drama, drawing heavily upon the original play's language and its traditional interpretations as expressing black "middle-class aspirations" (24). In this scene, Wolfe also includes elements from Shange's *colored girls*, inviting further comparison between the two plays. Importantly, the play's exploration of black stereotypes also provides a kind of meta-text that interrogates African American identity, simultaneously challenging the differing perspectives that black and white viewers might bring to the performance, a quality clearly noted in *Raisin*. Wolfe's exploration of domestic rituals, popular culture, styles and fads, hegemonic oppression in its many manifestations, and the underlying negotiation of double-consciousness inherent to the black experience all deserve comparison with Hansberry's formulation in *Raisin*.

As another family drama that follows Hansberry's centering of female community and authority, Pearl Cleage's *Flyin' West* (1992) shares at least as many if not more elements of characterization, structure, and thematic development with *Raisin* as Wilson's *Fences*. Also spanning three generations of African Americans, each generation in the play has a distinctly different experience in negotiating American racism. Whereas *Raisin* spans the historical changes marking the twentieth century, *Flyin' West* spans those marking the nineteenth century. Cleage's characters similarly parallel those in *Raisin*. Sophie, like Hansberry's Lena, is the play's dominating figure. Minnie, the youngest of the women, is at twenty-one close to the same age as Beneatha and similarly has been away to a "conservatory" for formal education (34). Similar to the way that Walter Lee loses much of the family's insurance payment in a risky enterprise, so too does Frank, the mulatto husband of Minnie, lose first his inheritance to processes of racism codified in law (54–55) and then his remaining money gambling with the white land speculators (47). Echoing Hansberry's description of a "hard-headed" and "mean" Big Walter (45), Cleage's Frank physically and emotionally abuses his wife (53), and later Fannie recalls how her own father physically abused her mother (51). Frank's plea for Minnie to support him in his efforts to sell her share of the land also parallels Walter Lee's attempts to get the support of his wife and his mother for the liquor store. Frank's desire to be white similarly parallels Walter Lee's fantasy of being a business executive dealing with office business (108). Further, Minnie's pregnancy and the risk Frank imposes in beating her (56–57) echoes Ruth's pregnancy in *Raisin* and the concerns it raises in the household. Whereas the Younger women move Walter Lee to reject Karl Lindner's offers to buy back their house to preserve the Clybourne Park racial homogeneity, Cleage signifies upon *Raisin* in that Sophie, Fannie, and Miss Leah preserve the black homogeneity of Nicodemus by poisoning Frank, preventing him from selling out to the white speculators (62–68).

What then continues to make Hansberry's *Raisin* relevant, and why does it resonate across and in certain ways define the African American dramatic tradition? In representing three different generations of African Americans at the approximate midpoint of the last century, Hansberry in effect accounts for race and social relations from across the entirety of the twentieth century, speaking to W.E.B. Du Bois's assertion that "the problem of the Twentieth Century is the problem of the color-line" (5) and thereby accounting for the great social change that defined the last century as well as the recurring manifestations of racism and oppression that continue to shape and inform the present. Out of this negotiation of stasis and change logically emerges an interrogation of the black experience in America, the question of being African and American and its many implications within the layered, simultaneous oppressions involving gender, class, race, sexuality, and nationality. As a result, further investigation may better position Hansberry's impact upon the African American dramatic and the larger literary and artistic traditions, a consideration that Hansberry certainly deserves.

Notes

1. Margaret Wilkerson recounts Hansberry's accomplishments and critical reception in "*The Sighted Eyes and Feeling Heart of Lorraine Hansberry*."
2. In "A Voice from the Streets," Samuel G. Freedman observes that "[s]everal critics have likened [*Fences*] to Arthur Miller's '*Death of a Salesman*,' centering as it does on a proud,

embittered patriarch, Troy Maxson, and his teen-age son, Cory" (36). Tom Scanlan's *Family, Drama, and American Dreams* (1978) compares *Raisin* to *Death of a Salesman* by way of the family drama in the American drama tradition.

3. Joan Herrington discusses Wilson's self-described influences in *"I Ain't Sorry for Nothin' I Done": August Wilson's Process of Playwriting* (20–40). Mark Rocha does the same in "August Wilson and the Four B's: Influences" (3–15).
4. Wilson, in calling for the establishment and support of an independent black theater, specifically names Euripides, Aeschylus, Sophocles, Shakespeare, Shaw, Ibsen, Chekov, O'Neill, Miller, and Williams as his influences from the Western drama tradition (11). Later, he positions himself within literary black nationalism as represented by "Ron Milner; Ed Bullins; Philip Hayes Dean; Richard Wesley, Lonne Elder, III; Sonia Sanchez; Barbara Ann Teer and Amiri Baraka," his self-described African American literary ancestors (20).
5. In "The Revolutionary Theatre," Baraka asserts that drama should help build a positive sense of black identity that resists the forces of white hegemony (210–15).
6. Larry Neal, in "The Black Arts Movement," describes the Black Arts Movement as being a logical outgrowth of the Black Power Movement to represent its "political values" dealing with "the art of politics" and the Black Arts Movement as addressing "the relationship between art and politics" (273).
7. Addison Gayle, in his introduction to *The Black Aesthetic* (1971), asserts that a major goal of the Black Arts Movement is to find an appropriate "critical methodology" for black artistic representation in that "unique art derived from unique cultural experiences mandates unique critical tools for evaluation" (xxiii–xxiv). In "Towards a Black Aesthetic," Hoyt Fuller writes, "The young writers of the black ghetto have set out in search of a black aesthetic, a system of isolating and evaluating the artistic works of black people which reflect the special character and imperatives of black experience" (9).
8. In another example published in a 1974 issue of *Negro American Literature Forum* , Robert Willis's "Anger and the Contemporary Black Theatre" states that Hansberry "left a legacy for the newer Black dramatists in that she pointed the way to a new direction, a newness in content and attitude, and a purpose for Black theatre" (213).
9. In *The Signifying Monkey (1988)*, Henry Louis Gates, Jr. describes the African American text as being "double-voiced" in the ways it draws upon and revises other texts, subverting and resisting while simultaneously reifying and reinscribing meaning (xxiv–xxvii).
10. In *The Souls of Black Folk*, Du Bois describes the "double-consciousness" inherent to the African American experience, observing that "this American world . . . yields [the Negro] no true self-consciousness. . . . [Thus] [o]ne ever feels his two-ness,—an American, a Negro; two souls, two thoughts, two unreconciled strivings; two warring ideals in one dark body, whose dogged strength alone keeps it from being torn asunder" (10–11).
11. Indicating the ways that *Raisin* resonated with black audiences, James Baldwin describes the "claustrophobic terror" that the play invokes (444).
12. In "*A Raisin in the Sun*: The Strong Black Woman as Acceptable Tyrant," Trudier Harris argues "that Mama Lena Younger is as much a problem in the lives of her family as whites are, and her influence is more immediate and perhaps operates at a more insidious level" (24).
13. *The Negro Family: The Case for National Action* (1965) published by the U.S. Department of

Labor, also known as the Moynihan Report, argues that a central problem of keeping the "vast numbers of the unskilled, poorly educated city working class" in recurring cycles of poverty and crime "is that the Negro family in the urban ghettos is crumbling" (screen 1). Rather than addressing the multiple layers of oppression imposed by ongoing historical governmental and societal practices that prevent poor blacks from accessing American educational, health care, and employment opportunities, the report blames the black poor for failing "to save" themselves (screen 1).

14. In her overview of "Folk Literature," Trudier Harris describes the man of words tradition as the empowerment that results from the verbal and creative dexterity as well as the competition demonstrated in the different folk forms—the dozens, toasts, storytelling, the blues, and preaching—of the African American oral tradition (282–86).
15. See Dolan Hubbard's "Sermons and Preaching" for a concise overview of the tradition.
16. Zora Neale Hurston describes the power and authority of the storyteller in *Mules and Men* (1935), referring to those being particularly adept liars. In the "Introduction," she indicates that stories and storytelling are a form of resistance in the ways that they demonstrate how the weak or marginalized—be they animals, men and women, or the devil himself—outsmart and triumph over the strong and advantaged (1–4).
17. According to Matthew 12:40: "For as Jonas was three days and three nights in the whale's belly; so shall the Son of man be three days and three nights in the heart of the earth." See also Jonah 1:17–2:10.
18. In *Raisin*, when Walter Lee asks his son, Travis, what he wants to be when he grows up, the child states, "Sometimes Mama asks me that too. And sometimes when I tell her I just want to be like you—she says she don't want me to be like that and sometimes she says she does." (108). Wilson clearly echoes this statement at the end of *Fences*.
19. Amiri Baraka summarizes these early criticisms in his tribute to Hansberry, "A Critical Reevaluation: A *Raisin in the Sun*'s Enduring Passion," published in the twenty-fifth anniversary edition of *Raisin* (19–20).
20. In "'The Crookeds with the Straights': Fences, Race, and the Politics of Adaptation," Michael Awkward lists the thematic and structural commonalities shared between *Fences* and Miller's *Death of a Salesman*, observing, "Wilson's play would not have been possible in its present form without the precursoral presence of Miller's canonical white American middle-class family drama" (n.14, 228).

Works Cited

Awkward, Michael. "'The Crookeds with the Straights': Fences, Race, and the Politics of Adaptation." *May All Your Fences Have Gates: Essays on the Drama of August Wilson*. Ed. Alan Nadel. Iowa City: University of Iowa Press, 1994. 205–29.

Baldwin, James. "Sweet Lorraine." 1969. *The Price of the Ticket: Collected Nonfiction 1948–1985*. New York: St. Martin's, 1985. 443–47.

Baraka, Amiri. "The Revolutionary Theatre." *Home: Social Essays*. New York: Morrow, 1966. 210–15.

———. "A Critical Reevaluation: *A Raisin in the Sun*'s Enduring Passion." *A Raisin in the Sun and The Sign in Sidney Brustein's Window*. Ed. Robert Nemiroff. New York: New American Library, 1987. 9–20.

Childress, Alice. *Wedding Band: A Love/Hate Story in Black and White*. New York: Samuel French, 1973.

Cleage, Pearl. *Flyin' West*. New York: Dramatists Play Services, 1995.

Du Bois, W.E.B. *The Souls of Black Folk*. 1903. Ed. Henry Louis Gates Jr. and Terri Hume Oliver. New York: Norton, 1999.

Ellison, Ralph. *Invisible Man*. 1952. New York: Vintage, 1995.

Freedman, Samuel G. "A Voice from the Streets: August Wilson's Plays Portray the Sound and Feel of Black Poverty." *New York Times Magazine* March 15, 1987: 36–50. Accessed January 31, 2006 <http://proquest.umi.com>.

Fuller, Hoyt. "Towards a Black Aesthetic." *The Black Aesthetic*. New York: Doubleday, 1971. 3–16.

Gates, Henry Louis Jr. *The Signifying Monkey: A Theory of African-American Literary Criticism*. New York: Oxford University Press, 1988.

Gayle, Addison Jr. "Introduction." *The Black Aesthetic*. New York: Doubleday, 1971. xivi–xxiv.

Hansberry, Lorraine. *To Be Young, Gifted and Black: Lorraine Hansberry in Her Own Words*. Adapt. Robert Nemiroff. Englewood Cliffs, NJ: Prentice-Hall, 1969.

———. *A Raisin in the Sun*. 1959. New York: Vintage, 1994.

Harris, Trudier. "Folk Literature." *The Oxford Companion to African American Literature*. Ed. William L. Andrews, Frances Smith Foster, and Trudier Harris. New York: Oxford University Press, 1997. 282–86.

———. "A Raisin in the Sun: The Strong Black Woman as Acceptable Tyrant." *Saints, Sinners, Saviors: Strong Black Women in African American Literature*. New York: Palgrave, 2001.

Herrington, Joan. *"I Ain't Sorry for Nothin' I Done": August Wilson's Process of Playwriting*. New York: Limelight, 1998.

Hubbard, Dolan. "Sermons and Preaching." *The Oxford Companion to African American Literature*. Ed. William L. Andrews, Frances Smith Foster, and Trudier Harris. New York: Oxford University Press, 1997. 648–52.

Hurston, Zora Neale. *Mules and Men*. 1935. New York: Harper Perennial, 1990.

Kappel, Lawrence ed. *Readings on A Raisin in the Sun*. San Diego: Greenhaven Press, 2001.

Kennedy, Adrienne. *Funnyhouse of a Negro: A Play in One Act*. New York: Samuel French, 1969.

———. *The Alexander Plays*. Minneapolis: University of Minnesota Press, 1992.

Livingston, Dinah. "Cool August: Mr. Wilson's Red-Hot Blues." *Conversations with August Wilson*. Ed. Jackson R. Bryer and Mary C. Hartig. Jackson: University Press of Mississippi, 2006. 38–60.

Lyons, Bonnie. "An Interview with August Wilson." *Conversations with August Wilson*. Ed. Jackson R. Bryer and Mary C. Hartig. Jackson: University Press of Mississippi, 2006. 204–222.

Miller, Arthur. *Death of a Salesman*. 1949. New York: Penguin, 1976.

Mitchell, Loften. "I Work Here to Please You." *The Black Aesthetic*. New York: Doubleday, 1971. 290–305.

Neal, Larry. "The Black Arts Movement." *The Black Aesthetic*. New York: Doubleday, 1971. 272–90.

Pettengill, Richard. "The Historical Perspective: An Interview with August Wilson." *Conversations with August Wilson*. Ed. Jackson R. Bryer and Mary C. Hartig. Jackson: University Press of Mississippi, 2006. 155–71

Rocha, Mark W. "August Wilson and the Four B's: Influences." *August Wilson: A Casebook*. Ed. Marilyn Elkins. New York: Garland, 2000. 3–16.

Rosen, Carol. "August Wilson: Bard of the Blues." *Conversations with August Wilson*. Ed. Jackson R. Bryer and Mary C. Hartig. Jackson: University Press of Mississippi, 2006. 188–203.

Savran, David. "August Wilson." *Conversations with August Wilson*. Ed. Jackson R. Bryer and Mary C. Hartig. Jackson: University Press of Mississippi, 2006. 19–37.

Scanlan, Tom. *Family, Drama, and American Dreams*. Westport, CT: Greenwood Press, 1978.

Shange, Ntozake. *for colored girls who have considered suicide/ when the rainbow is enuf*. 1976. New York: Scribner Poetry, 1997.

Shannon, Sandra G. *The Dramatic Vision of August Wilson*. Washington DC: Howard University Press, 1995.

Shannon, Sandra G. and Dana A. Williams. "A Conversation with August Wilson." *August Wilson and Black Aesthetics*. Ed. Dana A. Williams and Sandra G. Shannon. New York: Palgrave Macmillan, 2004. 187–95.

Sheppard, Vera. "August Wilson: An Interview." *Conversations with August Wilson*. Ed. Jackson R. Bryer and Mary C. Hartig. Jackson: University Press of Mississippi, 2006. 101–17.

U.S. Department of Labor. *The Negro Family: The Case for National Action*. Washington DC: GPO, 1965. June 29, 2006 <http://www.dol.gov/oasam/programs/history/webid-meynihan.htm>.

Watlington, Dennis. "Hurdling Fences." *Conversations with August Wilson*. Ed. Jackson R. Bryer and Mary C. Hartig. Jackson: University Press of Mississippi, 2006. 81–89.

Wilkerson, Margaret B. "The Sighted Eyes and Feeling Heart of Lorraine Hansberry." *Black American Literature Forum* 17 (1983): 8–13. May 12, 2006 <http://www.jstor.org/search>.

Willis, Robert J. "Anger and the Contemporary Black Theatre." *Negro American Literature Forum* 8 (1974): 213–16. June 17, 2006 <http://www.jstor.org/search>.

Wilson, August. *Fences*. New York: Samuel French, 1986.

———. *The Ground on Which I Stand*. New York: Theatre Communications Group, 2001.

Wolfe, George C. *The Colored Museum*. New York: Broadway Play Publishing, 1985.

9

Folding and Unfolding History

Identity Fabrication in Suzan-Lori Parks's *Topdog/Underdog*

JENNIFER LARSON

Gwendolyn Brooks's Satin-Legs Smith "sheds, with his pajamas, shabby days"; his closet is a "vault," personified as having "innards" that are his glorious "wonder-suits" (43–44). Satin Legs Smith's clothes do not just influence his mood. They also help define his identity and express his emotions. They are at times "sarcastic," "cocky and determined as his pride," or even "hysterical" (44). Yet, Satin-Legs Smith is so much more than his clothes; he is also a lover, a dancer, and a man struggling, for "the pasts of his ancestors lean against/Him. Crowd him. Fog out his identity" (46).[1]

In Suzan-Lori Parks's *Topdog/Underdog* (2002), articles of clothing take on similar functions vis-à-vis characters' identities. Both Lincoln and Booth believe that switching identities involves merely taking off old or putting on new clothes, as an actor puts on a costume to get into character for a performance and then leaves that costume behind to return to his offstage life. Although this taking-off and putting-on approach to clothing applies most obviously to the Lincoln costume and Booth's "boosted" suits, other articles of clothing—such as the father's left-behind garments and the mother's money-filled(?) stocking—also influence the brothers' perceptions of themselves and each other. Even the "suits" of the cards in the brothers' 3-Card Monty game symbolize elements of the brothers' identities. As a whole in the play, clothes highlight the fluidity, exteriority, and superficiality of identity, especially in its relationship to history and memory, for as Lincoln and Booth recall national history and even their own pasts, clothes dominate their discussions. Thus, clothes *un-*

"make the man" in *Topdog/Underdog* because they distract audiences' or characters' gazes from the interiors of themselves or the other characters and take these gazes to the exterior, the superficial. Ironically, in *Topdog/Underdog* the superficial becomes so prominent in the characters' lives that eventually, mask and wearer become hard to separate, and the clothes the brothers wear and engage actually come to irrevocably define them. So, clothes also "(re)make the man," as the clothes and costumes in Booth's and Lincoln's lives come not only to signify elements of their identities but also to help them live out the fates their names—Lincoln and Booth, Topdog and Underdog—imply.

When considering clothes in the play, we must remember that Parks designed the text to be staged as well as read, and that in a play, clothes are not just clothes, but are also costumes, with all the implications that come with that label. "Costumes" are more complicated than mere clothes because they must both reveal and hide an identity. In any play, the costume designer's role "is not to give the actors 'something to wear,' not to 'make them look pretty,' not even to 'dress the stage'; rather it is to aid in the interpretation of the play as a whole and of each character in the play. A good costume becomes part of the actor's characterization; it clothes the character properly, so that the audience is never aware of the dress as separate from the character" (Barton 49).[2] A writer may use a costume to highlight elements of a character, and a character may put on that costume within the play to hide or highlight elements of himself. Lincoln's Lincoln costume epitomizes this hiding and highlighting. As with many costumes, the pieces include both a clothing and a make-up, and/or mask, component. Although the makeup alone functions as a mask—a covering of the face—a costume as a whole is also a mask, covering an actor's identity with another in order to wholly obscure.

In *Topdog/Underdog*, the Lincoln costume moves beyond mere characterization to come alive with virulent or parasitic sentience, possessing or infecting the characters with which it comes into contact. This life grows both from the significance and meaning with which history has imbued the suit, top hat, and white face, as well as from the life that it usurps from its wearer, Lincoln. At the beginning, the play suggests that it matters not if the Lincoln impersonator at the arcade is white or black, so long as he wears the right clothes: the "fake old" Lincoln costume. This costume becomes an all-inclusive signifier of Lincoln-the-President and has a hypnotic effect on those who come into contact with it, charming them into believing that whoever wears the costume is actually Lincoln-the-President. For Lincoln, the costume's effect is internal; it distracts and disrupts his view of his true interior self. For others, the costume shifts the gaze away from Lincoln-himself and onto the merely superficial, the Lincoln costume.

This effect is most evident in Lincoln's interaction with the boy on the bus. Although Lincoln consistently asserts that he does not like to wear his costume outside of work, he decides to forgo this preference in favor of not missing the bus home. On the bus, he meets a boy who asks him for his autograph. Lincoln explains, "I pretended I didn't hear him at first. I'd had a long day. But he kept asking. Theyd just done Lincoln in history class and he knew all about him, he'd been to the arcade but, I dunno, for some reason he was tripping cause there was Honest Abe right beside him on the bus" (11). The boy asks for Lincoln's autograph without realizing the superficiality of the situation or noting the obvious paradox of a black man in whiteface dressed as Lincoln, alive and on a city bus.

The kid has "done Lincoln" in his class so he "knew all about him." He had even been to the arcade earlier that day to shoot the man he knew so well. Yet, he cannot separate Lincoln-the-President from a Lincoln impersonator—he does not know actual history from a disparate facsimile. The play thus problematizes conventional historical knowledge and the modes of imparting it upon or sharing it with others, especially youth. Through the deceptive effects of the Lincoln costume, *Topdog/Underdog* shows history to be fluid and unstable because it allows itself to be so easily transferred onto an unrealistic paradigm that borders on the absurd—a black man in white face dressed up as Lincoln-the-President. As the play will later explore again with the arcade shooters, the sole way to make this paradigm viable rests on the boy's ability to focus exclusively on the Lincoln costume—time, place, and race must fade away. Subsequently, this boy's fluid and unstable version of historical knowledge, sanctioned by his whiteness, renders Lincoln's blackness—and thus a defining element of his identity—insignificant, or rather, invisible.

Throughout the play, with varying degrees of success, Lincoln himself struggles with this distinction between his own identity and that of Lincoln-the-President. At the beginning, Lincoln seems anxious to separate himself from the character that he plays. Like *Invisible Man's* jaded Vet, who advises the naïve protagonist to "play the game, but don't believe in it" (Ellison 153), Lincoln believes that he can be Lincoln and Lincoln-the-President because he thinks the costume is simply part of a con. When he realizes that he can make money off the boy on the bus, he considers asking for five dollars "cause of the Lincoln connection" but, he says, "something in me made me ask for 10" (11). That "something" is the player or trickster Lincoln that is—at least at this point in the play—totally distinct from Lincoln-the-President.

This early separation between Lincoln-himself and Lincoln-the-President becomes even more evident as Lincoln continues his story: "All he had was a *20.* So I took the 20 and told him to meet me on the bus tomorrow and Honest Abe would give him the change" (12). Lincoln knows that he is not honest nor is he Abe (Lincoln-the-President). Knowing that the next day he would ride the bus without his costume, invisible as Lincoln-himself (just a black man on a city bus), he completes his con of the rich boy to his own financial gain. Lincoln is making money from this scheme facilitated by the Lincoln costume, but the implications for black identity are grim. He is in danger of falling into the trap that Houston Baker believes characterizes Ellison's Trueblood. In *Invisible Man*, Trueblood becomes a kind of minstrel whose masking leads him to be ostracized by his own community and embraced by the white because he "has indeed accepted the profit motive that gave birth to the mask in the first place" (Baker 193).

Yet, Lincoln imagines that, like his predecessor, he will leave his Lincoln costume behind one day and walk off the job. He says:

> I said to myself thats exactly what I would do: wear it out and then leave it hanging there and not come back. But until then, I would make a living at it. But it dont make me. Worn suit coat, not even worn by the fool that Im supposed to be playing, but making fools out of all those folks who come crowding in for they chance to play at something great. Fake beard. Top hat. Dont make me into no Lincoln. I was Lincoln on my own before any of that. (30)

This early Lincoln provides a marked contrast to the Lincoln we see at the end of the play who does not, or perhaps cannot, remove the Lincoln costume. Here, at the beginning of the play, Lincoln asserts his personal identity clearly and distinctly. He also points out the historical inaccuracies and paradoxes inherent in the suit and emphasizes that for him, the Lincoln gig is just another hustle. He mocks his shooters' notions of historical transference.

Of course, Lincoln is not wearing the Lincoln costume when he speaks these lines in scene 1. He is not under its spell. He realizes here that the clothes alone are insignificant. The clothes are "fake" and "not even worn by the fool that Im supposed to be playing." These lines suggest that the characters in the play inscribe the clothes and costumes of *Topdog/Underdog* with the meaning, weight, and power that they take on in the play. Even if Lincoln wore Lincoln-the-President's actual suit, the suit itself would not carry meaning: the clothes themselves did not witness history; the wearer did. The clothes themselves are just empty signifiers; they are just cloth. Like a word, a name, or a mask, the audience brings the meaning to them and imbues them with significance based on experience. Historicized and racialized memory give the Lincoln costume both meaning and life.

Other African American writers, most notably Jamaica Kincaid, have exposed "clothing's ability to preserve within itself a sort of memory and to transmit that memory to successive wearers" (Matos 847). But, in *Topdog/Underdog*, the significance does not transfer from wearer to wearer—it is not the former impersonator that affects Lincoln. Rather, significance transfers exclusively from clothes to character based on the meaning put onto the clothes by that specific character. The character need not even put on the clothes, just interact with them. This transference applies to Lincoln's costume as well as all other articles of clothing in the play.

Neither Lincoln nor Booth wear their father's suits (Booth only imagines that he does) or their mother's money-filled(?) stocking, and the suits that Booth steals are new; previous wearers may have tried them on, but their influence on the imbued meaning of the boosted suits could only be fleeting.

The first time we see Lincoln, he has just come home from work wearing his Lincoln costume. The stage directions tell us that even though Lincoln sneaks up on Booth, "the presence of Lincoln doesnt surprise him, the Lincoln costume does" (9). In the lines that follow, Booth continues to express his revulsion, without explaining the root cause of it. Yet, Booth clearly, at least at this moment, does not express revulsion for Lincoln-himself—his past or present actions—but for the effects of the Lincoln costume, with all of its racial and historical baggage. In addition to calling his brother a "shiteating motherfucking pathetic limpdick uncle tom" (21), signaling not only emasculation but also racial assimilation,[3] Booth calls Lincoln "all spooked out and shit" (9) and tells him, "take off that damn coat, man, you make me nervous standing there looking like a spook, and damn that face paint, take it off" (11). In African American culture and literature, the term "spook"—evoked most famously by Sam Greenlee's 1972 novel *The Spook Who Sat by the Door*—can signify spy as well as a more pejorative, racialized insult. It also implies ghostlike spectrality, the ghosts of Lincoln-the-President as well as the brothers' familial past. So, when Booth repeats the term "spook," he layers these various meanings onto Lincoln. Though Lincoln is only wearing a costume and seems himself oblivious to its effects at this point in the play, Booth perceives that the costume completely demeans his brother. At best, Lincoln is a ghost, a shadow of himself who has given up his chosen profession as a card dealer and become reduced to the haunting image of a dead president and a dark era in American history. At worst, he is completely stripped of his identity, unrecognizable and undesirable even to his own brother; or, he is spy, a white man's pawn infiltrating his people. This conversation also foreshadows the merging of Lincoln and Lincoln-the-President later in the play as well as Lincoln's death at Booth's hand. Thus the play indicates early on the inevitability of the brothers' fates, fates anticipated by superficial, external elements—their names and Lincoln's costume.

Booth also expresses concern that seeing Lincoln in the costume will cause Grace to leave him. He explains, "She sees you in that getup its gonna reflect bad on me. She coulda seen you coming down the street. Shit. Could be standing outside right now taking her ring off and throwing it on the sidewalk" (10). The effects of the Lincoln costume are not limited to Lincoln and Booth. The clothes emanate an unpleasant aura, so powerful it can, theoretically, even negate the love of a woman. Yet, we never see Grace. Like the mother and the angry shooting housewives, she is always off-stage or remembered—a ghost or specter essentially invisible herself. If she indeed does not exist beyond Booth's imagination, then she can be read to represent the slippage of Booth's identity into insanity as well as his hope—for love, happiness, and, as her name implies, salvation. By claiming that the Lincoln costume has the power to negate Grace's love and her presence, Booth is essentially claiming that the costume—with all of its negative connotations about the past and the present—chases away any hope that he might have for the future.

Lincoln himself alludes to the negative aura of the Lincoln costume when he awakens in scene 4 still in his costume after sleeping in it. Although the previous scene begins the same way with no mention from Lincoln, this time, he is upset. After relieving himself, "He claws at his Lincoln getup, removing it and tearing it in the process. He strips down to his t-shirt and shorts" (54). He explains, "Hate falling asleep in this damn shit," and launches into an extended soliloquy in which he imagines killing his employer and reminisces fondly of his days as a hustler (54). Remarkably, in this soliloquy Lincoln oscillates, even within individual paragraphs, between the first, second, and third person, indicating that he struggles with self-definition and perspective: "Got yrself a good job. And when the arcade lets you go yll get another good job. I dont gotta spend my whole life hustling. Theres more to Link than that. More to me than some cheap hustle. More to life than cheating some idiot out of his paycheck or his life savings" (55). The shift in reactions to the Lincoln costume between the beginning of scene 3 and the beginning of scene 4 can be read as part of this struggle. The opening stage directions of scene 3 tell us only that Lincoln "is horrific, bleary eyed and hungover, in his full Lincoln regalia" (38). Thus, in this early moment, just one scene previous, Lincoln shows no fear or revulsion for the costume. So, we can assume that the events in the remainder of scene 3 catalyze some kind of change in Lincoln, change that brings him to the revulsion that we see at the beginning of scene 4 and the identity crisis that follows it.

Structurally, scene 3 is the center of the play. After Booth details his date with Grace, the action turns to Lincoln's description of his daily assassination at the arcade, and *(Rest)*s fill this description. Parks explains in "Elements of Style" excerpted at the front of the play that *(Rest)*s indicate "where the figures experience their pure true simple state" (3). Thus, in Lincoln's description of his daily assassination, we can assume that we hear the uninhibited thoughts of Lincoln, the "real deal" about his job as a Lincoln impersonator. He says, "Its pretty dark. To keep the illusion of the whole thing/ *(Rest)*" (49). We now see the emotional toll that Lincoln's job is taking on him. Dressed as Lincoln-the-President, he dies countless times a day, and he witnesses this assassination—his own assassination. But, he is a disembodied witness:

> But on thuh wall opposite where I sit theres a little electrical box, like a fuse box. Silver metal. Its got uh dent in it like somebody hit it with they fist. Big old dent so everything in it gets reflected upside down. Like yr looking in uh spoon. And thats where I can see um. The assassins.

> *(Rest)*
> [. . .] Me looking at him upside down and him looking at me looking like Lincoln. Then he shoots.
> *(Rest)* (49–50)

He sees his murder, but in reverse, upside down, and in a costume. Lincoln's gaze is on the reflection of his would-be assassin, but the assassin's gaze is on Lincoln "looking like Lincoln" in the Lincoln costume. And even though he is dressed as Lincoln-the-President, the murder is real to him because it is he, Lincoln, who is alive, not Lincoln-the-President:

> And there he is. Standing behind me. Standing in position. Standing upside down. Theres some feet shapes on the floor so he knows just where he oughta stand. So he wont miss. Thuh gun is always cold. Winter or summer thuh gun is always cold. And when the gun touches me he can feel that Im warm and he knows Im alive. And if Im alive then he can shoot me dead. And for a minute, with him hanging back there behind me, its real.
> *(Rest)* (50)

The assassins rely on sensing Lincoln's life—the softness of live tissue, the reaction of warm flesh to the cold metal barrel of the gun—to recreate Lincoln-the-President's death for sport; they resurrect Lincoln-the-President, through Lincoln, just to kill him again. However, Lincoln's black body only appears to bring Lincoln-the-President back to life for the assassins, for, as Lincoln intuits in this scene, the historical incongruities—again time, place, and race—can only suggest that they are shooting Lincoln-himself.

To make the imaginative leap to Lincoln-the-President, the arcade shooters must rely on Lincoln's invisibility as well as a completely constructed and superficial historical reality. Lincoln's dress, his Lincoln costume, rationalizes this construction and their shooting. The Lincoln costume allows them to believe that Lincoln-the-President is not dead and that they can remake history or place themselves within it by shooting a live version of him, even if that version is a black man in white face. Based on Lincoln's description, the dummy replacement of him *will* likely fail because the assassins will not be able to feel its life. The Lincoln costume truly functions here as a kind of possession or parasite; the suit feeds off the "historical" shooters but it needs a live host to thrive.

In this passage, Lincoln's descriptions of his assassins' clothes also deserve attention. The aggregate of these descriptions implies that a wide variety of Americans, young and old, male and female, come to the arcade to shoot Lincoln, to participate in historical re-creation. Thus, the play explores a variety of motivations for shooting a black man dressed as Lincoln-the-President. The businessmen come in "dress shoes," implying wealth and formality or power; killing Lincoln, for them, kills competition from African American businesses or businessmen (49). This wealth, formality, and power also highlight the disparity between Lincoln's socioeconomic status and their own. Children also come, but in "school uniforms"—implying education as well as conformity (50). Their presence not only reaffirms that children learn a skewed and corrupting view of history in school, as suggested earlier in the play by the boy on the bus, but also that white hegemonic views of race—indeed even the desire to kill a black man—are systematically instilled in American youth. The tourists in "theme park t-shirts," add a disturbing performative entertainment element, reminiscent of Parks's use of another Lincoln impersonator in her earlier work, *The America Play* (1994). Through that Lincoln impersonator, Haike Frank writes, "Parks suggests that our image of America is only representation. We influence and distort our perception of reality with premade concepts that are handed down from generation to generation without being reflected upon. Consequently, it is easy to understand how Abraham Lincoln is reduced to the tall man with the beard and stovepipe hat who was murdered in the theater" (16).[4] Fake or superficial history can be more easily packaged as fun.

The shooters sanction their desire to kill a black man by disguising it as the desire to participate in historical re-creation and by shifting Lincoln-the-President's identity onto Lincoln. The costume transforms him and allows the re-creation of history in addition to the rewriting of it with a new black victim. Even though Lincoln's blackness removes the authenticity of re-creating Lincoln-the-President, the assassins indeed still participate in historical recreation because, by writing in this black victim, they are essentially becoming members of a lynch mob, lining up to kill a black man. Day after day, they lynch him, killing him by rendering him everyday more invisible to himself because of his invisibility to them; with each shot, they slowly kill Lincoln by contributing to his transition into the real assassinated.

For they can, of course, see Lincoln's blackness. He wears only white*face* and they come from behind him, in full view of his black neck. But this very blackness renders Lincoln-himself invisible and allows the assassin's gaze to shift exclusively to the costume to give meaning to their actions. As Ellison's narrator explains with the "tall blond man" with whom he fights in the street, there are two types of seeing—one superficial, that allows a white stranger to insult a black man that bumps into him, another more meaningful, that cannot *see* the same rage-filled black man kicking and punching him. Invisible man remembers, "One night I accidentally bumped into a man, and perhaps because of the near darkness he saw me and called me an insulting name" (4). But as invisible man holds the stranger and starts "to slit his throat," he explains, "it occurred to me that the man had not *seen* me, actually" (4). Similarly, Lincoln's assassins see him, but they don't *see* him. They see that he is a black man, and thus they reduce him to a set of superficial and pejorative stereotypes—a laborer or a minstrel—and render him expendable. They do not *see* that he is Lincoln, a brother, a poor man who is struggling to survive and who is allowing himself to be killed to do so.

But there is also a black man who comes to the arcade, a man who sees beyond the costume. The brothers' brief exchange about this man oozes with ambiguity. For example, Booth asks Lincoln if the man is "a brother" and if the man knows that Lincoln is "a brother" (34). Lincoln answers both questions indecisively, highlighting the ultimate permeability of racial lines. Booth also calls this man Lincoln's "Best Customer" and is careful to ask Lincoln whether this black customer actually shoots. "He shoot you?" Booth inquires; Lincoln replies, "He shot Honest Abe, yeah" (33–34). In his answer to this inquiry, complicated by the threat of intraracial violence, Lincoln again seeks to draw a clear line between himself and Lincoln-the-President. He evokes the "Honest Abe" moniker he used when "hustling" the school boy on the bus, indicating a desire to inscribe his Lincoln arcade gig as just another con.

In his whispers to Lincoln, the shooter captures the same essence of superficiality implied by the play's use of clothing up to this point. He asks, "Does thuh show stop when no ones watching or does thuh show go on?" and tells Lincoln, "Yr only yrself [. . .] when no ones watching" (34). These whispered utterances highlight the performative nature of identity in *Topdog/Underdog*—who the brothers are changes based on who their audiences want and/or expect them to be. Under the white gaze, wearing the Lincoln mask, Lincoln is invisible. When he is with Booth, he is the Topdog, and he must perform the guarded big brother role that the volatile Underdog expects.[5] The only time we see Lincoln "when no ones watching" is scene 4. Here Booth is onstage, but he is "fast asleep, dead to the world" (54). Scene 4 consists entirely of Lincoln's monologue—or dialogue with himself—and as previously described, proves to be the most tumultuous scene in terms of Lincoln's identity.

Immediately before this scene, at the end of scene 3, Booth and Lincoln practice adding "spicy shit" to Lincoln's death scene (50). This practice at first amuses the brothers, but the mood changes significantly when Booth yells, "I am the assassin! *I am Booth!!* Come on man this is life and death! Go all out!" (52). Although he has only just shot Lincoln, dressed as Lincoln-the-President, with a pretend gun, Booth has internalized his role as Booth-the-actor, the assassin. The brothers could have just as easily practiced this scene without the Lincoln costume. The action is not physically contingent upon it. Yet, Lincoln puts on his costume expressly for this practice, waits for Booth, and then continues to wear it for a full scene, indicating that the action must be at least emotionally contingent upon it. Booth screaming "I am the assassin!" breaks down a psychological barrier between Lincoln's life and Lincoln-the-President's life and makes the superficial costume very real. At this point, Lincoln cannot separate himself from Lincoln-the-President because of the overwhelming superficial historical similarities. Booth's taking up of the Booth-the-actor role for the first time in the play compounds the effects of the Lincoln costume; the dominating superficiality, inspired by the Lincoln costume itself, has completely obscured both brothers' identities—both for themselves and for each other. In essence, the costume "creates" a new Booth that is Booth-the-actor. By the end of the play, Booth, as he slowly makes his full transition to assassin, will be completely unable to separate himself from the legacy of Booth-the-actor, the assassin after whom he is named.

The last line of Lincoln's scene 1 "Emancipation" proclamation—"I was Lincoln on my own before any of that"—though intended to assert independence from his costume, does leave room for this type of complication between the brothers. The grammar of this line suggests no difference between the first Lincoln and the second, and it creates a kind of equation between Lincoln and Lincoln-the-President. As Lincoln has been working at his job for some time, the equation could describe the cumulative effects of impersonating Lincoln-the-President; or, it could suggest something more historical. Simply by naming the brothers Lincoln and Booth (though the father meant it to be "a joke"), the play suggests interconnectivity within history and identity. Lincoln—as an American and especially as an African American—must have a set of cultural assumptions, though likely superficial or apocryphal, about Lincoln-the-President, "The Great Emancipator." The black Lincoln would have internalized those assumptions in some way because of his name and his brother's, even if only because of others' (such as the arcade owners' and perhaps even their parents') treatment of them. A brother and sister named Jack and Jill, for example, would likely have trouble not internalizing their nursery rhyme legacy, especially because of their peers' inevitable ruthless taunting. The Lincoln costume takes Lincoln further into the interconnectivity between himself and the historically loaded, yet still superficial, signifier "Lincoln," and the assassinations take him even further.

Indeed, when both brothers are disturbed by the reaction—the gruesome death scene—that comes after Booth screams "I am the assassin," Lincoln delivers one of the play's most poignant and memorable sets of lines: "People are funny about they Lincoln shit. Its historical. People like they historical shit in a certain way. They like it to unfold the way they folded it up. Neatly like a book. Not raggedy and bloody and screaming" (52). Although Lincoln is framing this metaphor with the image of a book, the language and the image do not match. We open and close books, not fold and unfold them. The point, of course, conveys clearly regardless: the history that we read in books is sanitized and superficial. But Lincoln's "folding" and "unfolding" applies more aptly to fabric, specifically clothing and especially his Lincoln costume. The Lincoln costume highlights that audiences will believe in, if not wholly prefer, an unbelievable Lincoln impersonator, a black man in whiteface dressed as Lincoln-the-President who dies quietly, only to come back to life again for the next customer to kill. When Booth becomes the assassin at the end of scene 3, Lincoln can no longer fold history, or the Lincoln costume, back up and put it away the way he found it; he cannot leave the suit behind. He claws desperately at the costume in scene 4 because the history is no longer superficial; it is deeply personal.

The play itself nearly immediately implies the application of this "folding and unfolding" metaphor to costume. The next set of lines pertains explicitly to the Lincoln costume and Lincoln's personal struggles with it. After a *(Rest)*, Lincoln continues, "I am uh brother playing Lincoln. Its uh stretch for anyones imagination. And it aint easy for me neither. Every day I put on that shit, I leave my own shit at the door and I put on that shit and I go out there and make it work. I make it look easy but its hard. That shit is hard. But it works. Cause I work it" (52). Here Lincoln more clearly acknowledges the personal identity sacrifice and self-displacement needed to put on the costume. He realizes here that in "[leaving his] own shit at the door" to put on the Lincoln costume, part of his own identity is being usurped by Lincoln-the-President's. He attempts to position himself as a master of masking, a skill—at least in the form *Invisible Man*'s grandfather describes—that can be very powerful and subversive if used correctly, but the subversive elements and the fulfillment that comes therewith are missing from Lincoln's mask. Rather, he again points only to the detrimental effects. He acknowledges the toll that the Lincoln costume takes on him when he must leave himself behind in order to put it on, thereby rendering himself invisible. Also, in admitting that "a brother playing Lincoln" would be "uh stretch" for his audience, he shows he has recognized that the assassins cannot logically believe that they are killing Lincoln-the-President; they are there to kill him. Lincoln thus identifies the role he plays in his own assassination. He has willingly accepted the superficiality that defines his invisibility—a superficiality that only "works" because he works it, plays it like a 3-Card Monty game. Having achieved this realization, the next time we see Lincoln wake up in his costume, at the beginning of scene 4, he tears it off—but not for long.

Lincoln's dualistic relationship with the Lincoln costume only deepens as the play draws to its close. When the arcade fires him, Lincoln comes home wearing part of the costume—the "frock coat"—and carrying the rest in a bag (60). He soon puts the entire suit back on so that Booth can take a picture of him in it, and he remains in the costume for the rest of his play, and as such, for the rest of his life (90). His co-dependence on the Lincoln costume shows in that he even ponders going back to beg for his job. To this, Booth responds, "Link. Yr free. Dont go crawling back. Yr free at last!" (62). By evoking the Emancipation Proclamation and the words of Dr. King, the play makes Lincoln's struggle timeless and equates his struggle with the Lincoln costume to a struggle for civil rights and personal freedom. But as in Dr. King's speech, these rights and freedoms, at least for Lincoln and Booth, are still just a dream. The brothers are bound by all that the costume signifies: revisionist history, slavery, racism, double-consciousness, poverty, and even their own personalities.

Lincoln coming home, fired, with his suit is especially significant because at the beginning of the play, as mentioned above, he insists he will leave it behind when he leaves his job. This gesture of leaving the clothes behind parallels both his father's and his mother's abandonments, both of which are memorized in the play by the clothes each parent left behind. The play links the father especially almost directly to the Lincoln costume in Lincoln's mind. After talking about his "fake old" work costume, Lincoln—following a *(Rest)*—makes the connection to his father: "Remember how Dads clothes used to hang in the closet?" (29). Booth then adds, "Until you took em outside and burned em./ *(Rest)*/ He had some nice stuff. What he didnt spend on booze he spent on women. What he didnt spend on them two he spent on clothes. He had some nice stuff. I would look at his stuff and calculate thuh how long it would take till I was big enough to fit it. Then you went and burned it all up." Lincoln responds, "I got tired of looking at em without him in em" and after another *(Rest)*, returns to the Lincoln suit: "They said the fella before me—he took off the getup one day, hung it up real nice, and never came back" (29).

This connection between the father and Lincoln-the-President highlights the formative role that both have played in Lincoln's identity as well as Booth's. Booth thinks that he can grow into being a man like his father, simply by growing into his clothes—thus transferring his father's identity onto himself. Lincoln, on the other hand, complicates the father's legacy. In other works, as Nicole Matos explains in her essay on the role of clothing in Jamaica Kincaid's novels, "The generic rebellion of destroying clothing often becomes paired with another, more specific rebellion, something absolutely, expressly forbidden" (Matos 850). *Topdog/Underdog* adopts a similar paradigm, but revises it subtly. Instead of exclusively signaling rebellion, Lincoln's motives are more paradoxical. In burning the Father's clothes, Lincoln both affirms and denies clothing's ability to imbue identity. For example, when Booth asks, "Whyd he leave his clothes though? Even drunks gotta wear clothes," Lincoln responds, "Whyd he leave his clothes whyd he leave us? He was uh drunk bro. He—whatever, right? I mean, you aint gonna figure it out by thinking about it. Just call it one of thuh great unsolved mysteries of existence" (89). Lincoln's response takes the emphasis away from the father's clothes and transfers it back on to where it belongs, the father's actions. The clothes cannot stand for the father because they are just a shell. "Without him in em," they are just an empty signifier. Yet, the clothes hold some significance, for they still can signal his absence and the pain associated therewith. If the clothes were truly meaningless, Lincoln would not need to burn them or allow them to hang around for so long before burning them.

This paradoxical relationship with his father's clothes mirrors the duality Lincoln fights when putting on the Lincoln costume. Indeed, in turning immediately from the father's empty suit to the empty Lincoln costume, the play equates the two absences, suggesting that "The Great Emancipator" is also missing, or has left the brothers specifically and black America in general. Rather than reject and burn Lincoln's clothes, as he does with his father's, Lincoln steps into them and attempts to play the role of Lincoln-the-President. This more politically and socially minded motivation resurfaces again at the end of the play when Lincoln puts on his costume and mask for the last time. In this final scene, Lincoln's whiteface mask signals impending civil war. He applies the white paint for Booth's photo in "two thin smears" that look "more like war paint than whiteface" (91). Although the play leaves his motives for such application somewhat ambiguous, Lincoln *will* battle his brother in an epic clash of ideologies and battle for power. This historical resonance suggests that even more than a domestic father, Lincoln needs a political leader. He cannot leave the Lincoln suit empty because to do so has social as well as personal implications—it leaves America without an emancipator, and more immediately, it leaves him and Booth without the money to survive and liberate themselves from poverty.

At the same time as Lincoln discusses leaving his costume behind and the father leaving his clothes behind, the men are dressing up in Booth's boosted suits. Booth steals predominantly clothes and accessories, superficial items that can easily be exchanged for others. Booth is essentially shopping (or shoplifting) for new identities, and his true identity remains mysterious. The play identifies him, on the character list page, as the Underdog to his brother and tells us very little else about him outside of his relationship to Lincoln. He tries to steal Lincoln's wife, and the first time we see him on stage alone—at the play's opening—he is playing Lincoln's game, 3-Card Monty. The only other time we see him on stage alone, at the beginning of scene 2, he "comes in looking like he is bundled up against the cold" in layers of boosted clothes (25). Booth proceeds to peel off the layers of clothing, and though we would expect to see Booth himself in this scene, since there is "no one watching," we see only layer upon layer of stolen clothes. And, his actions evoke humor, which "hides" him even more. As he peels off each layer of stolen identity, we never see the true Booth, only more clothes. Under his coat "he wears a very nice new suit. He removes the jacket and pants revealing another new suit underneath. The suits still have the price tags on them" (25). It is clear that Booth does remove the second suit at some point, since he later "lays one suit out on Lincolns easy chair" and another "on his own bed" (25). But, the stage directions do not tell us what Booth should be wearing under the second suit with the price tag—what he was wearing underneath all the layers, what he was wearing before he put on the first item he stole—nor do they express how or when he should remove the second suit with the price tag still on it. Thus, the written text of the play leaves Booth's final identity ambiguous, fluid—and essentially up to the audience or director to assign. Under the layers of superficial stolen identity, there is no deeper identity for Booth.

Also, since these actions are represented only in stage direction, this moment is a purely visual experience. Booth does not represent himself through language, but only through acts. His identity, then, can be read as strictly performative. This performance, however, reveals nothing beyond Booth's deliberate and artistic shoplifting skills, for the stage directions' disrobing description ends abruptly and without resolution when Lincoln enters the scene with his payload and they begin to role-play a Ma and Pa scene. The previous stage directions, then, serve only to highlight the superficiality of Booth's identity: it is entirely stolen.

Booth also steals His and Hers dressing gowns for himself and Grace to wear on their romantic date. Again, whether Grace even exists or still has a relationship with Booth fundamentally does not matter. In either case, his fascination with her and his linking of her with an article of clothing indicates further slippage of his identity; he is either faking wealth and privilege or falling further into insanity. When Grace fails to show up at the party that Booth has planned for them, and put on the costume that he has set out for her, we see, in essence, a failed fairy tale; Booth dresses up for the ball, but his princess never shows up. His vision of a perfect marriage to the woman of his dreams (whether she is make-believe or not) is thwarted. This fairy tale parallel allows us to situate *Topdog/Underdog* more firmly in the critical conversation about clothing's relevance in literature. Most scholars explore clothing's relationship to female characters exclusively, and, the "Cinderella Complex,"[6] as Mary Jane Lupton describes it, is a helpful paradigm through which to examine clothing's influence on women. Lupton defines the "Cinderella Complex" as "a dangerous cultural attitude towards women, digested early and constantly reinforced: By looking right, and dressing right, and attending the right dances, a woman can get out of working and be financially supported by, if not a prince, then at least a young male executive" (Lupton 409). Clothes then not only define identity, but also determine potential for success and marriage. In Booth's case, Grace signifies this success, and in failing to put on the identity he steals for her—thereby allowing him to put on the matching wardrobe—she thwarts his success.

So, although women are absent from the stage in the play, women's impact, influence, and valuation are not. Since clothing and the obsession therewith is typically socially defined as a women's concern, by making clothes a central concern for Lincoln and Booth, Parks not only challenges a stereotype, but also broadens—to include men—the scope of investigation into of the effects of society's image-consciousness on identity. Also, Parks consistently mentions in interviews that people think that the play is written by a man. Or, they question her credibility as a female artist writing about men.[7] Through clothes, then, Parks proves that audience expectations and overreliance on the importance of image can take its toll on any actor, male or female.

The play also foregrounds the feminine through the mother's money-filled(?) stocking, Booth's inheritance. This article of clothing, more expressly an undergarment and entirely feminized, becomes the fragile thread by which Booth's sanity, and perhaps his entire identity, hangs. In the Ma and Pa play, Booth plays the mother role, as he obviously identifies more with the mother in his family since she leaves him the inheritance despite the fact that he is the younger brother. Even at the beginning of the play, Booth threatens to gamble with this inheritance. However, Lincoln knows—at least at this point—that his brother is joking, and tells him, "Thats like saying you dont got no money cause you aint never gonna do nothing with it so its like you dont got it"—to which Booth retorts, "At least I still gots mines. You blew yrs" (17). Though on the surface the brothers are speaking of economic responsibility, they are also more subtly speaking of family ties. Lincoln, in spending his paternal inheritance, has at least started the process of dissociating himself from his father's legacy. Booth, in keeping the mother's money-filled(?) stocking, unsure of the monetary value of its contents, still defines himself in connection with this inheritance and, subsequently, his mother's abandonment. Therefore, when the brothers return to the subject later, Booth is again on the defensive as he describes the day his mother left and gave him the money-filled(?) stocking:

> She was putting her stuff in bags. She had all them nice suitcases but she was putting her stuff in bags.
> *(Rest)*
> Packing up her shit. She told me to look out for you. I told her I was the little brother and the big brother should look out after the little brother. She just said it again. That I should look out for you. Yeah. (21)

Thus, Booth's bequest from the mother is not exclusively economic. This matriarchal inheritance also gives him license to feel superior to Lincoln, for despite the fact that he is "the little brother," the mother designates him as the Topdog. Also, in the lines immediately following this description, Booth attempts to emasculate Lincoln by calling him a "shiteating motherfucking pathetic limpdick uncle tom" and screams "Here I am trying to earn a living and you standing in my way. YOU STANDING IN MY WAY, LINK!" (21). Contrary to any hopes that Lincoln might have of being a black "Great Emancipator," the mother's mandate, symbolized by the money-filled(?) stocking that accompanies it, binds Booth to Lincoln. Even though Lincoln actually supports his brother emotionally and financially,

Booth, seemingly based on the mother's final charge, makes his life and his identity contingent upon his brother's. The money-filled(?) stocking makes Lincoln a link, unseverable—save by death—that ties Booth to his brother.

Indeed, when that tie is severed, Lincoln dies. After Lincoln wins the money, the stage directions read simply, "Lincoln brings the knife down to cut the stocking" (107). Booth, previously laughing, stops the action with, "I popped her" and goes on to describe Grace's murder. Again, Grace's existence, already established as questionable, is irrelevant here. In killing his "grace," Booth has killed his hope and his capacity to forgive. So, he redefines himself again, telling his brother, "That Booth shit is over. 3-Cards thuh man now—" (108). By equating this murder and shift in personal definition with the threat of the money-filled(?) stocking's destruction, the play links elements of Booth's personality—most obviously his sanity and familial responsibility—to the article of clothing.

Seemingly sensing Booth's break with sanity, Lincoln tries to return the money-filled(?) stocking. Again, the stage directions read, "Lincoln brings the knife down to cut the stocking." But this time, "In a flash, Booth grabs Lincoln from behind. He pulls his gun and thrusts it into the left side of Lincolns neck. They stop there poised" (109). Lincoln then only utters one more word—"Dont"—before Booth kills him. Booth's impulsive murder of his brother in reaction to the threat of, or actual destruction of, the mother's money-filled(?) stocking imbues this article of clothing with multivalent meaning vis-à-vis the brothers' identities. First, the play questions the brother's common paternity through its focus on the mother's affairs. Lincoln gives voice to this suspicion earlier in this scene when he asks Booth, "I know we *brothers*, but is we really brothers, you know blood brothers or not." (103). By severing, or threatening to sever, the maternal tie, Lincoln removes any definitive familial tie to Booth. They are now just two *brothers* arguing over money and a con; there is no "link" connecting Booth to Lincoln or "standing in the way" of Booth getting his score.[8] When Lincoln takes possession of and possibly destroys the money-filled(?) stocking, he simultaneously invalidates and destroys the mother's mandate to Booth to watch over Lincoln. Booth is now a self-appointed Topdog with no sense of responsibility to the one he views as Underdog; thus, his vengeance is swift and bloody.

Ironically, it is at this point in the play, when Booth most vehemently and ruthlessly asserts his rejection of his name and of Lincoln, that he fulfills the elements of his identity that are most historically linked to Booth-the-actor. John Wilkes Booth-the-actor's words—"sic semper tyrannis" (as always to tyrants)—uttered upon shooting Abe Lincoln-the-President, suggest a power play; Booth now sees his brother just as Booth-the-actor saw Lincoln-the-President—as a ruthless demagogue poised and determined to destroy his identity and way of life. So, now he is Booth, killer of Lincoln. He is the assassin. Simply renaming himself does not secure 3-Card the separation he had envisioned. In the penultimate paragraph of the play, he shows that he finally understands this and expresses a still unfulfilled desire to break free: "Watch me close watch me close now: Ima go out there and make a name for myself that dont have nothing to do with you" (110). Yet again, he is determined to do so with Lincoln's game: 3-Card Monty.

With these lines, Booth also brings attention to another set of important suits in *Topdog/Underdog*, the "suits" of cards in the brothers' 3-Card Monty game. Three-Card Monty play not only opens and nearly closes the play, but also provides the narrative backdrop for Lincoln's pivotal soliloquy in scene 4. Card suits are divided into two groups, the red and black—clubs and spades versus hearts and diamonds. For the play's confidence men, Booth and Lincoln, these categories, more precisely, separate the winners from the losers. When Booth plays 3-Card Monty, the black card loses, and when Lincoln plays, the red card loses. These suits can be read as symbolic of each brother's identity. In trying to take on the role of "The Great Emancipator" by putting on the Lincoln suit, Lincoln privileges blackness and racial uplift. Lincoln is also the mouthpiece for the play's most astute observation about racial dynamics, expressed in terms of a card game:

> [. . .] you was in such a hurry to learn thuh last move that you didnt bother learning thuh first one. That was yr mistake. Cause its thuh first move that separates thuh Player from thuh Played. And thuh first move is to know that there aint no winning. Taadaa! It may look like you got a chance but the only time you pick right is when thuh man lets you. And when its thuh real deal, when its thuh real fucking deal, bro, and thuh moneys on the line, thats when the man wont want you picking right. He will want you picking wrong so he will make you pick wrong. (105–6)

In 3-Card Monty, Lincoln can win, but in life, he cannot. Racial discrimination has reduced him to poverty and lawlessness. White America, the play implies, is playing with a stacked deck, especially economically. Lincoln, then, looks for power wherever he can find it—even if it means playing the game, in Ellison's sense or in his own.

Booth, on the other hand, privileges violence—onstage and off—and looks to bloodshed and anger, both commonly associated with redness, when his brother and Grace do not fulfill the roles he has assigned them, or when, in Lincoln's case, Booth loses to a more worthy opponent. Also, in Booth's game, it is the heart that wins. The heart signals his dependence on the emotional, and perhaps even his complete rejection of the rational. The competition, and its bloody ending, links the 3-Card Monty play to the dozens tradition in which players must demonstrate verbal and intellectual prowess, and the competitor who first resorts to physical violence concedes to inferiority through his lack of self-control. Parks intersperses game play throughout *Topdog/Underdog,* and Booth loses the endgame, not only because

Lincoln is better at 3-Card Monty—especially since he uses emotional distraction to manipulate his brother—but also because Booth escalates the game from mere play, predominantly vocal, to physical violence and ultimately death. Equating 3-Card Monty with the dozens makes the struggle between Lincoln and Booth less personal and more essentially masculine and racial. When throwing the cards, Lincoln and Booth—on the surface just Link-the-stink and 3-Card, two street hustlers—compete to demonstrate their superiority. At the same time, they are also Lincoln and Booth, would-be assassinated and assassin, fighting to survive.

Overall, however, the play makes any analysis of identity difficult because the brothers, in many ways, seem be two sides of the same man. The stage then becomes a battlefield in which the two sides of his identity fight for dominance. Articles of clothing, in this interpretation, become intensely symbolic, linked to shards of fragmented and intense memory. As the stage-mind's players interact with these elements and are shaped by them, the overall identity—the aggregate of the stage-mind—evolves. When Lincoln dies, Booth initially claims his dominance through his unique possession of the money-filled(?) stocking—now called the "money-stocking" in the stage directions—his inheritance. But the play ends with screaming, an emotive release, rather than language. Only Booth and this money-stocking remain. There is no language, no card play, and no audience—just an insane, and perhaps unwilling, assassin alone with his left-behind article of clothing.

Notes

1. Gwendolyn Brooks, *Blacks*. Chicago: Third World Press, copyright, 1991. Reprinted by consent of Brooks Permissions. All rights reserved.
2. There is surprisingly little criticism on general methods of costume interpretation. However, work on costuming techniques provides a provocative bridge between the literary and the material. For example, in his essay "Research in Theatrical Costume," Patton Campbell writes, "The costume business is one of subterfuge" because even in the creation of a costume, a designer must invent methods to make the durable look fragile, the bold look subtle, and the new look old (287). This type of subterfuge, of course, is at work in *Topdog/Underdog*'s Lincoln costume.
3. Booth uses similar language in scene 3. Lincoln wears his Lincoln costume again, and Booth taunts, explicitly linking Lincoln's costume to his emasculation, "Yr dick, if it aint falled off yet, is hanging there between yr legs, little *whiteface* shriveled-up blank-shooting grub worm. As goes thuh man so goes thuh mans dick" (45, my emphasis).
4. Frank also goes on to say more about the relevance of entertainment culture in general. Frank believes that, in *The America Play,* "The fact that the public shows greater interest in Lincoln's murder than in his political speeches and, by implication, his political deeds, points to the dominance of fragmentation and the power of sensationalism in society. Additionally, this

implicitly criticizes television's instant replay, which allows and also forces us to view, for example, a NASCAR crash, the explosion of the Challenger, or the destruction of the federal building in Oklahoma City, over and over again. Thus, the image with its brutal and tragic moment, is engraved into our consciousness, yet it is also reduced by repetition into absurdity" (12). The play also "suggests that the next generation will only know Lincoln as an activity, as an element in an amusement park and thus, the life story of Lincoln risks being reduced completely to his death scene. This could be seen as a critique of the power of entertainment in modern American society. It could also be interpreted as the public's need to reduce historical figures to one dramatic item or movement, for instance, Julius Caesar saying 'Et tu Brute,' Adolf Hitler declaiming and mustached or John F. Kennedy being shot in the motorcade." (12)

5. Jeffery Wright, who played Lincoln both in *Topdog/Underdog's* 2001 debut at the Public Theatre and in its 2002 Broadway debut, reflects on the parallel relationship between Lincoln's role at his job and his role in his family: "I do like the whiteface Lincoln wears. I like the inflection of this subsistence mask that is seemingly necessary and at the same time suffocating. I like this struggle to maintain a societal relationship that requires an amputation or a facade. That a relationship with your brother is predicated on the suffocation of yourself" (Tate 2).
6. Lupton borrows this term from Collette Dowling's book of the same title.
7. In a *Christian Science Monitor* article, for example, Parks says, "It's also experimental as a woman to write a play that just involves two men and to write it so well that people think a man wrote it" (Fanger 2), and in the documentary *Topdog Diaries: An Intimate Portrait of Playwright Suzan-Lori Parks*, she claims to have been told, "You must have a dick."
8. This reading also reconciles my interpretation with Parks's assertions about her play, reported in *Crisis*: "It ain't about the white man," Parks says quietly. "It ain't about the legacy of slavery at all. It's about these two men who are brothers and don't get along. They love each other intensely and have come through so much together, and are at each other's throats almost all the time. And that is worth talking about, too" (Bryant 44).

Works Cited

Baker, Houston A. *Blues, Ideology, and Afro-American Literature: A Vernacular Theory.* Chicago: University of Chicago Press, 1984.

Barton, Lucy. "A Major in Costume." *Educational Theatre Journal* 2.1 (1950): 48–51.

Brooks, Gwendolyn. "The Sundays of Satin-Legs Smith." *Blacks.* Chicago: Third World Press, 1987, 43–48.

Bryant, Aaron. "Broadway, Her Way." *Crisis* 109.2 (2002): 43–45.

Campbell, Patton. "Research in Theatrical Costume." *Educational Theatre Journal* 19.2 (1967): 286–88.

Ellison, Ralph. *Invisible Man.* New York: Vintage, 1952.

Fanger, Iris. "Pulitzer Prize Winner Shakes Off Labels." *Christian Science Monitor* 12 April 2002: [3pp.]. Online edition. 17 February 2006 <http://www.csmonitor.com>.

Frank, Haike. "The Instability of Meaning in Suzan-Lori Parks's *The America Play.*" *American Drama* 11.2 (2002): 4–20.

Greenlee, Sam. *The Spook Who Sat by the Door.* London: Allison and Busby, 1969.

Lupton, Mary Jane. "Clothes and Closure in Three Novels by Black Women." *Black American Literature Forum* 20.4 (1986): 409–21.

Matos, Nicole C. "'The Difference Between the Two Bundles': Body and Cloth in the Works of Jamaica Kincaid." *Callaloo* 25.3 (2002): 844–56.

Parks, Suzan-Lori. *Topdog/Underdog*. New York: Theatre Communications Group, 2002.

Tate, Greg. "Lincoln in Whiteface: Don Cheadle and Jeffrey Wright, the Battling Brothers of *Topdog/Underdog*." *The Village Voice*, July 25 2001: [3pp.]. Online edition. February 17, 2006 <http://www.villagevoice.com>.

Topdog Diaries: An Intimate Portrait of Playwright Suzan-Lori Parks. Oren Jacoby, director. Image Entertainment, 2004.

10

"With Deliberate Calculation"

Money, Sex, and the Black Playwright in Suzan-Lori Parks's *Venus*

JENNIFER LARSON

Some form of the word "complicity" appears in nearly every critical and scholarly examination of Suzan Lori-Parks's *Venus* (1996), the fictionalized life story of Saartjie Baartman, The Venus Hottentot, who performed in England and France in the mid-nineteenth century. *Venus* follows a young South African woman (The Girl) who agrees to go to England to make "a mint" as an "exotic dancer" who shows off her ample buttocks and perhaps her genitals (20). Not long after her arrival in England, however, The Girl's "business partner" leaves her with the greedy Mother-Showman, who transforms The Girl into The Venus and puts her on display in a cage and charges admission to see her. The Venus is "rescued" by The Baron Docteur, a rich man with whom she has a love affair, but who eventually abandons her to die so that he can dissect her corpse and become a famous anatomist.

Most interpretive questions about the play and Parks's motive for creating it center on whether Parks and her version of The Venus Hottentot contribute to black female exploitation as well as whether Parks and her Venus are working for or against what critics generally describe as some version of oppressor, exploiter, colonizer, or white sexist and racist hegemony (and to what degree). These critics generally engage this question of complicity in the play with an eye toward either completely indicting Parks and her Venus or completely exonerating them. Yet, I argue in this chapter, the play suggests both.

In her essay "new black math" (2005) Parks presents a poetic manifesto on the nature of African American theater. She writes, "A black play is simple./ A black play is COMPLICATED" (583). These lines—one of many paradoxical descriptions in the essay—indicate that, for Parks, theatrical work is inherently contradictory and messy. So, in *Venus*, she and her Venus can be working within, as well as against, the forces that oppress them. The seemingly illogical nature of this paradox does not destabilize the linear narrative of the play or its revolutionary implications, because, as Parks suggests, "A black play is double voiced but rarely confused" ("new black math" 576).

So, in *Venus*, what appears to be complicity may be simultaneously read as subversive agency. The play's protagonist, The Venus,[1] acts with what Harriet Jacobs calls "deliberate calculation," opting for a life based on personal choice rather than external force. Parks's protagonist chooses potential fame and fortune in a form of exploitation she hopes she can live with over certain slavery as well as unknown and potentially unbearable exploitation. The play makes economics a central factor in this decision, and, significantly, in many of the meta-performative aspects of the play—including the greed that eventually leads to The Venus's death and "scientific" display. As such, *Venus* parallels the plight of The Venus, as well as other characters in the play, with that of the modern African American playwright. The modern playwright must choose between catering to the paying public—white and black—and thus allowing her plays to be seen (and read); or, the playwright can hope to be miraculously discovered but will more likely face obscurity. At the same time, however, by writing Baartman's story for the stage, the original site of her exploitation, and by profiting from the presentation of this story, Parks maps the theater as a productive and profitable (though still problematic) healing space for African American playwrights. *Venus* as a whole, then, reinforces Parks's descriptions of the paradoxical nature of black plays.

The Venus's agency on stage also reasserts and de-pathologizes the black female claim to sexual autonomy, a move that channels Jacobs's similar assertions in *Incidents in the Life of a Slave Girl* (1861). Jacobs's description of her "deliberate calculation" comes after she has decided to choose a lover—one whom she does not love—rather than be raped by her master. Similarly, The Venus still faces sexual exploitation in private and public, but her influence over the Baron Docteur and other men in the play does allow her some power and economic advantage that she ordinarily would not have. When their sexual deviance and greed become too potent even for her shameless sexuality to overcome, her agency—as well as her life—are lost.

Parks comes under heavy fire from critics such as Jean Young, who objects to what she sees as *Venus*'s ahistorical portrayal of "Baartman's complicity in her own exploitation" (699). Young argues that Parks's Venus "reifies the perverse imperialist mind set, and her mythic historical reconstruction subverts the voice of Saartjie

Baartman" (700). *New York Times* theater critic Ben Brantley agrees that Parks "doesn't present Baartman as just an uncomprehending victim," but he applauds this decision and the play's accessibility to a broad audience (3). Anne Davis Basting, on the other hand, citing Parks's repetition of the phrase "Do I have a choice?" and the presence of a flashing "no" sign in the Public Theatre's staging of the play, sees the characters in *Venus* as caught up in "physical and economic threats and the weighty momentum of colonialism and sexism" (225). The Venus certainly engages the imperial/hegemonic/white power with innovative and creative tactics, but these tactics are not historically unique.

Jacobs provides a model of a nineteenth-century woman who claimed agency through what some might call complicity—choosing a relationship with a white man. Complicity implies not only consent, but also, in it purest form, cooperation or collaboration in a completely malignant enterprise. Agency, on the other hand, most simply implies embracing the potential for action—with no moral judgment implied—that serves as an instrument to an end, especially a subversive end. So, in both Jacobs's and The Venus's case, we cannot definitely call their decisions complicity, for both the morality and the extent of their shares (monetary and otherwise) in the endeavor are questionable. Even if they were equal partners with their oppressors in an endeavor that might be judged evil, accepting this alliance could still be called agency and still be subversive if it brought them some measure of freedom.

The play addresses this agency/complicity at its opening and its closing. Near the beginning and the end of *Venus*, we find what can be read as the "bottom line," or the moral of the story. At the beginning of the play, the The Mans Brother, later The Mother-Showman, later The Grade School Chum—a conglomeration of three of the play's most despicable characters—speaks the lines. This conglomeration asserts, "Tail end of r tale for there must be an end/ is that Venus, Black Goddess, was shameless, she sinned or else/ completely unknowing of r godfearin ways she stood/ totally naked in her iron cage" (5). But later, in her penultimate utterance of the play, The Venus herself delivers a slightly revised and expanded version of the same lines. She offers:

> Tail end of the tale for there must be uh end/ is that Venus, Black Goddess, was shameless, she sinned or else/ completely unknowing thuh Godfearin ways she stood/ showing off her ass in her iron cage./ When Death met Love Death deathd Love/ and left Love tuh rot/ *au naturel* end for thuh Miss Hottentot./ Loves soul, which was tidy, hides in heaven, yes, thats it/ Loves corpse stands on show in a museum. Please/ visit. (161)

Both lines portray The Venus as an unrepentant sinner, standing before her spectators. Yet, both lines also highlight her captivity. She does not cower or hide, but she is, after all, in an "iron cage."

Considering the repetition and revision (what Parks calls "rep and rev")[2] between the two passages, however, reveals much more complexity. The Venus asserts her individuality by changing the "r" to "thuh," making it individual, rather than collective. At the same time, she resists letting the story define her, for she does not call it "my" tale. She makes a similar article change before "godfearin," which she also revises with capitalization to "Godfearin." This move not only channels The Venus's conversion to Christianity earlier in the play, but also moves the locus of moral power away from The Mother-Showman and the spectators to a higher, more holy, moral arbiter.

Also, both passages contain the word "shameless," but the characters uttering this word have used it differently throughout the play. The Mother-Showman, for example, tells one of her customers that The Venus's "heathen shame is real" and immediately turns to Venus to say, "Lets give these folks their moneys worth" (46). The Mother-Showman assumes that the exposed Venus, who refuses to remove the small cloth covering her genitals because "its custom" (29) and whose "face was streamed with tears" (47) as she stood in her cage, expressed shame through her modesty and sadness. When The Mother-Showman says "shameless," she asserts that The Venus has grown so accustomed to her shame, to being locked in a cage and stared at—or touched—by strangers, that she is numb to it. However, according to Harry Elam and Alice Rayner, "There is no moment, in fact, when Saartjie really does seem to accept her circumstances or her treatment as shameful. Terrible, filthy, miserable, brutal, but never shameful. In the refusal of shame, she maintains an innocence that is not complicity; if it is still within the systems of oppression, it is nevertheless resistant" (277). "Shame" implies that The Venus has complete control over the situation that puts her on stage and makes her a spectacle.[3] Although she comes to find agency *within* her situation, she never has power *over* it. Like Harriet Jacobs, who regrets the actions to which the "demon slavery" drives her, The Venus, or at least the authorial voice behind her, also seems to claim—in the words of her contemporary—that those "whose homes are protected by law" and "whose purity has been sheltered from childhood," should not "judge the poor desolate slave girl too severely!" (Jacobs 83–84).

For The Venus, what would be truly "disgraceful" would be "to go home penniless," and she finds her agency in the promise of economic prosperity (75). When the Man and The Brother present their scheme for an exotic exhibition in England to The Venus, then The Girl, and tell her of her central role and her supposed share in the profits, she dreams "I would have a house./ I would hire help./ I would be rich. Very rich./ Big bags of money!" but then asks "Do I have a choice? Id like to think on it." The Brother, like the Baron Docteur later in the play, only answers her question with a question: "Whats there to think on? Think of it as a vacation!/ 2 years of work take half the take./ Come back here rich. Its settled then" (17). From

The Girl, he demands another answer and thus clearly establishes himself as master of the conversation, and indeed, the entire situation. Even The Brother's comment that follows, "Think it over, Girl. Go on./ Think it all over," is phrased more like an order than a reassurance of actual choice (17). This is relevant, of course, because The Girl does have a choice, but—like Jacobs's choice—it is the choice between one evil and a lesser evil.

According to Young, one of the play's harshest critics, "Parks frames the scenario around Baartman (The Girl) in this regard: She is a liberated and sovereign individual, capable, willing, and with the authority to control her circumstances and make choices," and this is problematic because it minimizes The Girl's oppression and makes her appear fully complicit in this oppression (700). But again, agency or choice and complicity need not and should not be equated. The Girl's choices only include willingly going with the men, or, denying The Man and his Brother, which would likely have resulted either in her kidnapping or in her remaining a slave in Africa. If she signs their contract, she may get the fame and money (or at least a portion of it) they have promised in a country that might be more sympathetic to her oppression, for there, the men tell her, she could be "a Princess" and there will be "a whole street full" of women just like her (16). This, ultimately, is choice—though not complete freedom. When The Chorus of the Court asks, "Are you here of yr own free will/ or are you under some restraint?" The Venus evades the question and responds only with "Im here to make a mint" (75). She has embraced what little agency she has and is using it to move toward the more hopeful and potentially more economically viable option, but she will not call this "free will."

A look at Jacobs's history shows that such an unattractive choice was sometimes the only option available to a black woman in the nineteenth century and thus, Parks's depiction of The Venus might not be as ahistorical as Young alleges. Jacobs describes how she knew her situation was dire, for "The influences of slavery had had the same effect on me that they had on other young girls; they had made me prematurely knowing, concerning the evil ways of the world" (83). So, she writes, "I know what I did, and I did it with deliberate calculation" (83). She goes on to hail the minor liberation, "something akin to freedom" that comes from choice, in that "it seems less degrading to give one's self, than to submit to compulsion" (84–85). Jacobs also admits to an economic element of her agency: "Of a man who was not my master I could ask to have my children well supported; and in this case, I felt confident I should obtain the boon" (85–86). In her white lover, Jacobs—who knew she was destined for sexual oppression—finds a way to use her agency to secure her children's security, and perhaps even their freedom. Thus, in Jacobs, we find a model of nineteenth-century black womanhood that can help us understand *Venus*'s assertion of agency as subversive. In her version of "the bottom line," The Venus revises the earlier description of her standing "totally naked" to one of herself "showing off her ass," evoking the slang phrase for challenging authority with blatant defiance.[4] Elizabeth Brown-Gulliory examines this moment in conjunction with The Venus's earlier "Do I have a choice?" line which, she maintains:

> speaks volumes in identifying a woman, as figured in Parks's imagination, who conceivably could have chosen between subjugation by the Dutch colonizers in her native South Africa and exploitation with the possibility of some monetary reward in England and France. One way to read Venus—alias Saartjie—is as an insurgent female character who understands that though she remains an object of patronymic exchange, she also remains capable of resistance. Interestingly, borrowing from the black vernacular, Venus chooses to "show her ass" as a strategy of resistance. (194)

As the play goes on, it becomes clearer that The Girl/The Venus knows the limits of her choices. For example, when the Brother declares his desire for her after they arrive in England, The Girl responds, "Home?/ Love?/ You outta take me shopping. I need a new dress./ I cant be presented to society in this old thing" (23). Here the Girl questions or problematizes the options that seem to be available to her—but ultimately are not—and speaks declaratively of the only certainties she has known: greed and economic or sexual exploitation.[5] She uses her seduction for material gain, knowing that The Brother and The Baron Docteur will eventually abandon her. Problematizing the options also suggests that this material gain is not The Venus's ideal choice. "Scene 22: Counting the Take/ The Deal that Was" is one of the most obviously money-focused in the play as The Venus and The Mother Showman count the money—The Venus in multiples of ten, the Mother-Showman in hundreds. In this scene, The Venus mentions she could "spruce up" her performance by reading poetry. The Mother-Showman responds only with "Count!" indicating that The Venus's desire to express herself through poetry and art will remain unfulfilled because unlike her, the oppressor does not see it as economically viable (51).

Venus also ends her "bottom line" with a poetic addition: "When Death met Love Death deathd Love/ and left Love tuh rot/ *au naturel* end for thuh Miss Hottentot./ Loves soul, which was tidy, hides in heaven, yes, thats it/ Loves corpse stands on show in a museum. Please/ visit" (161). Parks returns to the issue of being "tidy" in "new black math," when she reflects on the changes that have shaped her understanding of black theater since the publication of a previous essay on the subject, "The Equation for Black People on Stage" (1995).[6] She writes that although there are some similarities in the conversations about the trajectory of the art and of her own aesthetic, there are also key differences: "I was tidy back then. And now Im tidier. Tidier today like a tidal wave" ("new black math" 576). What appears simple at first glance, this suggests, is actually overwhelming and potentially destructive or iconoclastic. The end of The Venus's bottom line, then, is just another paradox. Even as The Venus dies, a victim of the exploitation of her spectators, she still craves more viewers.

Herein lies one of the most compelling connections between The Venus and the African American playwright: the playwright needs, perhaps even craves, an audience. But as with The Venus, questions arise about the lengths to which a black playwright must go to attract this audience, to fill the theater seats with paying customers. Ultimately, the black playwright must sell black life, black history, and the black experience to a predominantly white audience, and so like The Venus, the playwright straddles the line between complicity and agency. Again, Parks explains the situation in terms of a paradox: "A black play knows that racerelations sell./ A black play knows that racerelations are a holding cell" ("new black math" 580). The very spectacle that makes "a mint" may be the spectacle that puts the writer and the audience in a metaphorical "iron cage."

In creating these parallels between The Venus and the playwright, it is difficult to make distinctions between Parks's agency, the historical Baartman's agency, and the fictionalized Baartman's agency. Young is one of the few critics who attempts to do so by drawing on court documents and other records. But so many critics insist on bringing Parks's intent into the discussion of the play—even though authorial intent is so often dismissed or unknown—that the trend begs additional examination. In addition, Parks's comments on the play are typically ambiguous. As with her other plays, her paradoxical and obtuse observations about *Venus* vary widely by interview and ultimately shed little light on interpretive issues, for they both discount and support nearly every possible critical perspective. Ironically, it is also in the context of discussing *Venus* that Parks denies her individual aesthetic. In "Tradition and the Individual Talent" (1999) Parks writes, "someone once told me, '*Venus* isn't really a Suzan-Lori Parks play.' To which I responded: 'There isn't any such thing as a Suzan-Lori Parks play'" (28–29). Parks's answer becomes more significant when we read *Venus* as a commentary on the theater audience's expectations, for here, Parks seemingly denies her aesthetic culpability in not meeting these expectations. In this essay, Parks goes on to criticize such fidelity in economic terms. She claims that "once Miss X buys into the existence of an Xian style of writing and once that purchase keeps her simply and stupidly repeating her last best hit, well, then Miss X gets really stinky—no matter in what genre she writes or in what camp she parks, naturalists, realists, avant-gardists, or experimentalists" (29).

So, why forsake avoiding intentional fallacy and look so much to the author and her intent in *Venus*? Aja Marneweck asserts, "In contemporary African American theatre, there is a strong link between feminist critical intention in the work of playwright Suzan-Lori Parks and issues of race and stereotype" (53). Ultimately, Marneweck believes that "the play was criticized as racist because there was no authorial voice challenging the stereotypes presented in the play" (54). In *Venus*, audiences want to hear the voice of Parks, one of the most celebrated, most visible, and most challenging modern African American writers. Yet, this desire proves ultimately insatiable, for to do so would undermine the more creative, subtly subversive elements of the play and let the audience off the hook, for "in many ways, the story makes the racism and sexism seem too obvious; the circus sideshow aspect more subtly demonstrates our inevitable complicity in viewing the body" (Elam and Rayner 272). The plays and shows within the play make it impossible to deny that *Venus*, at least in part, is about the nature of spectacle and, by extension, the creation of that spectacle. Thus, the play can be read as pertaining to Parks and her contemporaries and the audiences they seek/need.

Yet, Parks clearly and willingly surrenders control of her text to the reader, actor, and director in her *(Rest)*s and Spells,[7] which "directors should fill [. . .] as they best see fit" (*Venus* "Author's Note"), as well as the text she brackets for omission; at the same time, *Venus*'s form often feels very imposing. Her unique language, which Kimberly D. Dixon describes as "perfectly suited to act as a force on actor or audience" (54), evokes the politics of black vernacular—written and spoken—but Parks repeatedly denies that she is attempting to represent vernacular speech or the vernacular tradition. Brown-Guillory attributes this use of alternate word forms to Parks's thwarting of hegemonic models of discourse. She writes, "[Parks] rejects any attempt at representing the unrepresentable in European-based discourse," and "much of what her characters speak supplies a performative rendition of their splintered selves occupying a liminal space [. . .]" (195). Through her unconventional language and her ambiguous *(Rest)*s and Spells then, Parks actively rejects complicity with dominant power structures by rejecting those structures' linguistic and dramatic forms.

Economics becomes a factor in these formal concerns because in order for Parks's rejection to be its most potent, her art must find a wide audience and readership. And since in publishing, as Lyman points out, "cost, not nuance is of necessity a principle concern," Parks's very specific formatting stylistics may someday be edited out to trim the price of her volumes (96). In the meantime, though, these differences draw attention to her work, and situate her in a position of ultimate textual authority—she is the only one who can edit her manuscripts. From a nineteenth-century perspective, as Harriet Jacobs's and other narrators' histories remind us, this particular agency is precious. But from a Broadway perspective, a playwright who wants success must consider how to create a play that appeals to the widest theater-going audience. Parks writes in "Tradition and the Individual Talent" that young and old writers are "both trying to write the next Broadway hit while not listening to the voice that wants to write that small, challenging downtown play" and that these compromises signify the "horrid dead ends of writing" (30).

But Parks's most recent plays *have* been Broadway hits, and she has moved on to the other, perhaps even more insidious box office, the Hollywood box office, by writing screenplays for Oprah Winfrey and Spike Lee.[8] She may be aiming for "challenging," but she is certainly not aiming for "small." Plus, Broadway audiences, polls show, are predominately white and wealthy, and according to the most recent research sponsored by the National Endowment for the Arts, the percentage of the African American population that attends non-musical plays has actually declined since 1992.[9] According to the 1992 data, "Participation rates for African Americans more than doubled from 5.8 percent in 1982 to 12.0 percent in 1992," with most of the increase from non-profit theater (2). However, according to the 2002 report, this participation rate had declined to 7.1 percent of the African American population (16). African Americans, in 2002, constituted 6.6 percent of the non-musical play audience, on and off Broadway. In contrast, white viewers constituted 84.1 percent of the non-musical play audience in 2002 (14).

In his 1937 *Negro Poetry and Drama*, Sterling Brown writes of the fundamental importance of the black audience to a black playwright. "Without their own audience," he claims, "they are doubly handicapped" (139). In an interview with *Crisis* before the Broadway opening of *Topdog/Underdog* in 2002, neither Parks nor George C. Wolfe specifically mention the need to bring in black audiences, though both speak of a need for "new audiences" (qtd. in Bryant 44). Wolfe points to the stars of the production, Mos Def and Jeffrey Wright, "both artists who have had success with popular culture," as the main draw (qtd. in Bryant 44). In so doing, however, Wolfe seems to be banking on an audience that comes to the theater not because of an interest in the art on stage but because of an interest in the movie stars on stage. The audience that values "popular culture" will likely expect to see the stereotypes and distorted images of African Americans that popular culture perpetuates. This is exactly the kind of audience that Sterling Brown despised, the kind that "frequently wants flattery instead of representation, plaster saints instead of human beings, drawing rooms instead of the homes of the people" (123).

And this is just the type of audience, black and white, that *Venus* criticizes. *Venus* portrays them as a sex-crazed chorus who want their money's worth, fueling the Mother-Showman's greed and demanding "Gimmie gimmie back my buck!" when The Venus dies (5, 161). But rather than only indict the audience—though they do often transgress beyond the gaze—the play places blame on those who put The Venus on stage: The Mother Showman and The Baron Docteur. Thus, the play seems to indict Parks, as she puts *Venus* on stage. Elam and Rayner question "Parks's own use and display of Baartman's story: for she too is making money from a repetition and spectacle of Baartman, exploiting her even as she tries to help" (269). As part of her work, Parks makes The Venus and her own art the spectacle, and the success of the work is measured by box office returns, at least in some degree. The degree we choose determines the degree to which Parks and The Venus are complicit in their own exploitations.

Anne Basting is among a few critics who also parallel The Venus or Parks and The Negro Resurrectionist. She writes, "The Negro Resurrectionist/Watchman faces a decision similar to Venus's before him. Forced to promise delivery of her body for the autopsy, he ponders his limited choices: loss of his job and the certain ensuing poverty, or honoring the bones of the dead" (225). This decision is also reminiscent of the choices the black playwright faces, and indeed many black artists face, when choosing whether to write what will sell or what pays homage to what Parks calls "the numerous hard times" past and present ("new black math" 579). More specifically, Christopher Innes notes that "like her own character, the Negro Resurrectionist, [Parks] brings dead figures back to life on her stage in new configurations to liberate and re-appropriate history" (106). Neither Basting nor Innes, however, examines this relationship's more problematic aspects. It is the Negro Resurrectionist, after all, who sells Venus's body, damming her to an after-life of forced exhibition. To equate Parks and The Negro Resurrectionist, then, indicts Parks as one of Venus's oppressors, damning her—through the written and performed word—to still more involuntary display.

However, Parks is also granting The Venus the fame she desired, and Negro Resurrectionist can be read as a signification on Negro *Insurrectionist,* and therefore the character's name may point to Parks "bringing back" a call for a revolution against conventional views of The Venus and the theater. Parks obviously thwarts the standard form of the play both through her unconventional language and pauses as well as by having the play run through intermission.[10] Elam and Rayner align themselves with this more favorable perspective on Parks and suggest:

> Her position as a playwright echoes the positions of her characters in the sense that any kind of representation or category, performative or otherwise, will tend to imprison the truth of experience, or history, or resurrection by the very act of representation. Those who look for strictly realistic "accuracy" are unaware that such accuracy conceals the imaginary dimension of the story. It is easer to jail the truth than to resurrect it. (275)

They also read the intermission scene and The Baron Docteur's call to the audience as "reminiscent of the audience participation initiative enacted by black revolutionary theatre of the 1960s and early 1970s" (276). Parks is clearly aware of this tradition for in "new black math," her manifesto on the state of African American theater, she includes a section entitled "The Intermission," in which a militant character named Black Playwright tries to convince a Brother on the Corner and Sister on the Street to participate in her call to action, first by giving her money to make a literal call (on a pay phone) to John Brown, Nat Turner, and Sojouner Truth. The brother and sister listen, but again there is an implied paradox, for the section ends with Brother on the Corner asking "Whats she talking about now?" (581).

At the same time, Parks quickly indicates her desire to separate herself from the "holding cell" of "racerelations"; such a dependence, *Venus* suggests, is actually the burden of the oppressor, not the oppressed. Aaron Bryant highlights "Parks' belief that 'Blackness' can be explored on its own—that African Americans' existence is not defined by the presence of 'Whiteness,' that Black people's lives and concerns can extend beyond issues of race" (44). In Parks's words, "The Klan does not always have to be outside the door for Black people to have lives worthy of dramatic literature" ("An Equation for Black People" 19). Yet, *Venus*—in an argument similar to Toni Morrison's in *Playing in the Dark: Whiteness and the Literary Imagination* (1992)—makes it clear that for the oppressor the spectator-spectacle relationship is parasitic, with the spectators feeding off the spectacle's otherness. For example, when trying to draw in audiences for The Venus's show, The Mother-Showman shouts, "Ladies and Gents are you feeling lowly?/ Down in the dumps?/ Perhaps yr feelin that yr life is all for naught? Ive felt that way myself at times. /Come on inside and get yr spirits lifted./ One look at thisll make you feel like a King!" (45). Since this audience is a paying audience, The Venus's otherness and the disparity between her and her viewers is the source of the show's income, and it would have been the source of Venus's fame and fortune if either The Mother-Showman or The Brother had honored her contract. According to Parks, "A black play knows that when audiences read it primarily through the rubric of 'race relations,' that those audiences are suffering from an acute attack of white narcissism" ("new black math" 578). If this audience's needs parallel Broadway audiences' needs, then Parks's income also depends on giving the predominantly white audience the otherness they need for self-definition.

In *Venus*, a main component of this otherness is sexual, for the British and French audience—scientists and non-scientists—are fascinated by what they perceive as The Venus's aberrant sexual organs. Yet, the play writes against this aberration, instead using The Venus's sexuality to pathologize male sexuality. Both The Baron Docteur and The Chorus of 8 Anatomists expose themselves and masturbate publicly after looking at The Venus, and, earlier in the play, The Brother reveals that his sexual fulfillment is tied to Venus's exploitation. He admits, "I wanted you then and I want you now/ Thats partly why we've come here./ So I can love you properly./ Not like at home" (23). After promising her that he will buy her "the town" the next day, he begins groping her. She tries to protest but is cut off by his reassurances, which are couched in promises of fame.

The Venus thus uses her sexuality to achieve some degree of agency over The Brother and The Baron Docteur, but this agency also clearly has limits. Near the middle of the play, The Mother-Showman, especially remarkable because of her mixed-gender name, links money and sexual protection. When The Venus questions

The Mother-Showman's accounting and threatens to "be [her] own Boss make [her] own mint" (55), the Mother-Showman convinces her that there is nowhere for her to go where people will accept her and her way of life and that she needs protection from drunken white men. We find out later, however, that these men still rape her—regardless of The Mother Showman's "protection." In the end, it is The Venus's sexuality—more specifically, a sexually transmitted disease—that kills her. The Baron Docteur gives her Chlamydia, and seeing that her death is probable, he abandons her to imprisonment to hasten this death and his own fame since he will dissect her. The only power she had is rendered impotent by male sexuality and greed.

Sexuality, of course, is an important tool for the playwright because sex sells. The problem, of course, in Parks's case is that the sexuality upon which she capitalizes has traditionally been misrepresented. Sander Gilman calls representations such as the Venus Hottentot "icons." The problem with using these icons in literature, Gilman explains, is that "when individuals are shown within a work of art (no matter how broadly defined), the ideologically charged iconographic nature of the representation dominates" (204). The Venus Hottentot icon is so potent that "Sarah Bartmann's [sic] sexual parts, her genitalia and her buttocks, serve as the central image of the black female throughout the nineteenth century" (Gilman 216). In the play, the anatomists' emphasis on The Venus's sexual organs' postmortem "reflects the general nineteenth-century understanding of female sexuality as pathological: the female genitalia were of interest partly as examples of the various pathologies which could befall them but also because the female genitalia came to define the female for the nineteenth century" (Gilman 216). This emphasis is so intense, however, that it becomes pathological itself.

In the play, The Venus suggests that staging her sexuality is the best way to remove its malignancy, though with complicated implications. She asks, "If I bear thuh bad mark what better way to cleanse it off?/ Showing my sinful person as a caution to you all could,/ in the Lords eyes, be a sort of repentance" (76). According to S. E. Wilmer, Parks's restaging the Venus Hottentot icon is "ethical" and through it, she is "paying respect to those who have disappeared by re/making and staging their histories" (443). As such, she, like The Venus, is finding agency in a situation that traditionally denied agency to African American women. Again, however, this subversion is not simple, for immediately following the assertion of her desire to be on display, The Venus denies not only her shame, but also her blackness. She says, "[. . .] I could wash off my dark mark./ I came here black./ Give me the chance to leave here white" (76). This denial shows Venus engaging the white audience's desire to find self-definition in her, for she establishes herself as the opposite of whiteness and portrays racial definition as something that must be given by authority—in this case, the court. This denial also resonates with Parks's rejection of her aesthetic vis-à-vis *Venus*. By denying her individual role in the art, she puts The Venus and her body on stage alone and reduces the play to only a spectacle with "genitals that people think about long after the curtain comes down" ("new black math" 577).

If we try to use *Venus* as a kind of crystal ball for the future of black playwriting, the vision is cloudy. In her dying words, The Venus says, "dont look" (159), but in the final chorus she asks us to "please visit" and screams "kiss me!"—a cry for adoration and affection. She both shuns our participation and embraces it, cooperates and subverts. Parks herself offers a similar paradoxical forecast: "A black play is on broadway, the great white way./ A black play is not on broadway, and furthermore, aint studying no broadway./ A black play is coming soon to a theatre near you" ("new black math" 577). The pitfall of the paradox is that in each of Parks's scenarios the play is either unseen, or seen by the wrong audience, so the black playwright—like The Venus—has no home, no love, and no "mint," but there are plenty of critics, white and black, waiting to dissect her and her work.

Notes

1. In this chapter I will focus exclusively on Parks and her created characters, separate from the real Sarah Baartman. As such, I will refer to the play's protagonist as she is called in the play: "The Girl" and "The Venus." The play's use of the definite article for most character names is interesting as it both universalizes and individualizes the character. In addition to fueling the paradoxical nature of the play, this definite article highlights the fluidity of the Venus Hottentot's actual identity. Spellings of her actual name varied almost ubiquitously across critical and historical sources, and as Elizabeth Dryud Lyman points out, "Saartjie herself, referred to variously as 'The Girl,' 'Venus,' and 'The Hottentot Venus,' is never named in a speech attribution or addressed by another character in her given name" (96).
2. Defined in "from Elements of Style" as Parks's method for "working to create a dramatic text that departs from the linear narrative style to look and sound like a musical score" (9).
3. The Venus does speak of her shame during her trial, in the following exchange: The Chorus of the Court asks, "One more question, Girl, uh:/Have you ever been indecent?" The Venus responds (after a spell and a *(Rest)*): "'Indecent?'" (Parks's quotation marks); The Chorus of the Court: "Nasty"; The Venus: "Never./ No. I am just me."; The Chorus of the Court: "Whats that supposed to mean?!?!"; The Venus: "To hide yr shame is evil./ I show mine. Would you like to see?" (76).
4. A Chorus member early in the play indicates that The Venus's ass is "An ass to write home about./ Well worth the admission price" (7), which further connects this subversion to Parks's creation and to economics as well as echoes Parks in "new black math."
5. The Venus's relationship to "home" is another paradoxical element in the play. She first seems eager to leave. Then, near the middle of the play, she tells the Baron Docteur, "I dont wanna go back inny more./ I like yr company too much./ Besides, it was a shitty life" (105).

And finally, she ends the play thoroughly homesick: "I always dream of home/ in every spare minute./ It was a shitty shitty life but oh I miss it." (158). Young's essay provides a thorough description of the political situation in Africa during Saartjie Baartman's lifetime.

6. This essay is included in *The America Play and Other Works* (Theatre Communications Group, 1995).
7. Jennifer Johung, who examines "the intersections between the activities of writing and performing, as well as the interactions between the interpretation of the written marks on the page and the embodiment of the corporeal markings of performers onstage" (41), asserts that these "spells initiate a constant negotiation back and forth—a flickering between the absent subjectivity of the historical figure and the present subjectivity of the figure in Parks's play, and between the absent subjectivity inherent in figurative presence and the material presence of the body of the performer" (49). The spells thus give the reader/performer significant power over the production and its meaning.
8. Parks wrote the screenplay for Spike Lee's *Girl 6* (1996) and co-wrote Oprah Winfrey's film adaptation of *Their Eyes Were Watching God* (2005). Both movies met with mixed popular and critical reception.
9. The surveys were modeled on U.S. Census Bureau surveys in which around 17,000 adult subjects described their arts involvement via various media. In "new black math," Parks acknowledges the audience issues raised by such surveys, but subtly mocks the impact: "A black play takes into account that pollsters have found that black folks dont attend the theatres in numbers large enough to influence the selection of plays produced" (578).
10. Parks breaks down the barrier between playwright, actor, and reader earlier in the play when The Brother speaks a description nearly verbatim (only the order is reversed) from the stage directions (10). Though this repetition would seem to align the writer, Parks, with The Brother (one of The Girl's most prominent exploiters), the inversion actually positions her in opposition to him.

Works Cited

Basting, Anne Davis. "Venus." *Theatre Journal* 49.2 (1997): 223–25.

Brantley, Ben. "Of an Erotic Freak Show and the Lesson Therein." *New York Times* 145 (May 3, 1996): C2.

Brown, Sterling. *Negro Poetry and Drama and The Negro in American Fiction*. 1937. New York: Atheneum, 1969.

Brown-Guillory, Elizabeth. "Reconfiguring History: Migration, Memory, and (Re)Membering in Suzan-Lori Parks's Plays." *Southern Women Playwrights: New Essays in Literary History and Criticism*. Ed. Robert L. McDonald and Linda Rohrer Paige. Tuscaloosa: University of Alabama Press, 2002. 183–97.

Bryant, Aaron. "Broadway, Her Way." *New Crisis* 109.2 (March/April 2002): 43–45.

Dixon, Kimberly D., "An I Am Sheba Me Am (She Be Doo Be Wah Waaah Doo Wah) O(au)rality, Textuality and Performativity: African American Literature's Vernacular Theory and the Work of Suzan-Lori Parks." *Journal of American Drama and Theatre* 11.1 (1998): 49–66.

Elam, Harry J., Jr., and Alice Rayner. "Body Parts: Between Story and Spectacle in *Venus* by Suzan-Lori Parks." *Staging Resistance: Essays on Political Theater.* Ed. Jeanne Colleran and Jenny S. Spencer. Ann Arbor: University of Michigan Press, 1998. 265–82.

Gilman, Sander. "Black Bodies, White Bodies: Toward an Iconography of Female Sexuality in Late Nineteenth-Century Art, Medicine, and Literature. *Critical Inquiry* 12.1 (1985): 204-–42.

Innes, Christopher "Staging Black History: Re-Imagining Cultural Icons." *Race and Religion in Contemporary Theatre and Drama in English.* Ed. Bernhard Reitz. Trier, Germany: Wissenschaftlicher Verlag Trier, 1999. 95–107.

Jacobs, Harriet. *Incidents in the Life of a Slave Girl: Written by Herself.* Lydia Maria Child, ed. Boston: The Author, 1861.

Johung, Jennifer. "Figuring the 'Spells'/ Spelling the Figures: Suzan-Lori Parks 'Scene of Love (?)'" *Theatre Journal* 58.1 (2006): 39–52.

Lyman, Elizabeth Dyrud. "The Page Refigured: The Verbal and Visual Language of Suzan-Lori Parks's *Venus.*" *Performance Research* 7.1 (2002): 90–100.

Marneweck, Aja. "Staging Stereotype and Performing the Exotic Erotic: An Interrogation of Desire in the Texts of Parks and Kennedy." *South African Theatre Journal* 18 (2004): 50–64.

Morrison, Toni. *Playing in the Dark: Whiteness and the Literary Imagination.* Cambridge, MA: Harvard University Press, 1992.

National Endowment for the Arts. "Report 35: Executive Summary." *American Participation in Theatre.* New York, 1992.

———. *Research Division Report #45: 2002 Survey of Public Participation in the Arts.* New York, 2004.

Parks, Suzan-Lori. "An Equation for Black People Onstage." *The America Play and Other Works.* New York: Theatre Communications Group, 1995. 19–22.

———. "from The Elements of Style." *The America Play and Other Works.* New York: Theatre Communications Group, 1995. 6–18.

———. *Venus.* New York: Theatre Communications Group, 1997.

———. "Tradition and the Individual Talent." *Theater* 29.2 (1999): 26–33.

———. "new black math." *Theatre Journal* 57 (2005): 576–83.

Wilmer, S. E. "Restaging the Nation: The Work of Suzan-Lori Parks." *Modern Drama 43.3* (2000): 442–52.

Young, Jean. "The Re-Objectification and Re-Commodification of Saartjie Baartman in Suzan-Lori Parks's *Venus.*" *African American Review* 31.4 (1997): 699–708.

Contributors

Joy E. Cranshaw is pursuing her doctorate at the University of North Carolina at Chapel Hill, where she focuses on twentieth-century American multiethnic literature and queer theory, particularly in connection with questions of identity, subjectivity, and representation. She presented "Native of the Borderlands: Reading Louise Erdrich through a *Mestiza* Lens" at The University of Oklahoma Student Association of Graduate English Studies conference in 2006 and has since continued investigating the fruitfulness of applying Latina/o Studies paradigms to readings of Native American literary texts. She was awarded a University Merit Assistantship for her first year at the University of North Carolina and an Amherst College Fellowship for her second year. Prior to her current graduate study, she taught English in New York City public schools for three years and earned a master of arts degree in education from the City College of New York, CUNY. She remains deeply dedicated to adolescent education, and an adaptation of her master's thesis, "When I Was Upstate: Reading Experiences of Incarcerated Adolescents," is forthcoming in *Emerging Literacies*, edited by Alison J. Matika.

Rachelle S. Gold has taught at the University of California, Berkeley; North Carolina Central University; and the University of North Carolina, Chapel Hill; and is currently enrolled in the doctoral program in English and

Comparative Literature at the University of North Carolina, Chapel Hill. She has presented papers at the College Language Association, the American Culture Association, and the Northern California Renaissance Conference, and she was the keynote speaker for Black History Month at the University of the Pacific in 2001. A highlight of her academic career was being selected as one of two Outstanding Graduating Seniors from a class of five thousand students at her alma mater, San Jose State University. She later studied Latin at the University of California, Berkeley's summer intensive workshop, completed her master's degree in English literature at Indiana University, Bloomington, and finished a second master's degree in education at University of California, Berkeley. Her awards include University of California, Berkeley's Outstanding Graduate Student Instructor honor and the Black Theatre Network's 2006 S. Randolph Edmonds Young Scholars award. Before moving to Durham in 2002, she worked as assistant director of financial aid at Santa Clara University. An avid swimmer, she also enjoys taking nature walks with her boyfriend Jim, an honest auto mechanic, her dog Tennyson, and her friends Jim and Elizabeth Pearce.

Pamela Hamilton is pursuing her doctorate at the University of North Carolina at Chapel Hill, where she focuses on African American literature and is interested in representations of race in children's fiction. She is a graduate of the University of Mississippi, where she spent much of her time writing for the campus newspaper. As a writer for *The Daily Mississippian*, she covered everything from student body politics to crime on campus. She also served as editor-in-chief of the newspaper. When she wasn't working on the student paper, she spent much of her time reading books for literature courses at Rowan Oak, and she has especially fond memories of reading for a favorite class on William Faulkner novels. She was inducted into the Ole Miss Hall of Fame in 2002, one of the highest honors awarded to graduating seniors. Before beginning graduate study, she worked as a newswoman for *The Associated Press*, where she covered education in South Carolina, and as an intern for the editorial board of the *New York Times*, where she wrote mostly about issues in higher education.

John Hannah is a doctoral candidate in English and Comparative Literature at the University of North Carolina, Chapel Hill, with an interest in African American and Southern literature. Awarded a U.S. Army graduate fellowship, he earned his master of arts degree in English from University of North Carolina in 1993. From 1993 through 1996, he taught English at the U.S. Military Academy at West Point as an instructor and assistant professor of English. In 1994 and 1995, he served as the assistant course director of "Plebe English," West Point's first semester composition course, for which he developed all related syllabi, lesson plans, and instructional materials and conducted all related course administration. Selected to attend the Australian Army Staff College in 1997, he earned a master's of defense studies degree from the University of Canberra. From 1999 through 2001, he taught English at the U.S. Air Force Academy in Colorado Springs as an assistant professor of English. In 2004, he finished his military career at the Pentagon, retiring from the U.S. Army with over twenty years of service.

Trudier Harris is J. Carlyle Sitterson Professor and Associate Chair of English and Comparative Literature at the University of North Carolina at Chapel Hill, where she teaches courses in African American literature and folklore at undergraduate and graduate levels. Author and editor of more than twenty volumes, her most recently published scholarly volumes are *Saints, Sinners, Saviors: Strong Black Women in African American Literature* and *South of Tradition: Essays on African American Literature*. She is currently at work on "The Scary Mason-Dixon Line: African American Writers and the South." Her memoir, *Summer Snow: Reflections from a Black Daughter of the South* (Beacon, 2003), was selected to inaugurate the One-Book, One-Community Reading Program in Orange County, North Carolina in 2003–2004. In 2005, she won the University of North Carolina System Board of Governors' Award for Excellence in Teaching as well as the John Hurt Fisher Award from SAMLA for "distinguished achievement" over the course of her career.

Jennifer Larson is currently writing a dissertation on Suzan-Lori Parks's plays, novel, essays, and screenplays in the doctoral program in English and Comparative Literature at the University of North Carolina at Chapel Hill. In 2003, she earned a master's degree in English from the University of North Carolina at Charlotte. She has presented papers on Ralph Ellison's *Invisible Man,* William Faulkner's *Light in August,* Colson Whitehead's *John Henry Days*, D. J. Spooky's *Rebirth of a Nation*, and David Walker's *Appeal*. She is the contributing editor for the David Walker section of the *North Carolina Roots of African American Literature* collection (2006, University of North Carolina Press) and has contributed entries to *Writing African American Women* (2006, Greenwood) and the *African American National Biography* (forthcoming, Oxford University Press). She has received research awards from the Center for the Study of the American South for projects on John William DeForest and Frances Ellen Watkins Harper. She has also published numerous online features and summaries for *Documenting the American South*. She has taught literature and composition courses at the University of North Carolina at Chapel Hill and serves as the coordinator of the Connected Learning Program at the University of North Carolina's James M. Johnston Center for Undergraduate Excellence.

Matthew Luter is currently a student in the doctoral program in English and Comparative Literature at the University of North Carolina at Chapel Hill. He recently completed his Master's thesis on T. S. Eliot and Don DeLillo, "DeLillo's Waste Land / Eliot in the Underworld: Myth, History, and the Writer," part of which he presented at the University of Louisville's annual 20th Century Literature and Culture Conference. Other current research interests include the postmodern American novel and the fiction of the contemporary U.S. South, and a probable area of inquiry for a future dissertation will be the presence of the celebrity character in recent American fiction. A native of Laurel, Mississippi, he completed his undergraduate degree at Millsaps College, in Jackson, Mississippi, where he was inducted into Phi Beta Kappa.

Meredith M. Malburne, a doctoral student and Teaching Fellow at the University of North Carolina at Chapel Hill, is currently pursuing coursework in twentieth century American literature and literary theory. She is interested primarily in the literature of the 1930s–1960s, along with issues of representation, power, politics, and race. She presented "Borderlands and Exiles in Herman Melville's 'Benito Cereno'" at The University of Oklahoma Student Association of Graduate English Studies conference in 2006, and she continues to study the influence of Melville on authors such as Richard Wright. Her work on Langston Hughes's controversial 1931 visit to the University of North Carolina was accepted for presentation at the 2007 Conference on College Composition and Communication Convention. She holds a master of arts in English from Georgetown University, where she was a writing fellow and teaching assistant. While at Georgetown, she completed a thesis on the revolutionary and anti-lynching poetry and prose of Langston Hughes entitled "Lynching America: Refocusing Langston Hughes's Revolutionary Canon." She remained at Georgetown after receiving her degree, managing several academic programs and teaching in the John Carroll Scholars Program. She also holds a bachelor of arts in English and French from Wellesley College, where she graduated magna cum laude. She was a 2005 Andrew W. Mellon Fellowship national semifinalist, she is the coach of the English Department intramural softball team at the University of North Carolina, and she serves on the editorial board of the *Carolina Quarterly*.

Benjamin Sammons is a doctoral student in English and Comparative Literature at the University of North Carolina at Chapel Hill. Upon entering the M.A.

program at the University of North Carolina, he was awarded a Booker Fellowship by the Department of English. In 2005, he presented a paper entitled "Sound the Alarm: The Radical Politics of Racialized Aurality in W.E.B. Du Bois's *The Souls of Black Folk*" at the New Voices Conference hosted by Georgia State University. This paper, which evolved into a master's thesis, united his enduring interests in pragmatist aesthetics and racial politics. In his doctoral research, he will add to these concerns an investigation of class, especially representations of poverty, in twentieth-century American and African American literature. He looks forward to a pedagogical career that exposes the ethical underpinnings of these literatures while exploring their continuing capacity for cultural critique.

AFRICAN AMERICAN LITERATURE AND CULTURE

EXPANDING AND EXPLODING THE BOUNDARIES

General Editor
Carlyle V. Thompson

The purpose of this series is to present innovative, in-depth, and provocatively critical literary and cultural investigations of critical issues in African American literature and life. We welcome critiques of fiction, poetry, drama, film, sports, and popular culture. Of particular interest are literary and cultural analyses that involve contemporary psychoanalytical criticism, new historicism, deconstructionism, critical race theory, critical legal theory, and critical gender theory.

For additional information about this series or for the submission of manuscripts, please contact:

Peter Lang Publishing, Inc.
Acquisitions Department
29 Broadway, 18th floor
New York, New York 10006

To order other books in this series, please contact our Customer Service Department:

(800) 770-LANG (within the U.S.)
(212) 647-7706 (outside the U.S.)
(212) 647-7707 FAX

Or browse online by series:

www.peterlang.com